# JUDAISM IN CONTEMPORARY

# Judaism
# in
# Contemporary
# Context

## Enduring Issues and
## Chronic Crises

## Jacob Neusner

VALLENTINE MITCHELL
LONDON • PORTLAND, OR

First published in 2007 in Great Britain by
VALLENTINE MITCHELL
Suite 314, Premier House, 112–114 Station Road,
Edgware, Middlesex HA8 7BJ

and in the United States of America by
VALLENTINE MITCHELL
c/o ISBS, 920 NE 58th Avenue, Suite 300
Portland, OR 97213-3786

Website: www.vmbooks.com

British Library Cataloguing in Publication Data

Neusner, Jacob, 1932–
    Judaism in contemporary context : enduring issues and
    chronic crises
    1. Judaism – 20th century
    I. Title
    296'.09045

ISBN 978 0 85303 665 4 (cloth)
ISBN 978 0 85303 737 8 (paper)

Library of Congress Cataloging-in-Publication Data

A catalog record has been applied for

Printed in Great Britain by Biddles Ltd,
King's Lynn, Norfolk

# Contents

# Acknowledgements

My thanks go to the copyright holders of my papers, who have graciously given permission for me to reproduce them here. I have made an effort in good faith to locate them all. If I have omitted any, I request the copyright holder to communicate with me, and I shall make up the omission on the earliest possible occasion.

1. Can Judaism Survive the Twentieth Century?
   *Tikkun* 4 (1989), 38–42. © 1989: *Tikkun*, 2107 Van Nes Ave #302, San Francisco, CA 94109

2. We've Won; So What?
   *Moment* 2 (1977), 61–62. © 1977: *Moment Magazine*, 5208 38th St. NW, Washington, DC, 20015

3. Wanted, Dead or Alive
   *Moment* 4/3 (1979), 61–64. © 1979: *Moment Magazine*

4. Toward a Jewish Renewal: After the Flood, After the Rainbow
   *Moment* 3/5 (1978), 11–16. © 1978: *Moment Magazine*

5. Why I am Not an Ethnic Jew, Why I am a Religious Jew
   *Jewish Spectator* 61/3 (1996–97), 16–19. © 1997: *Jewish Spectator*, Friends of the Center for Jewish Living and Values, 439 Park Milano, Calabasas, CA 91302, and Mark Bleiweiss, POB 440, Telstone 90840, Israel

6. Since I'm Jewish, This Must be Judaism
   *Jewish Spectator* 64/2 (1999), 5–7. © 1999: *Jewish Spectator*

7. Stranger at Home: Myths in American Judaism
   *Forum* 39 (1980), 31–38. © 1980: *Forum*, World Zionist Organization, POB 92, Jerusalem, Israel

8. Who Is Israel?
   *National Review* 29/24 (1977), 714–716. © 1977: *National Review*, 215 Lexington Ave., New York, NY 10016

9. Zionism and 'the Jewish Problem'
   *Midstream* 15 (1969), 34–45. © 1969: *Midstream*, 633 Third Ave. 21st Fl, New York, NY 10017

10. Judaism and the Zionist Problem
    *Judaism* 19 (1970), 311–323. © 1970 American Jewish Congress, 15 E. 84th St., New York, NY 10028

# Preface

The past half-century has witnessed the advent of a new type of authoritative voice in the world of Judaism, the public intellectual, who ordinarily is a scholar of Judaism engaged by issues beyond the walls of the study. Representing only themselves and no organization or party or sect or institution within Judaism, these public intellectuals none the less embodied a vision of their own.

Taking myself as an instance, I was ordained a rabbi but never held a pulpit. For nearly five decades I have spoken out on Jewish issues, but never occupied an office in organized Judaism or in the secular Jewish community, and claimed no authority but reason. I did not buy a hearing for my opinions by lavish donations of money to pet causes. All I was, and am, is a professor of the study of Judaism, exercising academic freedom within the world of Judaism.

For this half-century now closed, no one knew what to make of the public intellectual. This new-model authority represented an unwelcome intrusion into the – until then – controlled discourse of the Jewish community. Synagogue rabbis in the USA were, and are, answerable to their boards of trustees. The European communal rabbis served the organized, government-recognized Jewish community. Their freedom of action and expression competed with their need for discretion and conciliation with lay leadership and its opinions. However, other rabbis have accorded a cool welcome indeed to someone beyond the constraints of rabbinical and synagogue and community politics. Secular office holders – the wealthy and their employees – within the institutions of the Jewish community found they could not control someone whose living they did not provide, someone indifferent to the preferment of Jewish community pressures. The public intellectuals, most of whom by far are professors, but now also including poets, playwrights, and most recently even blog publishers, have found ample media outlets for expressing opinion and solid grounds in learning for passing judgment on issues of Jewish concern. This new kind of participant in the public life of Judaism and of the Jewish community was not to be silenced and, however others might try, could not be ignored. As the decades passed, more and more public intellectuals within Judaism confronted Jewry with their claim of moral authority, one that was based upon, and exercised, the power of ideas.

A list of the articulate voices of the pioneering generation and its continuators in a second and even third generation of public intellectuals in scholarship and journalism would extend for many pages. Issues subjected to their analysis would fill still more. Even the types of Judaic public intellectuals are many. But in the beginning, in the late 1940s and 1950s, Jewish authority figures such as professors of Jewish Studies not in the employ of the organized Jewish communities were rare; the new kind of professor of Judaism, in his academic base, did not find in the affairs of the Jewish community and of living Judaism a worthy venue for engagement; some of them thought that caring about Judaism and Jewry compromised their academic credentials. Now, 50 years later, although the Jewish community has not made itself entirely comfortable with such independent voices, it has come a long way toward adapting itself to free-standing critics and to finding ways to co-opt some, cooperate with others and collaborate with still others in a common enterprise.

Participating in the debates of the community of Judaism challenges any thoughtful Jew. Public intellectuals take upon themselves a complex task. Issues require negotiation, both politically and intellectually. The authority of the sacred writings of Judaism demands dialogue between the current generation and those that have gone before. Above all, in our time, crises without precedent arise in the course of events. Certainly the age offered its own agendum. The generation that came to maturity after the Second World War witnessed both the impact of the Holocaust on Judaism and on the life of the Jewish people and the advent of the State of Israel. Reaching maturity at mid-century mark, that generation has had to confront urgent and unprecedented issues of politics, theology, and Jewish public policy.

The essays I have collected here, out of a much, much larger corpus of writings on public Jewish issues, form my contribution to a half-century of Jewish public life. From the 1950s to the present day I have served as one of those persistent public intellectuals of the English-speaking community of Judaism – only one, I stress, of many. In this book I have selected essays published over nearly fifty years from the later 1950s and earliest 1960s through the end of the twentieth century, that I hope retain more than personal or ephemeral interest, and may sustain a second reading long after their publication. This is for two reasons. First, the issues that occupied my concern persist for a new generation to confront. Second, there is a story of a generation now passing that remains to be told; the essays collected here form a contribution to the narrative. These concern both Judaism the religion viewed in its own terms, and also Judaism the amalgam of religious and ethnic components viewed in the political setting of the Jewish people, with special reference to the English-speaking component of that people. These enduring issues are captured by the words 'Holocaust' and 'State of Israel'. The impact of the Holocaust has defined the condition and consciousness of world Jewry from the Second World War onward. For not a few it takes the place of Judaism. So, too, the State of Israel and Zionism define paramount parts of that amalgam. For many, these two substitute for Judaism. The Holocaust, Zionism, and the State of Israel represent claims upon the consciousness and conscience of the Diaspora that none would contemplate dismissing.

As a young American in the nascent decade of the Cold War, I saw the Holocaust as a catastrophic historic event, but not as a source of lessons for Jewish public policy. I saw the State of Israel as a given, a matter of on-going engagement, but not as the center of the life and consciousness of the Diaspora. I took an independent stance, and so begin with the issue that captures the condition of Judaism in the English-speaking Diaspora: freedom, and what it means to practice Judaism in a free society. The two givens of that essay are that we live in a free society and that it is not a society defined mainly by Jews: both statements are data of the American or Canadian or British or Australian or South African or New Zealand Jewish existence, but not of the Jews then imprisoned in the USSR, who did not enjoy freedom to practice Judaism, nor of the Jews of the State of Israel, who did not live out the lives of a minority in a majority culture that set the conditions of acceptable difference. Today, the Jews of the former USSR enjoy the freedom that we do, and the Jews of the State of Israel are frequently reminded of their minority status among their neighbors. For our part, in the English-speaking world, we have learned that freedom has its costs, but that minority status offers its compensations too. An evocative symbol is offered by intermarriage, the indicator of freedom, the measure of minority acceptance by diverse majorities.

By 'Judaism' people quite reasonably mean not only a religion pure and simple, defined in the model by which other religions are defined, but also a religion that is *sui generis* (as all religions are in some way or other). For its part, Judaism then emerges as a religious culture of an ethnic group, the Jews, or even simply a Jewish counterpart to the ethnicity of other ethnic groups. Thus Judaism the religion, in the second group of essays, which form the shank of the book, exists not only in its own terms but in relationship to the politics and ethnic character of the Jewish people. The Holocaust and the advent of the State of Israel present a problem to that Diaspora, because they also form definitions of Jewish peoplehood that contradict the givens of the Diaspora: secure citizenship and primary loyalty to the nationality and culture, beginning with the English language, of the USA, Canada, Britain, South Africa, Australia, or New Zealand. This set of essays is diverse but not, I hope, diffuse, since a few established issues predominate: Zionism and the State of Israel, the Holocaust, the condition of the organized Jewish community, and religion versus secularity in Jewish consciousness. Above all, I wrote these essays for a community of readers – not leaders, except in sensibility and consciousness, engaged in the reform of the organized Jewish community. What we wanted to accomplish in the 1950s and early 1960s we came to see fully realized by the later 1970s: the initial reform was in place. Then we began to criticize our own ideas: 'we've won, so what?'

What was new and challenging extended to my profession: professor of the study of Judaism within the academic study of religion unfolding in American, Canadian, and British higher education in this same half-century. When I came along, there were very few secular academic posts in any aspect of Jewish learning; now there are many. How to account for the expansion of the 1960s and 1970s?

Just as the post-war, Cold War generation was responding to the political challenge of the age, so the same generation confronted the cultural challenge to which the academic study of religion responded. The USA and its allies required the intellectual equipment to respond to the cultural diversity of the international alliance; imperialism no longer served as the medium of world order. How to deal with difference? Anthropology offered one set of answers, the comparative study of religion, another. As departments of Religious Studies took shape in substantial numbers in US, Canadian, British, Australian, and New Zealand universities, Judaism presented itself as a candidate for inclusion – and was invited in. But what, *about* Judaism, was to be studied in the new context? No models existed, much experimentation was required. Just as the departments of Religious Studies evolved out of the model of the Protestant Divinity School but then took their own course, so it was natural, to begin with, to come to undergraduate education with the secular program of the Jewish seminaries and Hebrew teachers' colleges: Hebrew language, Jewish history – all presented in the disguise of facticity and objectivity. But a generation of then-young professors had by trial and error to create a curriculum for the new context of culture.

The fourth and briefest collection of essays presents some personal impressions: what I learned from observing contemporary communities in the course of teaching and lecturing here and there. For many decades I pursued a program of academic lectures in universities and Jewish communities throughout the world. I conclude with personal reflections on the condition of Judaism and the Jewish people in the State of Israel, South Africa, Minneapolis, Minnesota, and Tübingen. The impressions are immediate and fresh, therefore dated to the day on which they were written down — but curiously affecting, to me at least.

At the end, I reproduce the interview that the writer and editor, William Novak, conducted with me 20 years ago. Over time I have been interviewed by a variety of journalists, written about by reviewers, discussed in public contexts, from New Zealand to Brazil, Sweden to the State of Israel, and throughout the USA and Canada. Of all of the published results, Novak's is by far the most perceptive. It is the one piece of writing about me that represents me as I see myself and how I wish to be remembered in time to come.

In addition to the acknowledgements to the copyright holders for permission to reprint my essays, I wish to thank the editors of the journals that for a half-century made possible the conduct of public discourse in Judaism, and that part of the Jewish community that concerned itself with conflict in complex issues of culture. Among them I point to the late Steven Schwarzschild of *Judaism* in the 1960s and early 1970s, Leonard Fein, founder of *Moment* in the 1970s and early 1980s, and William Novak of *Response* and then *New Tradition*. They served as models, each in his own way, for the public intellectuals just then making their voices heard, as well as providing the medium for their messages. If there was then, and consequently now continues to flourish, a Jewish intellectual renaissance of Judaism in the US sector of the English-speaking Diaspora, they were the midwives.

**Jacob Neusner**
Research Professor of Theology
Institute of Advanced Theology
Bard College
Annandale-on-Hudson
NY 12504 USA
neusner@webjogger.net

# PART I
## JUDAISM IN ETHNIC CONTEXT

# 1 Can Judaism Survive the Twentieth Century?

*Tikkun* 4 (1989), 38–42

The twentieth century, until practically our own time in the early twenty-first century, has produced no important and influential Judaic systems. The well-established Judaisms that flourish today – Reform, Orthodox, and Conservative Judaism – all took shape in the nineteenth century, and in Germany. Secular Jewish socialism and Zionism also arose in the nineteenth century. How is it possible that one period produced a range of Judaic systems of enormous depth and breadth, systems that attracted mass support and changed many people's lives, while the next three-quarters of a century did not? Further, what are we now to expect, on the eve of the twenty-first century? I think we are on the threshold of another great age of system-building in Judaism.

## WHY NO NEW JUDAIC SYSTEMS FOR 75 YEARS?

Why no new Judaisms for so long? The stimulus for system-building surely should have come from the creation of the first Jewish state in 2,000 years. Yet the creation of this state yielded nothing more interesting than a flag and a rather domestic politics, not a worldview and a way of life such as the one the founders of the American republic, Madison and Hamilton, enunciated.

American Jewry presents the same picture. War and dislocation, migration and relocation; in the past, these phenomena generated and sustained system-building in Jewish societies. But the political changes affecting Jews in America, who became Jewish Americans in ways that Jews did not become Jewish Germans or Jewish Frenchmen or Jewish Englishmen and women, have yielded no encompassing systems.

Millions of people moved from one world to another, changed their language, their occupation, and virtually every other significant social and cultural aspect of their lives, and produced nothing more than a set of recapitulations of Judaic systems, serviceable under utterly different circumstances.

I see three reasons why no Judaic systems have emerged since the end of the nineteenth century. I do not claim that they provide all-encompassing explanations, but I do think they help us answer the question before us.

## The Holocaust

First of all, the demographic reason, which has two components. The most productive sector of world Jewry perished. Also, the conditions that brought about the great systemic creations vanished with the six million. Not only too many (one is too many!), but the wrong Jews died. What I mean is that Judaic systems emerged in Europe, not in America or in what was then Palestine; and, within Europe, these systems came from Central and Eastern European Jewry. The Jewish population in Eastern Europe was vast. It engaged in enormous amounts of learning; and what's more, it formed a self-aware community – not scattered and individual, but composed and bonded. In short, for the Jews that perished, being Jewish constituted a collective enterprise, not an individual predilection.

In the West, people tend to identify religion with belief, to the near exclusion of behavior, so religion is understood as a personal state of mind. Jews in the West tend to be concerned more with self than with society, less with culture and community than with conscience and character. Under such circumstances, system-building doesn't flourish, for systems speak of communities and create worlds of meaning, answer pressing public questions and produce broad answers.

Yet the demographic explanation cannot, by itself, suffice. After all, today's Jewish population produces massive communities, 300,000 here, half a million there. Both American Judaism and Israeli nationalism testify to the possibility of system-building even after the mass murder of European Jewry. When we consider, moreover, the strikingly unproductive character of large populations of Jews, the inert and passive ideology (such as it is) of the Jewish communities in France, Britain, South Africa, and the Soviet Union, for instance, it becomes clear that even where there are populations capable of generating and sustaining distinctive Judaic systems, none is in sight. So we must turn to yet another explanation.

## The Demise of Intellect

The as-yet-unappreciated factor of sheer ignorance, the profound pathos of Jews' illiteracy in all books but the books of the streets and marketplaces, is a second explanation for the decline of Jewish system-building. The Judaisms that survive focus on emotional or political concerns – readily available to all. They offer nothing of taste and judgment, intellect and reflection; nothing of tradition and traditional culture, nothing of the worlds in which words matter.

The systems of the nineteenth and twentieth centuries made constant reference to the Judaisms of the Torah, even when rejecting it. Jews received and used the heritage of human experience, captured as in amber, in the words of the Torah. They did not have to make things up afresh every morning or to rely only on that narrow range of human experience that is immediately accessible.

By contrast, Israeli nationalism and the American Judaism of Holocaust and Redemption – the two most influential systems that move Jews to action in the world today – scarcely concern themselves with this traditional focus. They emphasize only what is near at hand. They work with the raw materials made available by contemporary experience: emotions on the one hand, politics on the other. Access to realms beyond requires learning in literature; but the Judaic systems of the twentieth century do not regard the reading of books as a principal part of the Jewish way of life. The consequence is a strikingly abbreviated agenda of issues, a remarkably one-dimensional set of urgent questions.

The reason for this neglect is that today's Jews, especially in Western Europe, the Soviet Union, and the United States, but also in Canada, Australia, South Africa, Argentina, Brazil, and other areas, have lost all access to the Judaism of the dual Torah, oral and written, that sustained fifteen centuries of Jews before now. Jews in the European, African, and Australian worlds no longer regard 'being Jewish' as a matter of intellect, and, to the extent that they have a Jewish worldview, it has little connection to the Judaic canon.

American Jews specifically have focused their imaginative energies on the Holocaust, and have centered their eschatological fantasies on 'the beginning of our redemption' in the State of Israel. But they have not gone through the one, nor have they chosen to participate in the other. Not having lived through the mass murder of European Jewry, American Jews have restated the problem of evil in unanswerable form and have then transformed that problem into an obsession. Not choosing to settle in the State of Israel, they have defined redemption – the resolution of the problem of evil – in terms remote from their world. In short, American Judaism is plagued by focusing on a world in which its members do not live.

## The Triumph of Large-scale Organization

Third and distinct from the other two factors is the bureaucratization of Jewry that has resulted from its emphasis on immediately accessible political and emotional concerns. Jews who place little value on matters of intellect and learning are placed in organizational positions of power, while those more reflective Jews are given little influence. This stratification prevents system-building, because intellectuals are the people who create religious systems. Administrators are not, and when they need ideas they simply hire publicists and journalists who churn out propaganda.

This emphasis on bureaucrats is hardly surprising. In an age in which, to survive at all, Jews had to address the issues of politics and economics, and to build a state (in Israel) and a massive and effective set of organizations capable of collective political action (in the United States), politicians, not sages, were needed. Though these politicians did their task as well as one might have hoped, we should not lose sight of the cost. The end of the remarkable age of Judaic system-building may prove to be a more calamitous consequence of the destruction of European Jewry than anyone has yet realized. Not just Jews, but the Jewish spirit as well, may have suffocated in the gas chambers.

## THE END OF THE JUDAISMS OF THE NINETEENTH CENTURY

Among the six great Judaisms of the first third of the twentieth century, all have lost their nerve and none retains vitality. Jewish socialism-cum-Yiddishism is a victim of the Holocaust. Zionism has no important message that is not already available from the Judaism of Holocaust and redemption. Reform, Reconstructionist, Orthodox, and Conservative Judaisms have all lost power.

Reform Judaism, having sold its soul to the Judaism of Holocaust and Redemption, has lost the source of its energy in the prophetic tradition of Judaism. Western Orthodox Judaism answers questions about living by the Torah in modern society that few people wish to ask anymore. Those who want tradition and also a place in an open society find the answer in a variety of Judaisms. The diverse Orthodoxies now concur, with the exception of the minority around Yeshiva University, that to be Orthodox is to live segregated from and with scarcely veiled hostility to the rest of the Jewish and gentile worlds. Accordingly, everyone wants a place in the center, everyone espouses the ideal that we now identify with Conservative Judaism: that we wish to be Jewish in an integrated society and that we want our Judaism to infuse our lives as Americans with meaning. It is a mediating, healing, centrist, and moderate ideal; an ideal that teaches us to look to the Judaic religious tradition for guidance, but to make up our own minds, to live by something we call Judaism, but to accept the possibility of change where appropriate, necessary, or desirable.

The institutions of Conservative Judaism, however, are weak. They do not enjoy the financial support of Jewish lay people, and much of the Conservative rabbinate is alienated from the movement's central institution, the Jewish Theological Seminary. In fairness, however, the younger generation of Conservative rabbis is starting to overcome this alienation.

What of Reform Judaism? If I had to choose two words to characterize the contemporary state of Reform Judaism, they would be sloth and envy. I call Reform Judaism slothful because it has become lazy about developing its own virtues, and thus deprives all Judaisms of its invaluable gifts and insights. I call it envious because it sees virtue in others and despises itself. The single greatest and most urgent idea in the Jewish world today is the one idea that Reform Judaism has made its own and developed for us all – the idea that God loves all humanity, not only holy Israel.

Yet the movement still regards itself as second class and somehow less than a fully legitimate form of Judaism. By 'the movement' I do not mean a few theologians at Hebrew Union College who have set forth a solid and substantial rationale for Reform Judaism both in history (Michael A. Meyer) and theology (Jakob J. Petuchowski). I mean the vast number of pulpit rabbis and lay people who see Jews who are more observant and think of themselves as somehow inferior, who meet more learned Jews and think less of themselves.

Though less observance and less learning weaken Reform Judaism's claim to Jewish authenticity, I think Reform Judaism has a message to offer all Jews, including the most Orthodox of the Orthodox and the most nationalistic of the nationalists, a message that is more important than studying the Talmud or not eating lobster. Reform Judaism defines Judaism as a religion of respect and love for the other, as much as for the self. Reform Judaism teaches that God loves all people, emphasizes the parts of the Torah that deliver that message, and rejects bigotry and prejudice when practiced not only by gentiles but by Jews as well.

The single most urgent moral crisis facing Jewish communities today is the Jews' hostility toward the other, the outsider. The novelist Norman Mailer, writing in the *New York Times* in language reminiscent of the prophetic tradition, stated what I conceive to be the great contribution of Reform Judaism to the life of Jewry everywhere:

What made us great as a people is that we, of all ethnic groups, were the most concerned with the world's problems ... We understood as no other people how the concerns of the world were our concerns. The welfare of all the people of the world came before our own welfare ... The imperative to survive at all costs ... left us smaller, greedier, narrower, preternaturally touchy and self-seeking. We entered the true and essentially hopeless world of the politics of self-interest; 'is this good for the Jews?' became, for all too many of us, all of our politics.

Mailer concluded: 'the seed of any vital American future must still break through the century-old hard-pack of hate, contempt, corruption, guild, odium, and horror ... I am tired of living in the miasma of our indefinable and ongoing national shame.' I find in Mailer's comments that morally vital prophetic tradition that Reform Judaism – alone among contemporary Judaisms – espouses. All the worse that today Reform Judaism has lost its nerve. Just when Jewry needs what Reform Judaism has always stood for, the message is muffled.

Speaking to the Council of Reform and Liberal Rabbis in London last year, Israeli Professor Yehoshafat Harkabi said that there is a crisis in our relationship to the gentiles. In a stunning public statement, Harkabi raised the possibility that 'the Jewish religion that hitherto has bolstered Jewish existence may become detrimental to it'. He pointed to manifestations of hostility against gentiles, formerly repressed, but ascendant in the past decade. In the State of Israel, in particular, that hostility takes such forms as these: Chief Rabbi Mordekhai Eliahu forbade Jews in the State of Israel to sell apartments to gentiles; a former chief rabbi ruled that Jews must burn their copies of the New Testament; Rabbi Eliezer Waldenburg, a scholar who has received the Israel Prize in Judaic Studies, declared that a gentile should not be permitted to live in Jerusalem; and the body of a gentile woman who lived as a Jew without official conversion was disinterred from a Jewish cemetery.

Explaining these and many other expressions of anti-gentile prejudice, Harkabi pointed out that these sentiments are not limited to the State of Israel, and he called for 'discarding those elements' of Judaism that instill or express hostility to outsiders. He said, 'Demonstrating to Orthodoxy that some of its rulings are liable to raise general opprobrium may facilitate the achievement of a modus vivendi between it and the other streams in contemporary Judaism.'

Where are we to find the corpus of ideas concerning gentiles to counter these appalling actions and opinions of the pseudo-messianic

Orthodoxy of the State of Israel? If in them, these days, it is mainly in Reform Judaism – a corps of rabbis bearing a moral concern and, more important, an intellectual system and structure that encourage the Jewish people to think both of itself and the other, to love not only itself but also the outsider. For this reason it is particularly tragic that the Reform movement has become lazy and envious, that it is insecure and accepting of views it should abhor.

And what of Orthodoxy? If the Reform movement exhibits a failure of nerve, Orthodoxy displays a failure of intellect. It is not that the Orthodox are stupid or wrong or venal, merely that their views are irrelevant to the great issues confronting today's world. Except for Yeshiva University Orthodoxy, all of the Orthodox Judaisms of the day (the *haredim*, or ultra-Orthodox, in various guises) exhibit the same enormous incapacity to speak to the Jewish condition.

This is not to suggest that the Orthodox are ignorant of the classical texts of Judaism or that they misrepresent their content. To the contrary, the representation of Torah-true Judaism by the *haredim* is sound on nearly every point. Knowledgeable people can quote chapter and verse of Talmudic writings in support of their position on all issues. That is precisely why the policies and program of the *haredim*, and therefore of the Judaism of the dual Torah, offer no meaningful option for Jews today. We must ask whether the Torah in its received or authentic or accurate version, as the *haredim* represent it, can serve in the twenty-first century. I think it cannot.

The Torah omits all systematic inquiry into the three critical matters of contemporary life: politics, economics, and science. Thus, any Judaism today that authentically realizes the Torah, oral and written, demands that Jews live only a partial life and that those Jews living in Israel dismantle the Jewish state. Jews living in the Diaspora, for their part, lacking a position on politics and economics and science, must simply retreat into ghettos, having no way to cope with the formative forces that shape the world today. The *haredim* want to make us all Amish, and the Jews are not going to agree, even though, right now, more than a few would like to walk out on the world as it is.

The three most powerful and formative forces in all of human civilization today are democracy, capitalism, and science; and on these three subjects the authentic, classical Judaism, accurately represented by the *haredim*, either has nothing at all to say or says the wrong things. The *haredim* can make their extravagant claims on the rest of us only by being parasites: we do the politics, the economics, and the science so they can live their private lives off in a corner.

If we are going to live in the twenty-first century, we require not only the Torah, but also economics, politics and science. World Jewry has no choice but to turn its back on the *haredim*. Would that God had made the world as simple as the *haredim* think it is. So fond farewell to the fantasy that the authentic Torah of Sinai, as the framers of the Babylonian Talmud read it in the seventh century, is, or can ever be, the authentic Torah of the twenty-first century. We shall do and we shall hear, indeed: *today*.

## AND YET: TOMORROW

Were the story to end with the creation of the new Judaisms of the nineteenth and early twentieth centuries, we would face an unhappy ending. But the advent of the twenty-first century marks the beginning of a new age of Judaic system-building. The vital signs are beginning to appear. I point to the formation of a distinctively Judaic politics, taking shape around *Tikkun* magazine, and another among the intellectuals of the right as well. These two intellectual perspectives present two of the three prerequisites of a vital Judaism: a worldview and a way of life. Both of them join the everyday and the here-and-now to an ideal in which people can find meaning in their life together. Whether these political Judaisms can take root in the social worlds of large numbers of Jews and thus constitute not merely theologies and life patterns but 'Israels' – that is, social entities – remains to be seen. Reform, Conservative, Reconstructionism, and western Orthodox Judaisms, as well as Zionism and Jewish socialism-Yiddishism, all formed not merely intellectual positions but social worlds. Their strength lay in transforming organizations into societies, so to speak. So far, *Tikkun* and *Commentary* express more than a viewpoint but less than a broad social movement.

I point further to the *havura* movement, the renewal of Reconstructionism with Arthur Waskow and Arthur Green, the development of an accessible Judaic mysticism by Zalman Schachter-Shalomi, and the development and framing of what we may call a feminist Judaism. Each of these extraordinarily vital religious formations gives promise of establishing a Judaism: a worldview, a way of life, realized within a social entity that calls itself (not necessarily exclusively) 'Israel'. All of these religious formations have identified urgent questions and presented answers that, to the framers, prove self-evidently valid. So I think the long period of no new Judaisms is coming to an end, though it is much too soon to tell which Judaisms, in North America at least, will inherit the greater part of Jewry.

The new Judaisms of the acutely contemporary age will succeed as we increasingly overcome the demographic and cultural catastrophe of the Holocaust. We have in North America a vast Jewish population increasingly capable of sustaining a variety of Judaisms, and we are facing a renewal of Jewish intellectual life in a way that might have stirred envy in even the proudest Jews of Germany and Poland between the wars. The possibility of the development of new Judaisms is helped by the decline of the power of the political and communal organizations that have dominated American-Jewish life in the twentieth century. The corporate model for organized Jewry has shown its limitations. The decay of B'nai B'rith; the demise, on the local scene, of organizations such as the American Jewish Congress; the retreat of the federations from the ideal of forming 'the organized Jewish community' and their transformation into mere fund-raising agencies – these are all indications of decreased organizational power. Jews no longer find interesting a Judaic existence consisting of going to a meeting to talk about something happening somewhere else. Merely giving money, for instance, to help another Jew help a third Jew settle in the State of Israel has lost all credibility. People want hands-on engagement, and the corporate model affords the opposite.

The rejection of the corporate model and the affirmation of the place of the individual at the center of activity now marks the mode of organization of every important new Judaism today. The *Tikkun* conference in New York City is an example of that fact. I see no clear counterpart on the political Judaism of the right, which seems to me to be fragmented in social circles such as those surrounding *Commentary*, the *National Review*, and *Chronicles*. Professors of Jewish origin in the new National Association of Scholars, for example, hardly form the counterpart to the social formation made visible at the *Tikkun* conference. In this regard, the left has provided the right with a model.

We no longer live in what Max Weber called a bureaucratic 'iron cage', and the fulfillment of our calling to be Israel comes only through our immediate and complete engagement with our highest spiritual and cultural values – whatever our Judaism tells us these are. We have, in other words, survived the twentieth century.

# 2 We've Won; So What?

*Moment* 2 (1977), 61–62

W e asked the federations to be instruments of Jewish survival, instead of engines of assimilationism, and they are.

We demanded that the United Jewish Appeal (UJA) build the Jewish loyalties of younger people, rather than relying on the Jewish loyalties of the older generation, and it does. We looked for means of achieving meaningful social relationships within Jewish community structures, and, in my case, I called for the re-creation of the ancient *havurot*, which I translated, 'fellowships'. Lo, we have *havurot*, and some even call themselves 'fellowships'.

We wanted to see the Holocaust remembered, and so it is. We sought to focus on Zionist perspectives as the center of Jewish community discourse, with the issue of Israel at the heart of our collective life. There it stands, at the very center.

We pleaded for the improvement of Jewish education and for attracting talented young people into careers in that field, for greatly increasing the support of Jewish education on the part of federations and welfare funds. We have been heard. We wanted more help for Hillel. All over the country, federations take a hand in the revival and improvement of Hillel on the campuses. We wanted Jewish learning to percolate upward to the campuses. In virtually all important universities at which sizable numbers of Jewish students are located it is possible to take many worthwhile courses in Jewish subjects.

Shall I continue? The list is very long. Back in the 1950s, 20 years ago, a handful of lonely voices, taking seriously the religious revival, the 'return of the third generation', yet concerned at the same time with 'the vanishing Jew', wanted the Jewish community to become both Jewish and Judaic. In those days we used to analyze the allocations of federations and demonstrate how the money of Jewry is used to starve institutions and organizations that make Jews Jewish and to support those that are non-sectarian. There were jokes about the three religions of democracy: Catholicism, Protestantism, and non-sectarianism. We appealed to the memory of the Holocaust. We evoked the achievements of the State of Israel. We called forth recognition of the meaning of our own historical experience – Holocaust, rebuilding.

And they listened to us. That is not to say any one of our small number was heard. It is only that the things we repeated in articles in obscure places and in important ones, in speeches in every Jewish setting, began to make sense to many people. We were the first to say what, in time, many would be glad to hear, what would, in time, become an almost conventional wisdom.

I do not think we can be more of a *Jewish* Jewish community than we are now. Obviously, we have yet much progress to make along the paths we currently travel. But it is difficult to think of any goal we envisioned 20 years ago that is not by now part of the institutional routine of the organized Jewish community. All the words we proposed as fighting slogans are now clichés, because our slogans have become programs. Our agendum has been adopted. Among the doers and makers of Jewry, what to us was fresh and important has become the norm – and even normal.

For two decades I was a minor prophet of this Judaic renaissance. I now find all that I have described above accurate – and disappointing and empty. I have the unhappy sense that the things I laid before all who would listen 20 years ago were not the right things. I have been a false prophet, and I know it now. What I prophesied and preached has come to pass, but what has come to pass is not really very important. The measure of true prophecy, we recall, is that what the true prophet says will be comes to be. These things which 20 years have brought into being are what I wanted them to be. But they do not mean what I thought they would mean.

How so? I have a sense that we have come just about as far as an ideology of Jewishness-as-survival can take us. There are large gaps in our inner lives as Jews that are yet to be filled. All of the positive programs and policies have not really attended to those inner questions which await attention. What I have in mind is not complicated. I am moved by the renewal of Jewishness and the resurgence, even, of Judaism. But why do I feel a sense of distance and emptiness, incompletion, when I should perceive fulfillment? We did not want to be the last Jews on earth – in North America, at least – and we are not. We have won. But what have we won?

What does it mean to us to be Jews and part of a continuity of Jews? When we have done our Jewish thing, how are we changed? How are we deeper people and wiser people? How are our lives more serene, our inner beings more whole and complete? We asked, and we were answered. But did we ask the right question? Now that we have done all that we can do to insure our endurance as a distinct and distinctive people on earth, *so what*? What is it that we want to sustain and why?

I have spent my scholarly life asking these questions of the most influential period and document in the history of Judaism. The period is Judaism in late antiquity, from the destruction of the Second Temple to the rise of Islam; the document is the Talmud. What is it all about in that terribly critical time and place? What is the meaning, in its setting, of that extraordinarily influential document?

As I reflect on the work of nearly two decades, I find in it some continuing themes, of which the most important is this: How is it that the inner life, the life of the mind of people who are learning, should have come to the fore as the single most important (though not the only) expression of piety and faith in Judaism? Why is it that Moses should be described as a rabbi, a man who learns Torah? Why is it that God should be portrayed as a master – not merely revealer – of Torah, and that the angels in heaven should be described as disciples of Torah?

Consider that the first seven centuries of our era saw the rise of the three great religions of the West: Christianity, Islam and the form of Judaism we have known. Keep in mind that, in the same period, the great and orderly polity of antiquity came to an end. Then you realize that it was in a time of revolutionary change that the classical definitions of what we want to sustain and the reasons for sustaining it took shape.

For Judaism not only says that the Jews should continue as a distinctive group. Its holy books also say *why* they should do so, and, still more important, *what* they should do as an enduring people. Now I do not suggest for one minute that the next stage in our collective adventure in North America consists of building more yeshivas or (among the modernists, like myself) going off and getting Ph.D.s in Judaic studies. I am only pointing out that there must be more of an answer than we have yet found to the question of what we do when we have succeeded in securing a fair measure of continuity.

I remember in the 1950s and 1960s that the one question I would hear wherever I lectured was, 'Why should I be Jewish?' I don't hear that question anymore. I suspect the reason is that those who wanted out have gotten out. I should guess that the intermarriage rate will now level off and perhaps even decline slightly. But I wish I now might hear the question, 'Now that we are Jewish and plan to stay that way, *so what*?' It is to answer that question that Judaic scholarship in all its forms, historical, theological, literary, is brought into being. I could not tell people why they should be Jewish, although somehow, it is clear, they know the answer. But I should be able to tell people what lay at the center and heart of Jewish existence for times past, and even suggest what may find a place in the heart and soul of Jewry now.

For I perceive, in all this success, this resurgent Jewishness and even rediscovered Judaism, an inner space, an emptiness that cannot and should not be filled solely by saving Soviet Jews, remembering the Holocaust and learning from it, making pilgrimages to the State of Israel, working for the federations, even by regular participation in synagogue life. The ideology of peoplehood-and-history, whether expressed in fund drives or in classrooms, calls for the giving of money and the learning of historical facts, is necessary. Its effects are laudable. Yet it is insufficient.

I am not sorry that we no longer ask: 'Why be Jewish?' In seeking to answer that question, we stumbled across ways of Jewishness that satisfied, for a time; learning how to be Jewish, asking 'why' became pointless. Now it is time for us to ask the next question, and to pursue the next answer: For what? How shall we remember and invent a Judaism that speaks not only to the necessity of survival of this great historic people, but that speaks also to the compelling needs of each individual Jew, of each of us who searches for meaning, for life, for understanding, for self?

# 3 Wanted, Dead or Alive
## Moment 4/3 (1979), 61–64

One of my sons, when he was a child and wanted to know how things were when I was his age, would ask: 'What were things like when you were alive?' Just as the young cannot imagine that their parents enjoy, or even know about, sex, so they cannot comprehend that their parents are alive in the same way in which they are alive.

About sex, they are wrong. About being alive, they have a point. My generation – the third generation of American Jewry – began somewhere, cared and dreamed and worried about some things, and is now finished. By and large, the things we wanted to make happen have happened, and the young see us as finished. I think they are right.

I grew up in West Hartford, Connecticut, a suburb of Hartford, when only a few Jews lived there. I remember, about being Jewish, only two things: first, I thought it was something to do only in private; and second, I wondered whether it would be done at all for very much longer.

I came, please understand, from a very Jewish – though not at all Judaic – family, so I was one of those who cared about being Jewish. I was, for example, one of the only people I knew who voted for Roosevelt in 1944 (as a sixth grader), which was a very Jewish thing to do in West Hartford (except when it was a very Irish thing to do). And I was one of the only people I knew who was aware that something of great importance was happening in 1948. Most of the Jewish kids I knew were not much interested in being Jewish and did a very good job of adjusting their appearance and behavior to match their lack of interest. My mother, a matriarch of the second generation, was proud of not having been born in 'Europe', which was less a place than a state of mind. (In our house, everything vulgar and tasteless was 'European'.) She called me Jackie, until my voice deepened and she switched to Jack. But it was only when I turned 21 and applied for my first passport that I discovered that my name, my only name, the name bestowed upon me at birth and hidden from me for more than two decades, was not Jackie, was not Jack, but was, in fact, Jacob.

Those few of us who thought about being Jewish, who were part of the generation that was too young for the the Second World War, too old for Vietnam, who missed Korea by virtue of student deferments, that seemed stuck in the cracks between great historical events, we worried about the Jewish future. We knew how few we were, and we knew how different we were from our grandparents, how far removed from the manifest wellsprings of faith and commitment and culture, and we could not imagine what a Jewish future might be built upon, from what new springs it would draw its strength.

Specifically, we could not know and did not guess that most of our friends, the ones who did not know and did not care, the ones who were busy 'waspifying' themselves, would one day marry Jews and join synagogues and temples and choose to live near other Jews and care about Israel and all the rest: that they would want to be Jews.

The mystery of the third generation: Jewish but not too Jewish. Not so Jewish that you stop being an American. We knew about that from our grandparents, who had remained too European ever to become Americans. Our parents tried to overcome the alienness, and succeeded. They became undifferentiated Americans, to everyone except themselves. We, in our turn, became for a time what our parents wanted us to be – undifferentiated Americans, to everyone, ourselves included.

Those of us who knew from early on that the Jews were supposed to last, who wanted the Jewish connection to survive, were, as I have said, few in number. I recall that one day, when I was in the ninth grade, I was walking along Farmington Avenue when a terrible thought occurred to me. A time would come, I realized, when the rabbi of our (Reform) temple would be dead, and my father, too, would die. Then I would be the last Jew on earth – or, at least, on Farmington Avenue in West Hartford. That was the day I decided to become a rabbi, a decision I promptly shared with the whole world. Years later, it is what those who knew me then most remember: 'He was the one who wanted to become a rabbi!'

What I really wanted to be and to become, of course, was a Jew. But I must have sensed that for our generation, being Jewish would require a special kind of effort and commitment. It had to become a vocation, because, left to flourish in a less explicit environment, it would not flourish at all. There being no longer a sustaining environment, it would wither. One had to set out to discover Judaism and self-consciously to make a Jew out of oneself, because we had neither encountered it nor been invited, nor, perhaps, even permitted to encounter it as we grew up.

The thing we wanted most was to be part of a community that would share our concern for 'being Jewish', whatever that might mean. In our day, that meant finding others who shared that most peculiar wish – in seminaries, in youth movements, in a few other scattered places. When we found those places, we used them to try to expand the Jewish possibility, to make the entire community a congenial place for our Jewish aspirations.

That is why the work of my generation is now over. We won the fight. Think about it: if there was an 'organized Jewish community' back when I was growing up, it was so remote that we never heard about it. In towns such as ours, federations did not yet exist or, if they did, scarcely thought of themselves as anything more than welfare agencies for the distressed. The Jewish community center was inaccessible, had no program that I can remember hearing of. There were few camps of Jewish content (though I went to a camp where everyone was Jewish), no youth movements to speak of (except for misfits). I never knew about the Sabbath; I never saw a sukkah. I remember how shocked I was, when I came to Oxford, to meet young Jews of intellectual distinction who knew the grace after meals – yes, the *birkat hamazon* – and said it. When I was at Harvard, the few observant Jews, almost all the sons of rabbis, were curiosities.

A Jewish community? To be built from what? Where were the people? Where were the models? That is what we wanted to know, and there was no answer save as we ourselves, we few, were ready to be the people, to provide the models. But to make that work, to make it last, to make it possible for our children to step easily into a living community, we had to develop a public agenda as well. We had to force the Jewish community to resolve its own ambivalence, in order, I suppose, so that we could resolve ours. Either become Jewish, really Jewish, whatever that might come to mean, be made to mean, or stop bothering, stop insisting on the difference, stop insisting even on survival.

Accordingly, we approached the community back in the late 1940s and early 1950s with a very peculiar set of demands. I remember, for instance, my earliest writings on the budgets of Jewish federations, published in my father's newspaper (the *Connecticut Jewish Ledger*, which we subsequently sold). I analyzed the budgets of the federation from year to year, and wondered in print what was Jewish about them or it. Later on, our group – for we became a kind of group, we few – went on to ask what was Jewish about Jewish community centers, and again, we found remarkably few answers. We wanted more attention to be paid to the State of Israel than was paid back then, before the earthquakes and revolutions that transfixed the entire community. Ah, there was so much that we wanted!

And we got it. We got it all. We were right to want it; we were right to get it. For the third generation, for the generation that married Jewish but did not know why, that wanted Jewish but did not know how, we provided the structure of organizations and the intellectual underpinnings that today serve as the foundation of organized Jewry in this country. My own three 'projects' were the reform of federations, the formation of *havurot* and the development of Jewish studies in universities. The federations have now become principal vehicles of Jewish expression and continuity; *havurot* multiply and are fruitful; and Jewish studies in universities, both quantitatively and qualitatively, have achieved distinction.

But what we wanted and needed and achieved, we wanted and needed for ourselves, not for those to come. What we accomplished was in response to our own agenda, an agenda that grew out of our own distinctive experience as the third generation. The world of our children is paradoxically different from our own. For them, being Jewish is much less a given than it had been for our parents, less to our parents than to our grandparents. But at the very same time, the *crafting* of Jewish lives, of a Jewish life, is no longer the laborious, idiosyncratic effort it was for us. They have available to them a Jewish education far richer than we had. Schools, summer camps, youth programs, and, of course, the State of Israel – a set of educational resources that is rich beyond anything we dreamed of. As well as an intermarriage rate larger than we imagined we could bear. As well as a growing number of converts to Judaism. Paradoxes all the time.

Paradoxes that will not be resolved until the fourth generation matures. I am inclined to be hopeful, for that is my nature, but I am also mindful of Arthur Hertzberg's warning: 'There is more passion for Jerusalem and more loyalty to Judaism in the American Jewish community today than we shall have in a decade, *if we do not do some radical things now.*' I agree with Hertzberg, but I also think that we, who are no longer alive, are not the ones to do the things that now want doing, or even to say very much about what those things might be. It is for the living to name those things and to do them, because the things that are to be done, whatever they are, will have to respond to the agenda of need of a generation that was framed by different experiences from our own and is defined by different needs. I do not see that there is much for 'the organized Jewish community' to do these days except not to block or to blight the things that still-unheard-of-names will soon be proposing, perhaps even demanding.

Here I am, about to pass the torch. But first, as they say, a word of advice, from the rocking chair to the runner: don't make the mistakes that I, or others like me, made.

We all got sucked into the value system of the organized community, as it existed in our day. We took seriously what we were not and apologized for what we were. We pretended to think, and some of us even came to think, that there is something more important than ideas. We, who spend our lives in classrooms and in libraries, in studies, pulpits, editorial offices, the places where intellectuals do their work, learned a whole new vocabulary, chose to play on alien turf. We were intellectuals out to reshape the world we loved, the Jewish world, but we neglected our own gifts of intellect and heart, our own vocabulary. Instead, we raised issues of material and mass, issues to which we had nothing special to contribute.

What, after all, were the foci of the reforms we proposed and effected? They had to do with the spending of money, the building of institutions, the ordering of priorities. We wanted the federations to spend their money on consequential things, Jewish things. So they did. And we have learned that money is not the answer. We wanted the synagogues to organize themselves in ways that related to the individual and his needs, in this time, in this place, to permit the formation of groups where people would not feel lost. So they did. We have now learned that organizing an institution in one rather than in another is not the answer. We wanted the community to focus its attention on the great cultural resource represented by the State of Israel, to pay attention, as it had not adequately in the 1940s and 1950s, to the political requirements of Zionism. So it did. We have now learned that our salvation does not lie in the east. The important thing to remember is that we were not frustrated in the pursuit of our goals. Our disappointments derive from other sources, not from our failure but from our success.

How is it that we were so very successful? Chiefly, we came to the community with what it already was coming to know. We were just a bit early on the scene. Even without us, the passionate reformers of the 1950s and 1960s, the things that we like to think we had a hand in making happen, would have happened. They might have taken a bit longer, but they would have happened. The community is in the hands of practical and effective and intelligent people, both lay and professional. They had as much good will as we and as much constructive purpose. They, too, understood what needed to be done, and they did it. They drew on what they had: money and organizational skill.

What we should have known all along, but are only now coming to see, is that neither money nor organization can secure our future. And when we chose to play on alien turf, we added only another layer of veneer to the House of Israel in America, a house that still has no solid foundation. I am not saying that we were wrong to make the choices that we made. I am saying only that those choices are no longer the choices that need making, and it is disheartening to encounter so many, third and fourth generation alike, who persist in fighting yesterday's wars. Our victory in those wars makes possible a new war. To win that war, too, intellectuals will have to stick to their lasts.

The new war is to shape an idea, not a shared consensus, but a consensus worth sharing. There is simply no corpus of intellectually consequential ideas about what it means to be a Jew, here and now, in this time and in this place, to which Jewry today has access. The ideas the rabbis preach must come from somewhere; the policies expressed in federation meetings have to begin with someone. If theology and ideology for contemporary Jewry were merely what people pretend – a conventional apologetic, a ritual of excuses – it might not matter. But ideas do move people; without ideas, people will not move. They will merely twitch, pretending life.

What people think really matters. How embarrassing to have to write these words. Yet the words are no longer obvious. They are not obvious to the formers and shapers of Jewry, because we, who formed the corpus of ideas, of theology and ideology, over the last 30 years, behaved as if they were secondary and actions were primary. As, perhaps they were – for a time. We did not invite the shapers and movers to our turf; we eagerly invaded theirs. We led them to believe that in their distance from the life of the Jewish intellect, from Jewish ideas, in their remove from the soul of Judaism, they could and should do those things that would secure a worthy Jewish present and a viable vision of a Jewish future. They looked to us for ideas; and we talked to them of money and how to spend it.

They had power, and we imagined ourselves impotent. So when they invited us to join them, that is exactly what we did, forgetting that if all we had to offer was a pale imitation of the resources they already had, they would not have wanted or needed to invite us. They did not know how to ask the question, and we did not hear the question they did not ask, the only question we might have been able to answer with some authority. We were too enamored with the trappings. So we lost our voice; we answered other questions, questions whose answers were already known, questions that mattered but that did not require us to answer them. We behaved like directors of agencies: asked for money, competed for money, and offered nothing of what we knew. Pretended to have sophistication. Lost our nerve, our sense of self.

Ideas come first. Vision takes precedence. The educated heart is what creates and shapes our energies to act. Did not the State of Israel begin in the minds of dissatisfied intellectuals? Was it not born as an idea? Was it not shaped by first-class minds? Long before there was a Jewish state, there was the idea of a Jewish state, and there would never have been a Jewish state without that idea. An idea: mostly talk – but what a conversation, and what an impact!

So it is with the great movements of every age. They start in our minds, not in our bellies (*pace* the Communists and the federations alike), not in our bank accounts. And when intellectuals are responsible for events, it is because they develop ideas that are compelling, not because they aspire to positions of power. The seductive attraction of high office subverts the far greater power that intellectuals who do not deny themselves might exercise.

That is the advice: do not be other than what you are. In this context, let those with ideas remain true to their hearts, their minds, their intellects. We are a people to whom a book is an event, a rare insight, an occasion for celebration. I think, for example, of Abram Heschel, who in the late 1950s laid forth an intellectual heritage still not adequately interpreted or understood. His monumental intellectual achievements of that period received no hearing either then or later. It was during the 1960s that he became a public figure and gained a vast and impressive hearing – but not for his distinctive intellectual contribution. I cannot blame him, but I think we would be better off today had he pursued, in his last years, those lines of thought and modes of reflection that in a few brief years yielded *Man Is Not Alone* and *God in Search of Man*. Heschel's public power was vastly greater in the 1960s than it had been in the 1950s. But it was a different kind of power, and it yielded different products, and all of them have now evaporated.

The plain fact is that the future of American Jewry will not be decided by the synagogues, the federations, the centers, the day schools, the hospitals, the American Jewish Committees and the Anti-Defamation Leagues. Nor will it be settled by raising another billion dollars for the State of Israel, nor even a billion for Jewish education and culture. The future of American Jewry will be decided, for better or worse, by the ideas that American Jews have and come to have regarding their future. It will be settled by what the fourth generation manages to achieve by way of a set of ideas. We of the third generation built a building, and that was an important thing to do. It is time now to place a foundation under that building. That has yet to be done. And that foundation does not take dollars. It takes words, and ideas.

# 4 Toward a Jewish Renewal: After the Flood, After the Rainbow

*Moment* 3/5 (1978), 11–16

Last month, 'Holocaust'. This month, Israel Independence Day. A coupling in time that reflects with uncanny accuracy the contemporary Jewish understanding, an understanding that has come to inform virtually every aspect of our communal life – that Jewish life is the story of Holocaust-to-redemption.

What does it mean to be an American Jew these days? For many people, the definition is remarkably straightforward: it means to accept the Holocaust-to-Redemption myth as central to one's theology, even to one's psychology. It means to be seized by the death-and-resurrection metaphor, and to view the world through its lenses. It could scarcely be otherwise. In all of Jewish time, there are not a dozen dates that will be remembered so long as there are Jews to remember things, and two of those dates occurred within our own living memory. It is entirely natural that our lives have been shaped by the events that those dates mark. And it is entirely understandable that in shaping, there has been distortion. We can hardly expect that those still in the thrall of the events will manage the perspective that only distance permits. But that does not free us from the need to ask not only what it means to be a Jew in contemporary America, but also what it *might* mean, what it *should* mean.

## HOW WE GOT HERE

Ours is the fourth generation. It is different from what we have known until now. Assimilation is no longer an interesting or an attractive ideology. By and large, those who wanted out of Jewish life are gone. At the same time, oddly, marriage to non-Jews has become an open (and increasingly popular) choice for those who have stayed Jews. Nor is that choice any longer attended by the guild and recrimination that it invariably invoked a short time ago. More often than not, the non-Jew is received into the Jewish family with relative ease. These apparently contradictory trends describe the world of the fourth generation: unashamedly Jewish, unself-consciously American, open to whatever the world has to say, but still unclear about what to listen for or even how to hear.

How is it that we have come to receive the non-Jew into our midst with such ease? It is because to join the Jewish group is to join a world not very different from the world the non-Jew has left. Indeed, the differences between ourselves and our non-Jewish neighbors have become so trivial that we do a better job, on the whole, of assimilating non-Jews into our midst than of assimilating Russian and Israeli Jews. That, plainly, is because being Jewish is not nearly so distinctive as it once was. It hardly involves profound changes of outlook or behavior; mostly, it implies a shift in cultural and social ambience. The shift, on the whole, is to a higher social, economic, and cultural status; to marry a Jew is to marry up. To marry a non-Jew is also to bring into the Jewish fold people whose knowledge, background and commitment are not much different from the prevailing norms of the Jewish community, and sometimes even to produce fresh energies for the community.

So here we are, in a time of renewed enthusiasm, profound and completed acculturation, substantial non-ideological assimilation, and genuine social integration – a mass of contradictions that provide the context for the next decade of American Jewish life.

It comes as something of a surprise, of course. When, in the crucible of Vietnam, American young people turned against that white, Protestant, middle-class conventional conception of our society which had in their eyes proved its moral bankruptcy, substantial numbers turned instead to their own ethnic roots, with the blacks leading the way. In the light of the third generation of Jewish consensus, one might have predicted that Jews would follow this trend lamely, if at all. For the third generation, which flourished from the end of World War II to the end of the Vietnam War, had adopted as its working slogan, 'Be Jewish – but not too Jewish.' Why 'Be Jewish?' Because anti-Semitism was still a problem; to cease to be Jewish would have been dishonorable. Why 'not too Jewish?' Because that would mean barring access to the American dream. The promised land cannot be entered by those with foreign accents.

But the children of the third generation could not fail to see the contradiction. Some resolved it by not being Jewish at all, a more attractive option during a time when anti-Semitism did not appear to be a clear or present danger. Others chose instead to be massively and militantly Jewish. Whatever the blacks could do, they could do better. But like the Russian Jews who want to be Jewish, their motive has outstripped their competence. The best they have been able to do is to experiment with the forms of 'being Jewish', an experiment that is often religious in its style and empty in its substance. Blacks want soul food? Then we shall have kosher food, and if that proves too difficult, then at least bagels on Sunday. The issue for this generation of good intention was not Judaism but, instead, the visible symbols and signs of 'being Jewish'. The striking modes of Jewishness they have adopted show clearly the results of the assimilation that has gone before.

Thus, one sign of 'being Jewish' that many of the young have adopted is the wearing of the *kippah* under all circumstances. Normally, when we see a *kippah*, we feel entitled to assume many other forms of observance – at least, one would suppose, eating kosher food and observing all aspects of the Sabbath. What, then, are we to make when we see a *kippah*-ed head bent over a hamburger at the local McDonald's? Or what of a group of American kids wearing *kippot* riding the bus in Tel Aviv on the Sabbath?

### WHERE WE ARE: THE HOLOCAUST

The adoption of superficial religious symbols is only one form, and not the most popular, for the new Jewish self-expression. Instead, the majority of newly revived Jews, of whatever age, have adopted as their central path of access to Judaism the Holocaust-to-redemption myth. This tale, with its obvious moral, is drummed into our heads by every medium of Jewish communication. It has become our fixation, the source of our metaphor as of our self-understanding, the primary energizer of Jewish life and the primary axiom of Jewish logic.

How did the Holocaust become so powerful a symbol? Before 1967, it was not. A whole generation had refused to pay attention, to be reminded, to confront. How is it that so suddenly there is a genuine popular response to Jewish theologians who create what they call 'Holocaust theologies', and who hold solemn meetings in cathedrals on 'Judaism after Auschwitz' and the like?

The answer lies in the 1967 War and in the weeks that preceded it. During those weeks, we feared the worst. Unlike others whose fears are born of fantasy, ours are born of memory. We have a name for our worst fears, and the name we have is Auschwitz. In those weeks of May and June, we foresaw the end of the Jewish state, and even – some thought – the end of the Jewish people. We trembled, and we knew, out of our own experience, the fear of destruction. We knew the sense of Auschwitz.

Then, even as we were feeling terror, we knew triumph. The

Holocaust was not merely averted; it was over, it would no longer be
the central theme of Jewish life. We had entered the post-Holocaust
era. And what is that era save the time of salvation, of the Messiah?
When we returned to the Wall, Jewish history as we had known it
came to an end. The fact that the 1967 War created as many problems
as it solved, that the triumph of arms led to a spirit of imperial tri-
umphalism for which, in the end, both the State of Israel and the
Jewish people are still paying the price, facts that were perceived by
only a few.

Then it was that theologians, journalists, publicists, fund-raisers,
organizers, speakers, novelists – the whole phalanx of Jewish public
relations – took up the theme of salvation through politics, the fan-
tastic and hopeless pronouncement of beginning of redemption. A
Messianic fervor swept over the Jewish people, both there and here,
and on that fervor were built the flawed structures of consciousness
and culture that today we see about us. Anyone who could cite a few
passages from Scripture and put on a good cry in public became a
Judaic theologian, and the more tears, the more profound he seemed
to be.

It is a mark of the assimilation expressed through ethnic assertion
that the old Jewish reservation about Messianism is scarcely remembered. To understand our people's long history of nay-saying in the
face of false Messiahs, both Jewish and gentile, we have to know our
people's equally long history of yea-saying to Torah and its claim to
sanctify the present and to regain in the here-and-now a foretaste of
eternity.

Holocaust-and-redemption theology is easy and appeals to people
with no access to Jewish piety, learning, tradition. Further, the powerful appeal well serves the interests of people who know precisely what
they want from our community – the fund-raisers.

So they organize their ghoulish trips to Auschwitz and to
Jerusalem, make the memory of dead people into an instrument
for the guilt and coercion of the living, and represent Judaism as a
religion for cemeteries and battlefields. Judaism, a religion of the
present and the future, affirms life and looks not to Auschwitz, but to
Sinai. But the Judaism of Sinai has not been heard from much these
days, and the life-giving symbols and signs of Torah have been
obscured by clouds of death and hot air. Hitler is represented as a negative symbol, rather than Moses as a positive one. So we are told we
should be Jewish not because God has called us into being, but in
order to spite Hitler.

A more spurious argument has never been put forth onto the stage of Judaic thought, a more ignorant and destructive conception of the wellsprings of Judaism has never been drawn before our people's eyes. But many were served, ignoramuses pretending to be learned, fund-raisers seeking easy access to emotions, as well as people of good intention who had no clear notion of what they had to do to achieve their good intention to be Jewish again.

### WHERE WE ARE: THE REDEMPTION

There is, yet, the other half of the Holocaust-and-redemption theory of Jewish existence, the redemption part. This, of course, has been expressed in the notion that the State of Israel has solved the Jewish problem, has given us reason to be Jewish and therefore serves as the center and the focus of Jewish consciousness. Once more it is obvious that that idea has well-served the practical administrators of Jewry. But it also has spoken to, and for, the Jewish masses, among whom I include myself. To a very real measure our Jewish lives respond first and foremost to what is happening in Jerusalem, and Judaism, as well as contemporary Jewish politics, surely teaches that that is an authentic and healthy Jewish emotion.

Yet it also is the best evidence for my thesis that we are both ethnically assertive and profoundly assimilated. When we get past the fund-raising (and, it is clear, no successful Jewish fund-raising in America and Canada is possible without a massive Israeli component), we must ask: To what extent does the State of Israel, its religion, culture, and intellectual life, shape or even contribute to the shaping of American and Canadian Jewish life?

I find the answer ambiguous. On the one side all of us come to life when the State of Israel is in crisis. The response to the 1967 and 1973 wars is very profound. The emotional commitment of the community surely was tested and found to be authentic and real. On the other hand, when we transcend the emotional concern and begin to ask about cultural and intellectual aspects of American Jewish affairs, the picture is very different.

Thus: to what extent does American Jewry make use of modern Hebrew? We have not sent tens of thousands of young people to study in Israel for summers or for whole school years. If Hebrew was going to be a significant factor in our community, the opportunity is here. Yet with all the investment of young peoples' lives in the study of Hebrew both here and there, we may say that this language is not part of American-Jewish culture.

To what extent is American Jewry involved in the inner life of the

Israeli-Jewish world? Do we read its books and talk about them? Apart from a few novels in English, we certainly do not. Do we follow the everyday events of their politics and institutions? Only in the public press, along with other Americans. Do we gain access to Jewish classics through Israeli scholarship? Apart from a few scholars of European origin and a handful of archeologists and other biblical specialists, Israeli scholarship makes virtually no impact whatsoever on American Jewish intellectual life. It makes slight enough impact even upon the American Jewish scholars who read Hebrew and can mediate the results of Israeli scholarship to the American Jewish public.

In the vast growth of Jewish studies in American universities, the study of Israeli society and culture (when we omit reference to a semester of conversational Hebrew) is minimal. The students are not interested. Neither are their parents. Israeli studies do not form a considerable part of what we understand as Jewish studies, because, I suspect, they do not answer questions we propose to ask when we undertake Jewish Studies.

We need not mince words. Apart from our deep concern for the welfare of the State of Israel and its people, we really are not much interested in the State of Israel or in Zionism. We are all aware of how much the Arabs have done to make Zionism an important issue for the Jewish people, and for that we are grateful. But it is difficult to discern a renaissance of Zionist theory, a reconsideration of classical and perennial issues of Zionist thought, in the current renewal of Zionist loyalty.

So, if we American Jews are Zionists, that does not mean we want to say more than that we are Zionists. We do not for one minute propose to shape our thinking about ourselves in response to the issues of Zionist theory, past or present.


## THE FLAW

My thesis is clear. American Jews over the past decade have entered a period of Jewish assertion, but have yet to make up their minds about what it is that they propose to assert. What they do assert turns out, on close examination, to be a superficial and assimilated thing, even while it looks on the surface to be the most Jewish thing of all. Holocaust-and-redemption theories of Jewish assertion, chugging along with all the power of the mighty engines of Jewish organization al life, on the one side, and fed by the fuel of those deep Jewish emotions to which they appeal, on the other, lead nowhere. The reason is that their basic goal and direction do not relate to the realities in which American Jews live out their lives.

Holocaust-redemption theories speak of a world of historical events, of upheaval, of a world destroyed and recreated, of a human experience of degradation and restoration. But American Jews of the third and fourth generations know about such experiences only in books. They can be asked to pretend they were there, they can make pilgrimages and shiver in Auschwitz, or dance at the Wall. But these are vicarious emotions. We are confronted with a theory of Jewish existence which speaks of a world we do not know, and which carefully ignores the world we do inhabit.

We have lived in a peaceful, progressive, and reasonably prosperous country. The Jews in this country are not weak and persecuted. They are not in need of a refuge. They do not even know the meaning of anti-Semitism in its political sense, and their knowledge of racism is gained from newspapers. True, they do know discrimination and have experienced social and cultural anti-Semitism of various kinds, even the religious sort. But the anti-Semitism that led inexorably to Auschwitz – and therefore, also to Jerusalem – is not part of our experience, and theories of Jewish existence that explain a world of metahistorical evil and eschatological redemption simply do not refer to our humble reality at all.

That is why our theories of what is meant by being a Jew in contemporary America all emerge as flawed. They talk about experiences we have not had, except in our nightmares, and ask us to accept a redemption which does not save us from anything from which we need to be saved, nor promise us a salvation which solves the real problems we must confront.

### WHAT THEN?

First, whatever theory of Jewish existence we propose to shape must be relevant to our situation as human beings, as Jews, as a distinctive group of human beings who choose to be Jews. The particular point of relevance, moreover, must be to those profound human problems that all of us must solve, and which we have to confront together, if our being Jews is to matter at the deepest levels of our lives. Let us face honestly and squarely the very difficult fact that we pretend to ignore: we are deeply assimilated to this country and its life. Just as grotesque as are the Russian refuseniks, who dance in the streets on Simchat Torah, because they know it is a holiday, but are not quite sure what to make of it, so grotesque are we in our ways.

Yet, assimilated as we are, we do choose to be Jews, to assert our Jewishness and to give shape to our lives through Judaism. That too is a difficult fact, which we of course take for granted: as deeply as we are part of the common life, so profoundly do we exhibit signs of being a distinctive group. These then are the parameters of theory. I do not know how we shall fill those outlines with color and meaning. I do know that theories of Jewish existence that ignore who and where and what we are will never serve us for very long.

Second, however, we propose to explore the meaning of our Jewishness and ask what it means to be a Jew here and now, but this exploration – the hard work of learning and discovery – must be done by all of us, not only by a few on behalf of many. Our character as highly educated men and women, our careers at the upper levels of society and politics and economy and industry and education, our commitment to freedom and free thought, our acknowledgement of our independence and our respect for our own judgments – these traits cannot be ignored when we undertake the quest, in the sources of Judaism and of Jewish culture, for a usable past and a credible future.

If there is anything pernicious in the Holocaust-and-redemption theory of Jewish existence, it is that it leaves the ordinary folk with no worthwhile tasks, no meaningful assignments. No theory of Jewish existence will speak to us which says only, 'Give and be saved. Cry and feel saved. Make a trip to Israel and be forever saved.' No theory of Jewish existence will persuade us of its sense which says only, 'Listen and do what you're told.' Nor will American Jews continue to concede that the true and authentic Jewish life is possible only elsewhere. If they do agree and yet stay just where they are, then their Jewishness will atrophy and die.

Before us all is the task of framing a vision and a hope, of shaping a purpose and a dream, worthy of our situation as Jews, relevant to our lives, appropriate to our condition as free and self-reliant men and women, and above all authentic to our calling as part of the Jewish people, the Israel that forms the center of human history and destiny.

# 5 Why I am Not an Ethnic Jew, Why I am a Religious Jew

Jewish Spectator 61/3 (1996–97), 16–19

I am not an ethnic Jew because ethnic Jewishness trivializes the Torah, turning commandments into customs, the sublime into mere ceremony. Ethnic Jewishness closes off all access to the Torah and (by definition) to God, who is made manifest in the Torah. And I am a religious Jew, that is to say, I practice Judaism because only in the practice of the faith do I gain access to what the faith conveys, which is knowledge of God as God wishes to be known. At stake in Judaism, a.k.a. the Torah, is humanity's encounter with God, and at stake in Jewishness is mere group continuity, lacking all transcendent standing and calling and purpose. Ethnic Jewishness recalls the psalmist's warning, 'if the Lord does not build the house, they labor in vain that build it'.

To practice Judaism, you must have a minyan (ten Jews), but to identify as an ethnic Jew (in the *Golah*, the Diaspora) you need only yourself, your personal life and preferences. Ethnic Jewishness defines the Jews as a group of people sharing a common ancestry and culture. The building block of ethnic Jewishness is the individual who possesses a Jewish heritage by reason of ancestry and possibly also through education and personal identity. But to be a Jew by religion, that is, to form that Israel of which Scripture and tradition and liturgy speak, you must be one of a minyan. Religious Judaism defines the Jews as 'Israel', meaning the kingdom of priests and holy people that assembled at Sinai and conducts its pilgrimage through history. The difference between the ethnic Jew and the religious Jew or Judaist – we may borrow from the great British scholar of Judaism, Raphael Loewe, the term 'Judaist', meaning a Jew who practices Judaism – is profound.

The ethnic Jew finds personal identification in 'being Jewish', and this may or may not have a bearing on community engagement. But the Judaist defines life in terms of family and community and takes up a position within 'Israel', the holy people, that is never utterly private, personal, or individual. The ethnic Jew appeals to a common history and a shared culture, the Judaist, to a divine vocation. The ethnic Jew identifies Jewishness through cultural and ethnic assimilation, learning to like the foods and sing the songs. For the religious Judaist, some-one enters Israel, the holy people, through an act of religious turning or conversion, a rite of supernatural weight (immersion or baptism, circumcision for males), and a confession of the faith witnessed by an appropriate Beth Din, rabbinical court.

What difference does it make whether Jews see themselves as an ethnic group or a religious community? At the present time, in North America, most Jews outside of small circles of Orthodoxy on the one side, and Reform on the other, see themselves as an ethnic group, part of which may practice a culture involving, or deriving from, a religion. They may belong to synagogues and participate on occasion in some rites, particularly rites of passage and those involving the home and the family. Consequently, ethnic Jews see the synagogue as a medium for the transmission of the ethnic culture to a new generation. But they find themselves alien from much that the synagogue does; they pick and choose, within the program of the synagogue, those occasions and events that fit the ethnic pattern they find affecting. Only a small part of the Jewish population of any city actually practices a Judaism, whether Orthodox or Reform or Conservative, within the framework of transcendence that Judaism means to evoke. Even observant Jews appeal to the concept of tradition, a secular and cultural category, in place of commandment. The rites represent what 'our people' has always done; this is how it has always been, and it carries its own historical imperative. When spoken in the name of religion by essentially secular Jews, the most paradoxical language that the tradition invokes is, 'who has sanctified us by his commandments and commanded us to ...' If you want to penetrate into the full extent of the ethnicization of Judaism the religion into the ethnic culture of a secular group, examine most of the sermons rabbis preach. On the holy days, in preference to theological themes, rabbis frequently choose political subjects having to do with the State of Israel or public policy in the United States.

American and Canadian Jews who regard themselves as loyalists and activists see themselves in the main as an ethnic group, rather than a religious community. Canadian Jewry, which Americans have always admired for its intense Jewishness, has carried the ethnicization of Judaism still further than have Jews in the USA. That is because Canada, since the Second World War, has gone farther than any other country in defining itself as an ethnic mosaic, preserving and honoring a vast number of cultures, privileging none but sustaining all. From a nation of two cultures – the English and the French – Canada has become a nation of many cultures, the first truly multcultural country in a post-nationalistic world. Ethnic difference now defines the norm. It is quite natural for Canadian Jews to sidestep all of the problems that religion carries in its wake and to define themselves in terms of the ethnic components of Jewishness, that is to say, involvement with the State of Israel, memorialization of the Holocaust, and the teaching of the history, traditions, languages, and cultures of the Jews as the substance of the Jewish ethnicity of the Canadian future. All of these components of Jewish ethnicity satisfy the requirements of culture: they are this-worldly, deal in facts not faith, and do not address matters of conscience, character, or consciousness in the way that the religion Judaism does.

American Jews also receive mixed messages. People understand that Americans will practice diverse religions or no religion at all. It is equally clear that the country finds itself dismayed when religious difference enters the public arena, and would on the whole prefer religion to be a personal and private matter, outside the framework of public policy. Americans expect people to differ about religion and accept that difference, but regard as illegitimate (the language used is 'un-American') any effort at introducing religion into public affairs. In regard to the legitimacy of ethnic difference, it is taken for granted that ethnicity will flourish, so long as all speak American English and share the common culture of the country. In private life, all will more or less conform to a single pattern, want the same things, define success in much the same way. How have American Jews responded? It is with a mixture of Judaism and Jewishness. We practice the religion Judaism at home and in family situations. But for public affairs, community activities, we have invented a version of secular Jewishness: Holocaust memorials, political action for the State of Israel.

Both Canadian and American secular Jewishness lays heavy emphasis on the matched symbolic structures and systems represented by the Holocaust, on the one side, and the State of Israel, on the other. We appeal to the Holocaust as the defining moment in the Jews' history, and the Holocaust is called upon to explain why we should be Jewish and do Jewish things – so as not to hand Hitler any more victories, so as to hear the commanding voice of Auschwitz, in the language of the Canadian-Israeli theologian Emil Fackenheim. We appeal to 'the centrality of Israel', meaning that we look to the State of Israel to fill with content the Jewishness that we espouse. To the Holocaust and to 'the centrality of Israel' the federations and welfare funds and United Jewish Appeal make their appeal, giving us in practical terms the counterpart to commandments, a this-worldly expression of an intangible but very real faith. We are thus called upon to give money, lobby for Israeli and Jewish ethnic concerns, and, in the USA, to practice liberal politics, all in the name of ethnic Jewishness. Trips to Israel, sequences of unsuccessful efforts to learn Hebrew, above all constant concern with Israeli politics and foreign policy – these form the substance of the public life of Jewry.

For most of my life I have accepted as inseparable both convictions: the ethnicity of the Jews and the religiosity of Judaism. I have also criticized the Jewishness of Holocaust and the State of Israel – the Jewishness of blood and iron – because it is a Jewishness focused upon a world we do not inhabit, experiences we have not had, a present that has little to do with us in our homeland, and a future that we cannot begin to imagine. Few of us, and none of our children, have experienced the Holocaust, and while we cherish the memory of those who were murdered and will always remember what happened, we speak of other peoples' world, not our own. The same is true of 'the centrality of Israel', which asks us to define as illegitimate our authentic existence in the everyday world and to aspire to live somewhere else, or, at least, to feel guilty and inferior for not living where we do not live. Both components of Jewish ethnicity I have argued lead elsewhere than to the core of our existence as human beings: where we live, how we live. Neither component addresses the critical issues of a human life: why we live and to what we aspire. Indeed, I even announced in the *Washington Post* (and, it turned out, many other newspapers in 20 languages), that 'America is the promised land, the best place to be a Jew.'

What I thought I was saying was, we live here. That means, we must think this is the best place to be a Jew, whatever we may say out of courtesy and dissimulation in public and to the Israelis. We have not got the slightest intention of emigrating to the State of Israel. Most of those who wanted out have gotten out. With three-quarters of a million Israelis in the USA, we may well claim Washington as our Jerusalem, and George Washington as our Moses. That's what I thought I was saying. What I thought I was doing was to call the bluff of everyone in organized Jewry, for I had committed a huge public heresy in saying out loud what everyone thinks, but no one cares to confess in public.

In that context, until very recently, I have found my place among the ethnic Jews who also practice Judaism. It is only now that I have come to call into question the very viability of the ethnic dimension and to ask myself whether, in affirming the ethnic along with the religious, we are able to practice Judaism at all. That is to say, I am not an ethnic Jew not because I do not feel the same sentiments, respond to the same emotions, like the same foods, enjoy the same pleasures, and cry at the same memories as everybody else. Nor do I reject ethnic Jewishness as an option for myself merely because I think it has manifestly failed in its mission, which is to make Jews Jewish and to keep them that way. Now that we have raised the first and second generations, with the highest rates of intermarriage American Jewry has ever known, I regard ethnic Jewishness as a colossal catastrophe. Every study has shown a clear correlation between practice of Judaism and low rates of intermarriage, indifference to Judaism and high ones. Ethnic Jewishness and all its works and ways have now to be rejected and dismantled. There is a different reason. *It is because I now wonder whether Jewish ethnicity may not make it impossible for us to practice Judaism at all.*

We hold, in the Torah (a.k.a. Judaism), the heritage of Sinai as prophets and sages have formulated that heritage. What takes place at Sinai is God's self-manifestation to humanity through the people gathered together for the encounter. For nearly the whole of recorded history, the holy community of the faithful, which calls itself 'Israel' and finds its record in Scripture (the written Torah), has celebrated that event of self-revelation with the response, 'we shall do and we shall obey'. The Torah, written and oral, then sets forth the details. It is in the details that God lives. In these sentences I believe I have summarized the affirmation of holy Israel through all time, the truth upon which rock we have built our polity. The language that I have just used must simply baffle the secular Jew, for whom the Torah is a history book (except when it can be shown not to contain history), a collection of facts that bear their own self-evident meaning. Such a Jew by definition does not know or seek God. The secular Jew uses the word 'Israel' to speak of the State of Israel and knows nothing of the sanctity of Israel, God's first love, that forms the foundation of the Torah that is Judaism. Then the details of the Torah – whether food taboos, time taboos, or marriage taboos – come forth as customs and ceremonies, some to be noted, some not, depending upon private tastes: lobster and shrimp through the year, matzah on Passover, for instance.

Secular Jewishness lacks context. If the context for Passover, which many observe, is the intrusion of the Eternal into time to meet Israel at Sinai, then what sense has the Haggadah to those who gather to celebrate a long ago event, which, as a matter of historical fact, probably never happened, and certainly did not happen the way the Torah says? To state matters more generally, taken one by one, the details make no sense; taken all together and all at once, they make a sublime statement. What fails, therefore transcends the fault of subjectivity, the picking and choosing; what lacks is comprehension of the whole, the very capacity to understand the detail in its context as part of a whole and complete statement. The event may be moving, but its message is lost.

Curiously, an acutely contemporary instance comes to us in the *Commentary* magazine symposium (August, 1996) on the condition of Jewish belief. In it, the editor astutely challenged a variety of Jews, nearly all of them claiming to practice the religion, Judaism, to show what kind of discourse they are capable of sustaining in conversation with the Torah. He asked questions of belief: do you believe thus and so, and he raised questions of politics and sociology as well as of theology. To some of its participants – Joseph Polak among the Orthodox, Lawrence Hoffman among the Reform, and myself – the editor's questions form a challenge: they ask not what *I* believe. Rather, I am not an 'I' but only part of a 'we', that is, 'we, Israel'. The sole authentic discourse sustained by the Torah insists on the 'we' that a minyan represents. But a fair number of the respondents missed the editor's subtlety and answered with that very 'I' that, on its own, transforms theological discourse into a mere response to a public opinion survey. In context, that marks the borders of an utterly secular, private, and personal realm. So people wrote not about knowing God in the Torah, but finding God (as though God were lost) in emotion or in personal discovery in nature or the like. Not a few of the players wrote as though Sinai had never taken place. From the perspective of the Torah, a fair number of those who wrote in *Commentary* cannot be called *talmideh hachamim*, and, much to my puzzlement, even some who in fact are great scholars of Judaism in our time wrote like *am haratzim*, people utterly ignorant of the Torah. So secular has Judaic public discourse become that even the acknowledged scholar communicates idiosyncratically and subjectively, like an ethnic Jew, with the capital 'I' at the head.

Some years back the great philosopher, Alisdair McIntyre, wrote an astonishing book in which he maintained that we have lost the power even to understand the classical writings of philosophy, so that we can no longer gain access to our tradition of ethics. We are in the position of chemists without the oxygen theory, of physicists who know no mathematics. We can do the experiments, but we cannot explain their results. It is that moment at which the great tradition is utterly lost and beyond recovery to which I refer when I claim that ethnic Jewishness has failed. Ethnic Judaism values tradition but not Torah, nationhood or peoplehood but not the Israel or the holy people called by God. Ethnic Jewishness seeks continuity with the old songs, the old foods, the old feelings, but it turns away from the ever-renewed encounter with the living God that gives the songs their power, the foods their flavor, the feelings their power to frame sensibility. That is not because religious Jews rarely intermarry, and ethnic Jews commonly do so. The ethnic connection can go forward, if the children choose, in the family heritage of a Jewish grandfather, as the Nazis said in the Nuremburg laws and as the State of Israel's citizenship statute on the 'ingathering of the exiles' has ruled. Ethnic Jewishness fails because it affords access to a tradition of which it can make no sense, to a continuity vacant of all human value, and to a peoplehood lacking any vocation beyond self-perpetuation.

I choose religious Judaism over secular Jewishness and I affirm my vocation within Israel, the holy people, but not within 'the Jewish people', whether nation or ethnic group. I find the core of this conclusion in the way in which our sages of blessed memory read the written Torah's account of the fall of Adam and Eve from Eden. Our sages see Israel as the counterpart to Adam and Eve, and they see the pattern of our existence in time ('history') as counterpart to the pattern of human destiny: the fall from Paradise. But then, so our sages maintain, Israel is not only the counterpart to Adam but also the opposite: in Eden humanity lost, but at Sinai humanity regained, that perfect relationship with God that prevailed at the moment of creation – the perfect Sabbath – when the Torah records: 'God saw all that He had made, and found it very good ... and God blessed the seventh day.' The sages proceed to tell us that, Israel's own story recapitulates the story of Adam and Eve, the exile from the land comparing with the exile from Eden. But, they hasten to add, with the Torah, Eden is regained, 'today, if you will it'.

# 6 Since I'm Jewish, This Must be Judaism

*Jewish Spectator* 64/2 (1999), 5–7

When religion becomes a matter of personal opinion, then morality gives way to impulse and whim, and sentimentality rules. Private religion appeals to the feeling of the moment and, under such conditions, learning and tradition no longer govern. What is gained by the relevance of the moment is vastly outweighed by what is lost.

The Reformation began the long process of rendering religion personal, climaxing in the privatization of the religious consciousness, the divorce of religion from the social order. The conviction that the 'I' forms the criterion of all things sublime – the grotesque 'Here-I-stand-I-can-do-no-other' misunderstanding of the Protestant conscience – echoes reformers' critiques of the corporate and public in religion. In the case of Evangelical Christianity, religious individualism insists that God intervenes in each individual's life.

In Reform Judaism, born in the heart of Evangelical Christian Prussian Germany, the stress on what the individual finds personally meaningful is sacrosanct. Both Evangelical Christianity and Reform Judaism secure a place for the radically isolated individual, for the integrity of the individual's conscience, for the individual's right to be wholly unique in the encounter with God. These tenets, more than most, characterize the religious bias of Americans in general, and the modern variations of Reform and Conservative Judaism in particular.

In the United States, with its stereotypical bias against history and tradition and social authority in favor of individual autonomy, there is an acute elevation of the individual. The practice of Judaism in contemporary America has shown the grotesque possibilities of the privatization of religion. Apparently everything begins with me, personally, this morning, here and now. It is the unique amalgam of the religious and the ethnic in the corporate life of Jewish Americans, who are Jewish and therefore regard themselves as primary data for the definition of Judaism that embodies these possibilities. If 'Judaism' is 'the religion of the Jewish people', then whatever religion the Jewish people practice is 'Judaism'. And then, get out of the way, because here comes do-it-yourself-Judaism that acknowledges no authority, tradition or communal structure.

A local synagogue in Clearwater, Florida, for example, has invented a new religious rite for itself. Thirty years ago, the rabbi started what he called 'the chain of tradition'. He gave silver ID bracelets to young people who were completing their religious education at the Temple. The soon-to-be graduates wore them. Then they linked their bracelets together and carried them to the altar; the bracelets were 'blessed' and then put into the ark, along with the scrolls of the Torah. There are now 571 bracelets linked together – so reports Maureen Byrne in the *St Petersburg Times*. The rabbi explained, 'It deepens my faith in the continuity of Judaism and the viability of the people. We speak of a chain of tradition in Judaism from generation to generation. We will pass on our tradition, one link at a time.'

Using this language, the rabbi invokes a key image of Judaism, 'a chain of tradition'. The notion of a chain reminds us of the teaching of Moses to Joshua, of Joshua to the prophets, of the prophets to the sages, and onward through time to the teachings of the rabbis of the Talmud – and then to us. But the tradition that is passed on in a chain from Sinai forward consists of religious teaching. 'Tradition' is not a trinket, but content. The Torah deems 'tradition', for example, to be Hillel's famous saying: 'If I am not for myself, who will be for me? And if I am only for myself, what am I? And if not now, when?' That is the heart of Judaism: substance. I do not believe that, in the centuries since Sinai, anyone before the rabbi in Clearwater ever imagined that by 'tradition' people could mean linking person A to person B to person C and putting their names on ID bracelets and making the bracelets into a chain – and placing the chain at the focal point of public worship, no less, 'one link at a time'.

There is a certain logic to this weird 'new tradition'. The rite conforms to the theory that Judaism is pretty much an ethnic culture, with some God-talk tacked on for the fastidious. It is not a matter of divine imperatives, whether about discipline in food or about discipline in sex. It is about customs and ceremonies, not kosher by the law of the Torah but kosher-style pickles and kosher-style hot dogs – not Judaic, but Jewish-style. If all that matters is my own initiative, the imperative of how I feel this morning, then what else should join the Torah in the holy ark if not an ID bracelet with my name on it? Certainly my holy 'self' seems to belong more in an individualized world than do the commandments of God at Sinai speaking at dawn and dusk in the rhythm of creation. In the language of Judaism, 'Israel' in this classic framework is not commanded to reproduce itself or to worry about its ethnic future. The destiny of the Jew is 'to love the Lord your God with all your heart, with all your soul, and with all your might'.

The Clearwater 'tradition' of 30 years' standing may trivialize, but at least it does not debase tradition. In Winnipeg a few years ago I saw another 'new tradition' at a certain synagogue and this one represents utter corruption. In most synagogues, the Torah scrolls are treated with utmost respect. The scrolls are carefully protected, kept in a sacred spot, removed for declamation with much solemnity, with the song, 'This is the Torah that Moses set before Israel at the command of the Lord.' It is not an object to be manhandled or joked with. To celebrate the festival of Simchat Torah (which means 'rejoicing over the Torah'), people read from the Torah and walk in procession around the synagogue carrying the holy scrolls and singing prayers.

In Winnipeg on the evening of Simchat Torah, in place of the processions, the declamation, and the singing, the conservative rabbi removed the Torah from the ark without prayer and song, and stretched it open entirely, from Genesis through Deuteronomy, the pieces of the parchment held by the entire congregation in a huge circle around the room. Then, wearing an Uncle Sam costume, the rabbi (apparently confusing this holiday with Purim) proceeded to jump around the room. Bouncing from place to place with enormous enthusiasm, he pointed to the passage in the Torah at which a given story took place: 'Look, here is the place where Abraham bound Isaac, there is the spot where Israel crossed the Red Sea, here are the Ten Commandments,' and so on around the room. I think a little rabbinical psychodrama was what the good rabbi had in mind. Instead of 'This Is Your Life!', pandering to the lowest possible common denominator of television's gaga-land, it was a 'This Is Where it Happened in the Torah!'

Here is not ethnic whim, but rabbinical creativity, another 'new tradition'. In general, people avoid touching the Torah's parchment altogether when reading it by using a hand-shaped pointer to keep the place. When the parchment begins to slip from the wooden handles, it is traditionally adjusted not by a bare hand, but by a hand covered with a tallit or prayer garment. If a scroll of the Torah falls to the floor, all those present are expected to fast in mourning for a period of time. If a scroll rips, the ripped parchment is not thrown out, but buried in a formal *geniza*, a special capsule designated for burying objects of holiness. The notion of stretching the entire scroll around a room, literally lowering the Torah to the floor, is a textbook desecration, and clearly an indication of the rabbi's ignorance about the true Jewish expressions of honor. This was no celebration of the Torah; it was a humiliation.

Not knowing what to expect, I had gone to the celebration with a

Jewish woman from Poland. She and I and those with us resolutely refused to join the circle. When we saw the jumping up and down with the scroll and the possibilities of damage and disgrace, not wanting to have to fast and not able to give a plausible warning, we left in horror. I later found out that many American synagogues practice this ritual, one that has spread in popularity in large part due to the internet.

If Judaism is what Jews do, then on what basis can I object to a 'new tradition?' The sanctity of a Torah scroll may be debased in the name of collective enthusiasm and rabbinical cheerleading, but who has the right to complain? I never could fathom the religious experience that people were expected to attain – all in the name of relevance and contemporaneity and personal engagement, I suppose. No one ever explained to me what was wrong with the traditional carrying of the Torah in procession, with song and prayer, in the first place.

If religion is how I feel this morning, then no tradition stands in judgment of what I do, no commandments guide my life, God is not invited to do more than pass an opinion, if that much. The religious community, the culture shaped by centuries of encounter with revelation, the social order formed of universally accepted morality – these weigh in the balance against the radically isolated individual whose conscience outweighs all else. That is why so many traditional circles conceive the Reformation to have represented a tragic calamity for the West, and why Orthodox Judaism in the State of Israel currently will not concede a place to the Reform and Conservative movements in the Jewish homeland.

# 7 Stranger at Home: Myths in American Judaism

*Forum* 39 (1980), 31–38

At issue is American Judaism, not the destruction of the Jews of Europe ('the Holocaust') or the creation of the Jewish State in the eastern Mediterranean (Zionism). But American Judaism, the world-view and way of life of the vast majority of Americans who regard themselves as Jews, shapes its conceptions of meaning out of the materials of events of Europe and the Near East.

Indeed, these events, far from America's shores and remote from American Jews' everyday experience, constitute the generative myth by which the generality of American Jews make sense of themselves and decide what to do with that (sizeable) part of themselves set aside for 'being Jewish'. Stating matters in this way, speaking of 'a part' of the life of an otherwise undifferentiated American, imposes too narrow limits upon our discourse. What is to be called 'the myth of Holocaust and redemption' shapes the day-to-day self-understanding of those who live within the myth. The myth dictates both percep-tions and deeds pertinent to the workaday world of ordinary folk. Thus a sizeable sector of American Jews sees the world along lines expressed within a vision of reality beginning in death, 'the Holocaust', and completed by resurrection of rebirth, 'Israel'.

I want to explore the puzzling frame of mind of people whose everyday vision of ordinary things is reshaped into a heightened, indeed mythic, mode of perception and being by reference to awful events they never witnessed, let alone experienced, and by the exis-tence of a place in which they surely do not plan to dwell or even to visit.

Why do people of the particular social and historical profile of American Jews, that is to say, fully acculturated Americans, with a considerable measure of educational accomplishment, yet occupying one of the lower rungs in the ladder of social esteem and forming, if not a pariah people, also no secure sector of the governing and highly regarded echelons of most towns and cities – why do such people urgently construct for themselves a world in which they do not live, an ark they do not plan to stock and float? Why do they draw upon experiences they have not had, and do not wish to have, for their generative symbols and organizing myths, definitive rites, and deeds of a holy way of life?

To begin with, let us ask the questions to which the myth of 'Holocaust and redemption' – the story of the extermination of European Jewry and the creation of the State of Israel – forms a compelling, and, to believers, self-evident, answer. Indeed, why the slaughter of the Jews of Europe should be turned into 'the Holocaust', a term with – again, to participants – self-evident (even 'unique') meanings and implications has to be found out in the context of the life of the people to whom those meanings and implications prove self-evidently unique.

The important questions to be answered by reference to that component of the normative myth have to be specified. Similarly, why American Jews sustain the contradictory position of deeming the State of Israel to be critical to their own existence as a distinctive, self-sustaining group in American society, and also insisting that they and their future find a permanent place within American society, has to be worked out. Here is a strange sort of civil religion indeed. What sort of Zionism can make sense within this contradictory position? For American Jews find themselves Americans in the streets of Jerusalem, but willfully Jews in their own and their neighbors' consciousness and imagination.

Being a minority, and, as I said, a not much admired and emulated minority, American Jews find themselves persistent strangers, strangers at home, whether the home is here or there, made to feel alien over there, yet more strange at home by what happens, always where they are not. What is puzzling is not that political events – the destruction of a group, the formation of a national state – should generate dislocation in society and thus in peoples' imagination. Social change yields symbol change. It is that the state of dislocation should be made into the permanent, and, if truth be told, normative, condition of a group. The killing of the bulk of Europe's Jews constitutes a social change of profound and lasting consequence. Setting up a Jewish state in the ancient homeland also presents a social change of equivalently fundamental character: social change is symbol change.

The shift in the symbolic life of those Jews fortunate enough to find their way to the Jewish state, the use of the destruction of European Jewry in the self-understanding of that state, the formation of a consequent symbolic structure, with its myth and rites of expression of that myth – these expressions in the context of Israel's civil religion are not difficult to describe and to explain. The incapacity of

American Jews to make sense of themselves in the aftermath of these events, except through the appropriation of exactly the same symbolic structure, myth, and rites – these, as I have said, define the critical problematic of American Judaism.

To state my case simply: if you want to understand Judaism in America, this is the question you must ask. For in the end it is a ubiquitous human dilemma taken up and expressed in a mere idiomatic way within American Judaism. But what that dilemma is and why it takes the forms it does and not some other forms, why, specifically, people choose to work out their sense of themselves and their society in terms essentially irrelevant to their ordinary world and everyday experience, are the questions that others will have to work out.

I can bring you only to the end of that turf on which I too live, the ground that is both not mine and not not-mine, the only land that I know, the only language that I speak, but which, language and land both, I am supposed to regard as someone else's. Why I should be a stranger where I think I should be at home, whether in Jerusalem or Providence, I cannot say. But powerful modes of determining society's norms, both there and here, both without and within, both social and deep within the heart, insist not that I cannot go home again, but that I am not supposed to have a home, not now, not ever, not where I am, and, in the nature of things, not anywhere else. The myth of 'Holocaust and redemption' expresses the persistent and powerful sense of dissonance, in particular, between where I am and the consciousness of who I want to be.

Who are those Jews who respond to the myth of Holocaust and redemption? They form the vast and vital center of American Jewry, a wall-to-wall consensus on the importance of the State of Israel to American Jews' own Judaism, and on the self-evident truths yielded by 'the Holocaust'. The Jews under discussion are those who do not wholly practice the disciplines of Judaism and yet who do not wholly neglect them. They take an active part in the life of the Jewish community, its synagogues, organizations, philanthropies, politics and other political activities, at the same time as living a life essentially void of the spirituality and sensibility of Judaism. They are a community of belief and behavior, for they respond in their guts in a single normative way to the world at large.

In deed and in word there is a deeply felt, profoundly compelling consensus among the American Jews of whom I speak, that is, among nearly everyone outside of the smallest groups of Orthodox observers, and yet including many of them too. This iron consensus involves, as I said, the twin notions of 'Holocaust' and 'redemption', bearing meanings everyone knows, leading to conclusions everyone has reached in advance. These are the Jews of whom I speak, and this is their 'Judaism', that is, their way of life and worldview.

The myth of 'Holocaust and redemption' takes the form that it does because it responds, in particular, to the issues of assimilation and self-hatred. 'The Holocaust' captures that sense of dislocation and fear of the rest of the world that is our lot. It expresses in an extreme way the potentialities or our pariah status. By itself, of course, the destruction of European Jewry could not serve as an organizing myth; the message is too stark and terrifying. But completed by the redemption of the founding and success of the State of Israel, 'the Holocaust' takes on a different dimension. The 'Holocaust' asks the question that the Zionism fulfilled in the State of Israel answers. The pariah people triumphs over its worst catastrophe and creates its home in its ancient homeland.

For American Jews, beset by the challenges of assimilation and overwhelmed with a sense of discomfort at their own (paltry) differences from the majority, *the myth of Holocaust and redemption serves both to express and to give remission from fear; it explains the necessity of being Jewish and places its actuality somewhere else.*

The same myth gives remission from the fear by its reference-point, the State of Israel, which is a refuge from the nameless fears of the pariah people; and at the same time, it gives a center and core to the meaning of being Jewish. In all, the myth as it is framed and believed in this country addresses itself to the human condition of American Jewry.

This is why the myth expresses those self-evident meanings that, nowadays, people perceive. What has happened to turn events of history into mythic theology is, I contend, to be located in the everyday context of the people for whom events become myth, history becomes theology. It is here, and not in the events that themselves constitute mere history; it is the circumstance of our own fears within American society and culture that has transformed the extermination of European Jewry into 'the Holocaust'. The reason is simply that it is in this country that 'the Holocaust' dominates Jewish public discourse and reliably evokes normative responses and emotions known in advance. In other words, since in American Judaism 'the Holocaust' constitutes one part of the paramount and stable structure of myth and ritual, it is in the context of American Judaism that 'the Holocaust' (and its counterpart, the redemption formed of Zionism) has to be described and interpreted.

The myth of 'the Holocaust' is that it was a unique event, which, despite its 'uniqueness', teaches compelling lessons about why Jews must be Jewish and, why, in consequence of that fact, they must do certain things known in advance (which have nothing to do with the extermination of European Jewry). The redemptive part of the myth maintains that the State of Israel is the 'guarantee' that the 'Holocaust' will not happen again, that it is this state and its achievements which give meaning and significance, even fulfillment, to 'the Holocaust'. The associated ritual is especially bound up in various activities, mostly of a financial character, sometimes of a political one, in support of the State of Israel. The rites of the redemptive myth involve attendance at ritual dinners at which money is given, or at least, where the myth is celebrated, endless cycles of work in that same cause, rehearsal of the faith to outsiders and marginal Jews, trips to the State of Israel. In all, the ritual is shaped within the definition of the meaning of 'being Jewish' around activities in celebration and support of the existence of the state.

If you want to know why be Jewish (the question answered by the myth), you have to remember (1) that the gentiles wiped out the Jews of Europe, and are not to be trusted, let alone joined; and (2) if 'Israel', meaning the State of Israel, had existed there would have been no 'Holocaust', so (3) for the sake of your personal safety, you have to 'support Israel'. Though you do not have to go and live there, it is a mark of piety to feel guilty for not living there (a piety remarkably rare in American Jewry).

This, then, is the myth under discussion, and, briefly noted, these are the accompanying, expressive rituals. All are in the service of making sense out of the distinctive group-life of an assimilated and chronically (but not acutely) self-hating group of Jews, and are at best marginal to their historical way of life and worldview, and to that of their ancestors, down to their grandparents.

The more important half of the regnant myth of American Judaism, as I said, is the part about redemption. This Zionist part speaks of the formation and maintenance of the State of Israel as the compensation and consolation for the death of nearly six million European Jews. While there are many American Jews to whom Zionism is simply unknown, in fact the redemptive valence imputed to the State of Israel in American Judaism constitutes a Zionist judgment. American Judaism must be deemed a wholly Zionist Judaism.

There can thus be no discussion of Zionism within the context of American Judaism without confronting that first and simplest judgment of Zionism upon world Jewry: all those Jews who do not live in the State of Israel are in exile from the State of Israel. The puzzling issue of why American Judaism is so Zionist lies in that formidable, inescapable issue, the issue of *Golah*, or exile. Around that awesome contradiction all the other discourse on Zionism in our community must circle, weaving and bobbing, drawing near and moving far. In the end, all discourse is obsessed and bound up with that simple obvious fact.

What sort of Zionists are we outside the State of Israel? What kind of Zionism do we think worth pursuing while engaged in a permanent exile? If I thought I had solid answers to these questions, I should offer them. I cannot find suitable replies. Nor is it my place to raise those equally intractable questions confronting my counterparts on the other side of the oceans: What sort of Zionism do you contemplate, outside of the nationalism of the State of Israel? If Zionism is principally, or only, identical with Israeli nationalism, then what do you have to say to the rest of the Jewish world, with its other nationalisms? And what to the rest of your own population, which is not Jewish at all? It is clear that there is a formidable beam in my eye, which magnifying the mote in the other person's eye will not remove.

Let us dwell on this difficult matter. Zionism maintains that Jews who do not live in the Jewish State are in exile. There is no escaping that simple allegation, which must call into question the facile affirmation of Zionism central to American Judaism. Zionism further declares that Jews who do not live in the State of Israel must aspire to migrate to that nation or, at the very least, raise their children as potential emigrants. On that position American Judaism chokes. Zionism moreover holds that all Jews must concede, indeed affirm, the centrality of Jerusalem, and of the State of Israel, in the life of Jews throughout the world. Zionism draws the necessary consequence that Jews who live outside of the State of Israel are in significant ways less 'good Jews' than the ones who live there.

All of these positions, commonplace in Israeli Zionism and certainly accepted, in benign verbal formulations to be sure, by American Jews, contradict the simple facts of the situation of American Jews and their Judaism. First, they do not think that they are in exile. Their Judaism makes no concession on that point. Second, they do not have the remotest thought of emigrating from America to the State of Israel. That is so even though in ceremonial occasions they may not protest when Israelis declare that to be their duty. Third, they may similarly make a ritual obeisance to the notion of 'the centrality of Israel', meaning of the State of Israel. They do so even understanding that this proposition carries with itself the corollary of the peripherality of the *Golah*, in general, and of the mighty community of

American Jews, in particular.

Looking at Zionism and its Israeli corollaries we should hardly predict that at the heart of the hope of American Judaism, lies so egregious, so contradictory, so remote a set of propositions as are found in Zionism. If, therefore, 'the Holocaust' accommodates so poorly as an explanation of the human existence of American Jews, the redemption – the salvific myth, hope, and rite – that is defined by Zionism fits still less well. There can be no accommodation, nor is it possible to adapt so intractable a vision of Jewish existence as the Zionist one to the commonplace realities of American Jews. The question to be faced then, is why 'the Holocaust' of long ago is identified with the faraway salvation of the State of Israel? Once more, we must ask what we learn about American Judaism and the social and imaginative world of American Jews from the particular mythic framework within which they live out their lives, by which they explain themselves.

To begin from the fundamental issue, I must raise the question of exile. If, after all, there is to be a Zionism, it must contain the principle of Zion. And Zion without non-Zion, a land without and 'outside-the-land', is not possible. One category creates the other. For Zion is exclusive and, in the nature of things, also wholly locative. There is no Zion in Heaven. It is here on earth, in the material reality of the land and State of Israel. So, too, there cannot be an 'exile' that is solelyinternal, an existential alienation given concrete, material reality merely by an aching heart.

True, alienation and exile are bedmates. But they are not one flesh, and Zionism speaks of the flesh, the this-worldly political fact of Jewish existence. So we must confront the simple question: Are American Jews (we) in exile? The real question is what use the notion – the Zionist notion – of exile may have for American Jews.

The vision of the world that so captures the attention of American Jews as to make the Zionist perception persuasive requires specification. Here, too, we have to try to make up or allude to the story never told – to retell the myth – that captures the matter. Once more it is the story of people who do this-worldly things but take onto their shoulders a prophet's cloak, a philosopher's mantle. It is the tale of people who with perfect confidence in their righteousness seek and pursue it. Yet it must be said that the aspect of the Jews' existence that is susceptible to the salvation afforded by the vision of 'Zion redeemed' and the salvific work of Zionism is not the whole. Zionism promises insufficient redemption. It solves only some of the problems, not all of the anguish of the human and Jewish condition.

Some may conclude that Zionism, taken seriously and not just given ritual assent, is hopelessly in contradiction with the facts of American Jewish existence. Indeed, that may well be so. But if it is so, it is also a countervailing fact that Zionism is the single most powerful and important movement in the history of the Jewish people in the present century. The creation of the State of Israel is universally acknowledged among Jews to be the single most important achievement of the Jewish people in this time – that, and not the human achievements of American Judaism.

So there can be no evasion of the Zionist challenge to American Judaism, the Zionist defiance of American Jewry's comfortable and complacent situation. On the contrary, a Zionist theory of American Jewry, if such can be coaxed out of the intractable, arid soil of Zionist slogans and ideologies, becomes necessary. For without a Zionist understanding of itself, American Jewry cannot draw into a single frame of reference its own sense, both of the circumstance of Jewry in this world, on the one side, and of the situation of itself in this country, on the other. But out of structural contradictions what sort of ideology is to emerge?

A Zionist approach to American-Jewish existence becomes possible when there is a hierarchy of concerns, a ladder leading upward, with many rungs. No Zionism can ask itself to deny the importance of taking up the life of the Jewish state. None can speak of a central point other than Jerusalem. Any Zionist theory that purports to deem Shaker Heights or Glencoe, Beverly Hills or Newton somehow to stand on that same elevated plane of Jewish and Judaic fulfillment as the Israeli towns of Rishon LeZion, Petach Tikvah, or Mevessaret Zion (First to Zion, Gate of Hope, Zion's Messenger), hardly deserves to be taken as a serious construction. There are givens, and these, in the present instance, define what would be ludicrous.

Zionism as an expression of Utopian ethnic loyalty and that alone clearly will not do. Zionism shorn of Zion is not possible. But a wholly locative Zionism, consisting solely of emigration and repeating only slogans about a centrality that all concede and none perceives, also is not useful. These are the boundaries of argument: utopian Zionism, an oxymoron, and locative Zionism, a necessity but an obstacle. To conclude: American Judaism lives a life separated from reality by a veil. American Judaism offers a life constructed around symbols that invoke other times and other places, a *Heilsgeshichte* discontinuous with itself.

The concrete and unmediated everyday Jewish life of the Israeli Jew stands in contrast to the ways of compromise and self-restraint, of small self-deceptions, petty pretense and few achievements of the Jews of America. The myth of 'Holocaust and redemption' accurately describes and evokes the everyday life of Israeli Jews, who day by day confront their own destruction but prepare for it, who concretely, in this world, experience their own achievements and glory in them too. But what reality does that same myth conjure, and what response do those same symbols of death and triumph over death evoke, for people who, in this same context, know a world of exile very like the one destroyed, but who then have formed no other?

American Judaism is founded upon living life through the lives of other people. It brings to the status of a remarkable, puzzling mode of existential being the same frame of mind that brings to football games people who never exercise at all. With the recognition that, at its foundation, American Judaism is the existential counterpart to a spectator sport, we reach the end of the argument. The 'myth of Holocaust and redemption' presents us with a Judaism for American Jews that is like ballet choreographed for clumsy oafs; a system of salvation by others, for others; an existential counterpart to sports as spectacles, not as exercises, not even for fun. Judaism in its American-Judaic formulation calls for love with a breaking heart, holding close with open arms.

It is the people, one people, which mends the broken heart and draws the open arms into closed embrace. For the costs of Zionism, so painfully totted up in these remarks, are to be balanced against the gains. There is, after all, the state, with its Jewish way of life, its Hebrew language, and, in our context of discourse, its remarkable presence and evocative power in the imagination of American Jewry. There is, again, that particular reading of the 'Jewish problem', solved now and (God willing) for all time to come by the Jewish state. These are not nothing. Against such gains, it is hard to find weighty the costs of paradox, contradiction, and, alas, recognition of our own self-deception – our inner contradictions nearing hypocrisy.

# PART II
## JUDAISM IN ZIONIST CONTEXT

# Who Is Israel?

*National Review* 29/24 (1977), 714–716

8

Is Zionism Judaism? If not, what *is* the relationship between Judaism and Zionism? To understand the attitudes of American Jews toward the State of Israel you need a taste for ambiguity and irony. The ambiguity is in the meaning of 'State' and 'Israel'; the irony, in the passionate engagement with the destiny of the 'holy land' on the part of people who are passionately American, deeply secular in the commonplace sense of the word, and uncommonly perplexed by the meaning of their own identity as Jews.

On the one side, the nearly unanimous concern for the welfare of the State of Israel – the Jewish state – on the part of American Jewry is interpreted as support of the old country by an ethnic group, with its parallels extending from Greek-American concern for Cyprus to the Anglo-American concern for Britain that led to our involvement in the First World War. Accordingly, Jews are an ethnic group and express a perfectly natural, and American, ethnic attitude.

On the other side, Jews themselves insist that they form a religious group, and that Zionism constitutes an integral expression of Judaism. It follows that Jews are a churchly community and that the State of Israel represents not their 'old country' (which it isn't), but their Vatican. This latter approach, of course, raises its own perplexities. Who ever heard of a Baptist national home? And when did Roman Catholics last demonstrate in behalf of papal governance of a slice of the Tiber's shore?

Yet if the perceived connection – indeed, the powerful sense of shared destiny – between the Jews of the American Diaspora and the State of Israel is not to be interpreted as religious, it surely is more than ethnic. The language associated with the State of Israel is the language of redemption. The hopes evoked are expressed in the imagery of classical Judaic Messianism. The ancient prayers for the restoration of Zion – meant, in olden times, to express the Messianic hope for the end of days – are today indistinguishable from prayers for the welfare of the State of Israel, containing phrases such as 'the beginning of the sprouting forth of redemption'.

But that merely leads to the further perplexed question of whether

Zionism is a Jewish mode of secular nationalism or a secular mode of Jewish Messianism. The millennial and chiliastic emotions; the invocation of prophetic images of the end of days; the association, with the State of Israel, of the destiny of 'the kingdom of priests and the holy people' of theological discourse; and the unnuanced allegation that 'Zionism is Judaism' – these argue for the latter view.

Yet what can be *religious* about a state? From the Protestant perspective, Judaism is engaged in a kind of neo-Erastianism; from the Roman Catholic perspective, the ancient Israel after the flesh has confused the city of God with the city of man. The principal western modes of Christianity scarcely understand this heightened sense of spirituality lavished by their Jewish friends and neighbors upon what to them is merely another secular state.

Unraveling the skein of ambiguity begins in the recognition that one man's act of religion is another man's secularism. What is an act of religious piety to a Roman Catholic is a work of idolatry to a Protestant of a certain sort. What Christians long ago declared a matter of private conscience – the eating of pork, for example – is of importance in Judaism and Islam. For 'religion' is a word that refers to different things for different 'religions'. The West fought for 100 years before it found peace in the secularization of the state. It took another 200 years to establish the proposition that nationality and religion are distinguished from one another. The distinction even now seems – in Holland, for example – to make no difference whatsoever.

By contrast, in the religions of the Middle East (Islam, Judaism, and the Oriental forms of Christianity), religion defines nationality, and nationality, religion. Consider the State of Israel, with its law that matters of personal status – marriage, divorce, and the like – are settled by the authorities of church, mosque, or synagogue. Not far away, in Lebanon, the 'Christian' armies seem incongruous to western Protestants and Catholics, and the use of the cross as a military emblem an anachronism (if not blasphemy). Indeed it is, except in the lands untouched by the Reformation and the Catholic Renaissance of the nascent centuries of our modernity.

Judaism, for its part, seriously entered the West only when large numbers of Jews migrated from the lands of Eastern Europe. In the vast Jewries of Poland, Ukraine, Lithuania, White Russia, Hungary and the south Slavic territories, to be a Jew was to dress in a certain way, as it was also for the diverse forms of Christian nationality. The Jews had their own language and vastly articulated culture, forming a distinctive nationality and religion as well. There was no separating the two. They were a nation of one religion, and theirs was a religion of one nation. Entering the West – and this means, principally, coming to America and Canada three generations ago – the Jews in 40 years had to accommodate themselves to 400 years of Western cultural history.

To begin with, the immigrants hardly tried. Their natural inclination was to continue life as if they had not been uprooted. Overcoming the deep sense both of being aliens and of alienation, they reconstructed as best they could the Yiddish civilization of the east on the sidewalks of New York. It was left to their children to become the real Americans, and they did – with a vengeance.

The second generation did not merely give up the heritage of the first – a thousand-year-old heritage of language, culture, and deeply spiritual values. It deliberately obliterated that ancient civilization through a conscious act of forgetting. The children not only spoke American, they became American by deliberately forgetting that they were also something else and by feigning ignorance of the fact that no one else believed they weren't. Other Americans, however, didn't perceive the Jewish Americans as very American. The decades of the second generation, from about 1920 to 1945, witnessed the exclusion of Jews from the mainstream of American life and the unembarrassed expression of anti-Semitism in institutions of cultural and economic life.

The third generation therefore put on a new cloak: to be American in all ways except religion. To be Jewish now meant to be a kind of American, differentiated solely by matters of religious faith. Judaism was understood to be a kind of religion not different in its deep structures and definitive traits from other American religions. Will Herberg spelled all this out in his classic work, *Protestant–Catholic–Jew*, showing that the three 'religions or democracy' had been forced into a common American mould. That other side of 'being Jewish' – the side excluded from the category of religion by the prevailing understanding of what a religion could contain and had to exclude – was kept hidden.

The consensus of the third generation, then, may be simply stated: 'To be Jewish, but not too much so'; not so much that one could not also find a place in the undifferentiated mass of Americans. It was this consensus that was to fall to pieces in the late 1960s. It was at that point, principally because of the traumas of 1967 and 1973, that Zionism became a definitive component of the American Jewish worldview. The children of the third generation took seriously what their parents had set forth rather casually. Inevitably, therefore, the fragile consensus had to break into its conflicting components. For some, not being too Jewish meant not being Jewish at all. The flow out of the Jewish community and into movements of political or religious redemption was torrential. For others, if one was to be Jewish at all, then that meant more than the moderation of learning, the suppression of passion, the benign formality of joining a synagogue but not taking too active a part in its religious activities.

The wheel had come full circle. The religious tradition of Judaism, with its insistence on the sanctification of the profane and the requirement of expressing God's will in each and every aspect of everyday life, overspread the limits of permitted religiosity.

The religious way of life defined by Judaism cannot be confined to the walls of the synagogue, on the one side, or to the limits of merely ethical behavior with one's fellow human beings, on the other. Praying and ethics are part of Judaism, but not the whole. Learning in Torah – the sanctification of the intellect in the service of God's Word – has some counterpart in Christianity, but outweighs all else in Judaism. The people of Israel, God's people, is simply not a church, and the meaning of being 'Israel' is not to be compared, in its intellectual problematic, to ecclesiology. And, it must be said, the place of the Messiah in the redemption of Israel and the study of Christology have nothing to do with each other.

Christians nonetheless may understand if they try to imagine how things would appear under the following aspect: Israel (meaning the Jewish people) is God's servant. The suffering of Israel bears meaning for the nations. The redemption of humanity depends upon Israel, whose suffering now will in time gain atonement for the sins of the world, and by whose redemption humanity will be redeemed. Reread Isaiah chapters 53 and 54 and understand that they refer to the Jewish people. At that point – if you can do it – you will enter into the imaginative context of Israel, the Jewish people.

Now back to the present. For a moment I will cease to describe, and will tell you my own sense of these matters. When I read those verses, I think only of the Israel after the flesh of which I am part: 'He was despised and rejected by men, a man of sorrows and acquainted with grief, and as one from whom men hide their faces; he was despised, and we esteemed him not.' Keep in mind the meaning of the extermination of millions of European Jews: 'Like a lamb that is led to the slaughter, and like a sheep that before its shearers is dumb, so he opened not his mouth. By oppression and judgment he was taken away; and as for his generation, who considered that he was cut off out of the land of the living, stricken for the transgression of my people?' Kierkegaard struggled with Abraham's willingness to sacrifice his son Isaac. But in our day Jews had to choose which of their children would live and which would die, and they were not one man but thousands and hundreds of thousands. Our people, by oppression and judgment, was taken away.

Among their friends and neighbors, who considered that train-loads of human cargoes crossed Europe to extinction in the east? Who was stricken when a million children, two or three or four years of age, were taken from their parents, and were shoveled directly into crematoria, without even prior asphyxiation? The silence of the good Europeans echoes in the silence of America and Britain. We read those words of Isaiah, understood by two millennia of Christians to refer to Jesus Christ, and we know of whom Isaiah spoke and what he prophesied, and not for one time and one generation only.

For us, therefore, the State of Israel is called by its rightful name, *Israel*. While Jews do not confuse the decisions of the Israeli parliament with the will of God, nearly all understand the state to be something like that 'diminished sanctity' of which Ezekiel spoke in the aftermath of the destruction of the First Temple in 586 BC. And all know that had there been no Holocaust, there also would be no state. None perceives the state as a mere this-worldly thing, convenient for relocating the remnants of European Jewry and the Jewish refugees from Arab states.

Yet, you rightly object, are you Jews not secular? Where are the stigmata of religiosity, to make credible your claim of religious significance for the State of Israel? If you have no religious convictions about other matters, then how are we to grasp what can be religious for you in this one thing? The question is fair; the answer not easy. For the bulk of western Jewry – exclusive of Orthodoxy and limited segments of non-Orthodox Judaism – will not concur that to be Jewish is to be a Judaist (that is, a practitioner of Judaism). Jews outside of the USA and Canada, and many here as well, do not acknowledge an inexorable tie between being Jewish and confessing Judaism.

At this point one's conception of secularity enters the picture. If you hold that secularity requires a wholly this-worldly and factual interpretation of life, then there is nothing secular about the intense engagement with 'being Jewish' – namely, with who is Israel – exhibited by the vast majority of secular Jews. If thirst for salvation and quest for redemption are marks of a truly religious spirit, then what is *not* religious about the Messianic hopes and heightened sense of participating in foreordained events characteristic of secular Jews?

If to give for humanitarian purposes is secular (as well as religious), but to sacrifice and focus one's whole being upon the object of sacrifice is a salvific mode of life, then the curiously practical and concrete ways in which Jews center their collective life upon support for the State of Israel surely bear salvific meaning. For the righteousness (bordering, alas, on self-righteousness) associated with the secular act of supporting the United Jewish Appeal or even Bonds for the State of Israel is not a secular fact. To those who do these deeds because of 'being Jewish', there is nothing secular about them. If you recall that Judaism for its part expresses its beliefs in concrete, practical deeds in the secular world, you will have to concede that, from the viewpoint of Judaism, those who see the UJA as a kind of shrine are not entirely incomprehensible.

That brings us back to where we started: the problem of understanding the feelings and attitudes of American Jews toward the State of Israel. The ambiguities remain, but we understand how they are generated. The irony of religious passions being lavished by mainly secular people upon a state which, like all other states, is a contingent and this-worldly fact, may now be richly enjoyed. Indeed, once you achieve an understanding of this rather curious phenomenon of the larger American culture, you are apt to see ironies and ambiguities where formerly you saw only what is obvious and given, even in the self-evident truths of your own situation.

# 9 Zionism and 'the Jewish Problem'

*Midstream* 15 (1969), 34–45

When Herzl proposed Zionism as the solution to the Jewish problem, the 'Zionism' of which he spoke and the 'Jewish problem' that he proposed to solve constituted chiefly political realities. But, as Arthur Hertzberg trenchantly argues in *The Zionist Idea*, Zionism actually represented not a merely secular and political ideology, but the transvaluation of Jewish values. If so, the same must be said of the 'Jewish problem' to which it addresses itself. Zionism as an external force faced the world, but what shall we say of its inner spirit? The inwardness of Zionism – its 'piety' and spirituality – is not to be comprehended by the world, but only by the Jew, for, like the Judaism it transformed and transcended, to the world it was worldly and political, stiff-necked and stubborn (in Christian theological terms), but to the Jew it was something other, not to be comprehended by the gentile.

In his celebrated correspondence with Eugen Rosenstock-Huessy, Franz Rosenzweig wrote:

> I find that everything that I want to write is something I can't express to you. For now I would have to show you Judaism from within, that is, to be able to show it to you in a hymn, just as you are able to show me, the outsider, Christianity. And for the very reason that you can do it, I cannot. Christianity has its soul in its externals; Judaism, on the outside, has only its hard protecting shell, and one can speak of its soul only from within˙ ...

Following Hertzberg, one can hardly see Zionism except as a new Judaism, a completely new view of all that had gone before and an utterly different conception of what should come hereafter. But this Zionism – neither spiritual nor political, but in a measure a unique amalgam of the spirit and the polis – is hidden by its hard protecting shell. What then can we say of its soul from within?

---

*\*Judaism Despite Christianity: The 'Letters on Christianity and Judaism' Between Eugen Rosenstock-Huessy and Franz Rosenzweig*, edited by Eugen Rosenstock-Huessy, University of Alabama Press, 1969, p. 133).

The Zionism of which I speak is the effort to realize through political means the hope supposed to have been lost in the time of Ezekiel, proclaimed imperishable in the time of Naphtali Herz Imber (1856–1909, the writer of Hatikvah), the continuous hope of restoration and renaissance first of the land of Israel, then of the people of Israel through the land, and finally, since 1948, of the people and the land together, wherever the people should be found. This Zionism did not come about at Basel, for its roots go back to the point in the ages at which Jewry first recognized, then rejected, its separation from the land. Zionism is the old-new Judaism, a Judaism transformed through old-new values. It is a set of paradoxes through which the secular and the religious, separated in the nineteenth century, were again fused – re-fused – in the twentieth. Zionism to be sure is a complex phenomenon; within it are tendencies that are apt to cancel each other out. But all forms of Zionism are subsumed under the definition offered here, which represents, I think, the lowest common denominator for all Zionist phenomena.

The Jewish problems that Zionism successfully solved were the consequence of the disintegration of what had been whole, the identity, consciousness, and the culture of the Jew. It was, as I said, Zionism which reconstructed the whole and reshaped the tradition in a wholly new heuristic framework.

In former times it was conventional to speak of the 'Jewish problem'. Most people understood that problem in political and economic terms. What shall we do about the vast Jewish populations of Eastern and Central Europe, which live a marginal economic life and have no place in the political structures of the several nations? Herzl proposed the Zionist solution to the 'Jewish problem'. Dubnow wished to solve the 'Jewish problem' by the creation of Jewish autonomous units in Europe. The Socialists and Communists proposed to solve the 'Jewish problem' by integration of Jewry into the movement of the international proletariat, and to complete the solution of the problems of the smaller group within those of the working classes.

Today we here less talk about the 'Jewish problem' because Hitler brought it to a final solution: by exterminating the masses of European Jews, he left unsolved no social, economic or political problems. The western Jewries are more or less well-integrated into the democratic societies. The State of Israel has no 'Jewish problem' in the classic sense. The oppressed communities remaining in Arab countries are relatively small, and the solution of their problems is to be found in migration to the West. So the 'Jewish problem' does not describe reality or evoke a recognized, real-life perplexity. (This does not mean that Jews do not have problems, or that gentiles do not have problems in relating to and understanding both Jews and Judaism.)

I shall concentrate on three aspects of the contemporary Jewish situation, all closely related, and all the result of secularism. The first is the crisis of identity, the second, the liberal dilemma, the third, the problem of self-hatred. The Jewish identity crisis may be simply stated: There is no consensus shared by most Jews about what a Jew is, how Judaism should be defined, what 'being Jewish' and 'Judaism' are supposed to mean for individuals and the community. The liberal dilemma is this: How can I espouse universal principles and yet remain part of a particular community? The problem of self-hatred needs little definition, but provokes much illustration, for many of the phenomena of contemporary Jewish life reflect the low self-esteem attached to being Jewish.

For Jews the secular revolution is not new. From the Haskalah, the Jewish Enlightenment or Emancipation in the eighteenth century onward, Jews have come forward to propose a non-religious inter-pretation of 'being Jewish', an interpretation divorced from the classic mythic structure of Judaism. The God-is-dead movement evoked little response among Jewish theologians and ideologists because they found nothing new in it. If the issue was naturalistic, instead of supernatural, theology then Jewish theologians had heard Mordecai Kaplan for generations. If the issue was atheism, it had been formulated by Jewish secularists, socialists and assimilationists in various ways from the mid-nineteenth century onward. If the secular revolution means that large numbers of people cease to look to religion, or to religious institutions, for the meaning of their lives and cease to practice religious traditions and to affirm religious beliefs, then this is neither news nor a revolution. Jews have participated in that sort of 'revolution' for two centuries. They have done so without ceasing to regard themselves, and to be regarded by others, as Jews. That does not mean that the Jews have found antidotes to the secular fever, but that by now they have a considerable heritage of experi-ence, a substantial corpus of cases and precedents, for what Christians find to be new and revolutionary: the loosing of the world from all religious and supernatural interpretations.

The secular revolution has imposed upon Jews a profound crisis of identity. In former times everyone knew who was a Jew and what being a Jew meant. A Jew was a member of a religious nation, living among other nations by its own laws, believing in Torah revealed at Sinai and in one God who had chosen Israel, and hoping for the coming of the

Messiah. The gentile world shared the philosophical presuppositions of Jewish beliefs. Everyone believed in God. Everyone believed in prophecy, in revelation, in the Jews' holy book. Everyone believed in the coming of the Messiah. Above all, everyone interpreted reality by supernaturalist principles. To be sure, groups differed on the nature of God, the particular prophets to be regarded as true, the book God had revealed. But these differences took place within a vast range of agreement.

When religious understandings of the world lost their hold on masses of western men, 'being Jewish' became as problematical as any other aspect of archaic reality. If to be Jewish meant to be part of a Jewish religious community, then when men ceased to believe in religious propositions, they ought to have ceased being Jewish. Yet that is not what happened. For several generations Jewish atheists and agnostics have continued to take an active role in the Jewish community – indeed, functionally to constitute the majority in it – and to have seen nothing unusual either in their participation in Jewish life or in their lack of religious commitment. Indeed, today the American Jewish community is nearly unique in interpreting 'being Jewish' primarily in religious, or at least in rhetorically religious, terms. Other Jewish communities see themselves as a community, a nation, a people, whether or not religion plays a role in defining what is particular about that community. The secular revolution immensely complicated the definition of Jewish identity, not only by breaking down the uniform classical definition, but also by supplying a variety of new, complex definitions in its place.

Today, therefore, if we ask ourselves, 'What are the components of "Jewishness"?' we are hard put to find an answer. What are the attitudes, associations, rituals both secular and religious, psychology and culture, that both Jews and others conceive to be Jewish? The truth is that today there is no such thing as a single Jewish identity, as there assuredly was in times past, an identity one could define in meaningful terms. Jewishness now is a function of various social and cultural settings, and is meaningful only in those settings.

The Jews obviously are not a nation in the accepted sense; but they also are hardly a people in the sense that an outsider can investigate or whose components of peoplehood they can understand. There is no 'Jewish way' of organizing experience and interpreting reality, although there was and is a Judaic way. There is no single Jewish ideology, indeed no single, unitary Jewish history, although there was once a cogent Judaic theology and a Judaic view of a unitary and meaningful progression of events to be called 'Jewish history'. Only if we impose upon discrete events of scarcely related groups in widely separated places and ages the concept of a single unitary history can we speak of 'Jewish history'. Jewish peoplehood in a concrete, secular, this-worldly historical sense is largely a matter of faith, that is, the construction of historians acting as theologians do in other settings. There once was a single Jewish ideological system, a coherent body of shared images, ideas and ideals, which provided for participants a coherent overall orientation in space and time, in means and ends. There once was such a system, but in the secular revolution it has collapsed.

It is indeed the secular revolution that has imposed on Jewry a lingering crisis of identity. Jews today may find in common a set of emotions and responses. These do not constitute an 'identity', but rather a set of common characteristics based upon differing verbal explanations and experiences. That does not mean no one knows what a Jew is. In particular settings Jews *can* be defined and understood in terms applicable to those settings. But as an abstraction the 'Jewish people' is a theological or ideological construct not to be imposed on disparate Jewish communities in various times and places. Lacking a common language and culture, even a common religion, the Jews do not have what they once had. Today Jewish identity varies so greatly that we need to reconsider the viability of the very concept of 'Jewishness' as a universal attribute, for today Jewishness cannot be defined in neutral, cultural terms.

If there are no inherent and essential Jewish qualities in the world, then nothing about 'being Jewish' is natural, to be taken for granted. Being Jewish becomes something one must achieve, define, strive for. It is today liberated from the forms and content of the recent past, from the 'culture Judaism' of the American and Canadian Jewish communities. If the artifacts of that 'culture Judaism' – matters of cuisine, or philanthropy, or cliquishness – are not part of some immutable and universal Jewish identity, then they may well be criticized from within, not merely abandoned and left behind in disgust. One can freely repudiate them in favor of other ways.

Omissions in contemporary Jewish 'identity' are as striking as the inclusions. Among the things taken for granted are a sense of group loyalty, a desire to transmit 'pride in Judaism' to the next generation, in all a desire to survive. But the identity of large numbers of Jews, whether they regard themselves as secular or not, does not include a concept of God, of the meaning of life, or the direction and purpose of history. The uncriticized, but widely accepted Jewish identity syndrome is formed of the remnants of the piety of the recent past, a piety one may best call residual, cultural and habitual, rather than self-conscious, critical and theological (or ideological). That identity is not even ethnic, but rather a conglomeration of traits picked up in diverse everyday experiences. It is certainly flat and one-dimensional, leaving Jews to wander in strange paths in search of the answers to the most fundamental human perplexities.

Why are Jews in the forefront of universal causes, to the exclusion of their own interest and identity? Charles Liebman, writing in *The Religious Situation 1969*, examines the reasons given for this phenomenon. He rejects the notion that Jewish liberalism, cosmopolitanism, and internationalism rest on 'traditional' Jewish values, for, he points out, it is the secular, not the religious, Jew who espouses cosmopolitanism. Jewish religious values in fact are folk-oriented rather than universalistic.

Liebman likewise rejects the view that the Jews' social status, far below what they might anticipate from their economic attainments, accounts for their attraction to the fringes of politics. This theory accounts, Liebman says, for Jewish radicalism rather than Jewish liberalism, that is, for only a small element of the community. Further, Jewish radicals normally abandon Jewish community life; the liberals dominate it.

A third explanation derives from the facts of history. Liberal parties supported the emancipation of the Jews; conservative ones opposed it. But in the USA this was not the case. Indeed, until the New Deal, Jews tended to be Republican, not Democrats or Socialists. Liebman posits that the appeal of liberalism is strong among Jews estranged from the religious tradition. This appeal, he says, 'lies in the search for a universalistic ethic to which a Jew can adhere *but* which is seemingly irrelevant to specific Jewish concerns and, unlike radical socialism, does not demand total commitment at the expense of all other values'.

Since the secular Enlightenment or Emancipation, Jews have constantly driven to free themselves from the condition that Judaism thrusts on them. This Liebman calls estrangement:

> The impetus for intellectual and religious reform among Jews, the adoption of new ideologies and life styles, but above all else the changing self-perception by the Jew of himself and his condition was not simply a desire to find amelioration from the physical oppression of the ghetto. It was rather a desire for emancipation from the very essence of the Jewish condition ... The Jew's problem with his alienation from the roots and traditions of the society.

Here is the point at which the phenomenon of secularization becomes important. Jews earlier knew they were different, estranged. But with the collapse of religious evaluations of difference, the Jews ceased to affirm that difference. Secularization changed the nature of the Jew's perception of his condition, transferred the estrangement from theology to the realm of contemporary culture and civilization.

Jews supported universal humanism and cosmopolitanism with a vengeance. They brought these ideals home to the community so that Jewish difference was played down. Look, for example, at the *Union Prayerbook*, and count the number of times the congregation prays for 'all mankind'. The *New Liberal Prayerbook* in England so emphasizes the universal to the exclusion of the particular that one might write to the English liberal rabbi responsible for the liturgy: 'Warm and affectionate regards to your wife and children, and to all mankind.' Liebman concludes:

> The Jew wished to be accepted as an equal in society *not* because he was a Jew, but because his Jewishness was *irrelevant*. Yet at the same time, the Jew refused to make his own Jewishness irrelevant ... He made ... contradictory demands on society. He wants to be accepted into the tradition of society without adapting to the society's dominant tradition. This constitutes the liberal dilemma: how to affirm universalism and remain particular.

Complex though the liberal identity of secular Jews is, it is still more complicated by the phenomena of anti-Semitism and consequent self-hatred. The 'Jewish problem' is most commonly phrased by young Jews as 'Why should I be Jewish? I believe in universal ideals – who needs particular ones as well?' Minorities feel themselves 'particular', see their traditions as 'ritual', and distinguish between the private, unique, and personal and the public, universal, and commonplace. Majorities do not. Standing at the center, not on the fringe, they accept the given. Marginal men such as the Jews regard the given as something to be criticized, elevated, in any event as distinguished from their own essential being.

Jews who ask, 'Why be Jewish', testify that 'being Jewish' somehow repels, separates a person from the things he wants. North American society, though it is opening up, still is not so open that men who are different from the majority can serenely and happily accept that difference. True, they frequently affirm it, but the affirmation contains such excessive protest that it is not much different from denial. The quintessential datum of American Jewish existence is anti-Semitism, along with uncertainty of status, denial of normality, and self-doubt. The results are many, but two stand out. Some over-emphasize their Jewishness, respond to it not naturally but excessively, to the exclusion of other parts of their being. Others question and implicitly deny it. The one compensates too much; the other finds no reward at all.

As Kurt Lewin pointed out (in *Resolving Social Conflicts. Selected Papers on Group Dynamics*, New York, 1948, p. 164): 'every under-privileged minority group is kept together not only by cohesive forces among its members but also by the boundary which the majority erects against the crossing of an individual from the minority to the majority group'. A member of an underprivileged group will try to gain in social status by joining the majority – to pass, to assimilate. The basic fact of life is this wish to cross the boundary, and hence, as Lewin says:

> he [the minority-group member] lives almost perpetually in a state of conflict and tension. He dislikes ... his own group because it is nothing but a burden to him ... A Jew of this type will dislike everything specifically Jewish, for he will see in it that which keeps him away from the majority for which he is longing.

Such a Jew is one who will constantly ask: 'Why be Jewish?', and who will see, or at least fantasize about, a common religion of humanity, universalism or universal values that transcend and incidentally obliterate, denominational and sectarian boundaries. It is no accident that the universal language, Esperanto, the universal movement, Communism, the universal psychology, Freudianism, all were in large measure attractive to marginal Jews.

True, Jews may find a place in social groups indifferent to their particularity as Jews. But a closer look shows that these groups are formed chiefly by deracinated, de-Judaized Jews, along with a few exceptionally liberal non-Jews standing in a similar relationship to their own origins. Jews do assimilate. They do try to blot out the marks of their particularity in ways more sophisticated, to be sure, than the ancient Hellenist Jews who submitted to painful operations to wipe away the marks of circumcision. But in doing so, they become not something else entirely, but another type of Jew. The real issue is never to be or not to be a Jew, any more than it is to be or not to be my father's son.

Lewin makes this wholly clear: 'It is not similarity or dissimilarity of individuals that constitutes a group, but interdependence of fate.' Jews brought up to suppose that being Jewish is chiefly, or only, a matter of religion think that through atheism they cease to be Jews, only to discover that disbelieving in God helps not at all. They still are Jews. They still are obsessed by that fact and compelled to confront it, whether under the name of Warren or of Weinstein, whether within the society of Jews or elsewhere.

Indeed, outside of that society Jewish consciousness becomes most intense. Among Jews one is a human being, with peculiarities and virtues of one's own. Among gentiles one is a Jew, with traits common to the group that has been rejected. That is probably why Jews still live in mostly Jewish neighborhoods and associate, outside of economic life, mostly with other Jews, whether or not these associations exhibit traits supposed to be Jewish. When crisis comes, as it frequently does, then no one doubts that he shares a common cause, a common fate, with other Jews. Then it is hardest to isolate oneself from Jews, because only among Jewry are these intense concerns shared.

The Jewish community has yet to face up to the self-hatred endemic in its life. Jews are subtle enough to explain they are too busy with non-Jewish activities to associate with Jews. Students coming to college do not say to themselves or others, 'I do not want to be a Jew, and now that I have the chance not to be, I shall take it.' They say, 'I do not like the Hillel rabbi; I am not religious so won't go to services; I am too busy with studies, dates, or political and social programs to participate in Jewish life.' From here it is a short step to the affirmation of transcendent, universal values, and the denial of a particular 'religious' identity. That those who take that step do so mostly with other Jews is, as I said, proof of the real intent.

The organized Jewish community differs not at all from the assimilationist sector of this student generation. Indeed, it shows the way. Leadership in Jewry is sought by talented and able people, particularly those whose talents and abilities do not produce commensurate results in the non-Jewish world. Status denied elsewhere is readily available, for the right reason, in Jewry, but in Jewry status is measured by the values of the gentile establishment.

Lewin says:

> In any group, those sections are apt to gain leadership which are more generally successful. In a minority group, individual members who are economically successful ... usually gain a higher degree of acceptance by the majority group. This places them culturally on the periphery of the underprivileged group and makes them more likely to be 'marginal' persons ...

Nevertheless, they are frequently called for leadership by the underprivileged group because of their status and power. They themselves are usually eager to accept the leading role in the minority, partly as a substitute for gaining status in the majority. As a result, we find the rather paradoxical phenomenon of what one might call 'the leader from the periphery'. Instead of having a group lead by people who are proud of the group, who wish to stay in it and to promote it, we see minority leaders who are lukewarm toward the group ...

This, I think is very much true of US Jewry.

American Jews want to be Jewish, but not too much so, not so much that they cannot just be 'people', part of the imaginary undifferentiated majority. Herein lies their pathology: they suppose that one can distinguish between one's Jewishness, humanity, personality, individuality, and religion. A human being, however, does not begin as part of an undifferentiated mass. Once he leaves the maternity ward, he goes to a home of real people with a history, a home that comes from somewhere and that was made by some specific people. He inherits the psychic, not to mention social and cultural, legacy of many generations.

What has Zionism to do with these Jewish problems? It is, after all, supposedly a secular movement, called 'secular Messianism', and the problems I have described are the consequences of secularity. How then has an alleged secular movement posited solutions to the challenges of secularity faced by the formerly religious community?

Zionism provides a reconstruction of Jewish identity, for it reaffirms the nationhood of Israel in the face of the disintegration of the religious bases of Jewish peoplehood. If in times past the Jews saw themselves as a people because they were the children of the promise, the children of Abraham, Isaac and Jacob, called together at Sinai, instructed by God through prophets, led by rabbis guided by the 'whole Torah' – written and oral – of Sinai, then with the end of a singularly religious self-consciousness, the people lost its understanding of itself. The fact is that the people remained a community of fate, but, until the flourishing of Zionism, the facts of its continued existence were deprived of a heuristic foundation. Jews continued as a group, but could not persuasively say why or what this meant. Zionism provided the explanation: the Jews indeed remain a people, but the foundation of their peoplehood lies in the unity of their concern for Zion, devotion to rebuilding the land and establishing Jewish sovereignty in it. The realities of continuing emotional and social commitment to Jewish 'grouphood' or separateness thus made sense. Mere secular difference, once seen to be destiny – '[the God] who has not made us like the nations' – once again stood forth as destiny.

Herein lies the ambiguity of Zionism. It was supposedly a secular movement, yet in reinterpreting the classic mythic structures of Judaism, it compromised its secularity and exposed its fundamental unity with the classic mythic being of Judaism. If, as I suggested, groups with like attributes do not necessarily represent 'peoples' or 'nations', and if the common attributes, in the Jewish case, are neither intrinsically Jewish (whatever that might mean) nor widely present to begin with, then the primary conviction of Zionism constitutes an extraordinary reaffirmation of the primary element in the classical mythic structure: salvation. What has happened in Zionism is that the old has been in one instant destroyed and resurrected. The holy people are no more, the national people take their place. How much has changed in the religious tradition, when the allegedly secular successor-continuator has preserved not only the essential perspective of the tradition, but done so pretty much in the tradition's own symbols and language?

Nor should it be supposed that the Zionist solution to the Jews' crisis of identity is a merely theological or ideological one. That is the practical result of Zionist success in conquering the Jewish community. For the middle and older generations, as everyone knows, the Zionist enterprise provided the primary vehicle for Jewish identity. The Reform solution to the identity problem – we are Americans by nationality, Jews by religion – was hardly congruent to the profound Jewish passion of the immigrant generations and their children. The former generations were *not* merely Jewish by religion. Religion was the least important aspect of their Jewishness. They deeply felt themselves to be Jewish in their bone and marrow and did not feel sufficiently marginal as Jews to *need* to affirm their Americanness/Judaism at all. Rather, they participated in a reality; they were in a situation so real and intimate as to make unnecessary such an uncomfortable, defensive affirmation. They did not doubt they were Americans. They did not need to explain what being Jewish had to do with it. Zionism was congruent to these realities, and because of that fact, being Jewish and being Zionist were inextricably joined together.

But how different is the newer generation? True, extreme aberrant Jewish elements in the New Left are prepared to turn against the State of Israel. But what seems to have weakened the New Left more than anything else, and caused its split into numerous bickering factions, is the defection of considerable numbers of Jewish radicals, unable to stomach both the crude anti-Semitism and the mindless pro-Nasserism of the Communist-line New Left groups. If this is so, we can only conclude that the younger generation is as viscerally Zionist as the older generations. The rock on which the New Left split was none other than 1967 Zion. I cannot think of more striking evidence of the persistence of the Zionist conception of Jewish identity among the younger generation.

The Zionist critique of the Jews' liberal dilemma is no less apt. Zionism has not stood against liberal causes and issues. On the contrary, Zionist socialists have stood at the forefront of the liberal cause, have struggled for the working-class ideals, have identified the working-class cause with their own. The record of Israeli and American Zionist thought on liberal issues is unambiguous and consistent. The liberalism of which Liebman writes is of a different order. It is a liberalism not born in Jewish nationhood, but despite and against it. The liberal cosmopolitan Jew, devoted to internationalist and universal causes to the exclusion of 'parochial' Jewish concerns, is no Zionist, but the opposite. He is a Jew acting out the consequences of deracination in the political arena. His universal liberalism takes the place of a profound commitment to the Jews and their welfare. Indeed, it is a liberalism that would like to deny that Jews have special, particular interests and needs to begin with. 'Struggling humanity' in all its forms but one claim his sympathy: when Jews suffer, they *have* to do so as part of undifferentiated humanity.

In so far as this Jewish liberalism was non-sectarian and hostile to the things that concern Jews as Jews – as in those Jewish welfare federations that articulately state their purpose as humanitarian to the exclusion of Judaism – Zionism has rejected that liberalism. It has done so because of its critical view of the Emancipation. Unlike the Jewish liberals, the Zionist saw the Emancipation as a problem, not a solution. He was dubious of its promises and aware of its hypocrisies. He saw Emancipation as a threat to Jewry and in slight measure a benefit for Jews. The Jews' problem was that Emancipation represented de-Judaization. The price of admission to the roots and traditions of the Jew, according to Zionist thought.

At the same time the Zionist stood between the religious party, which utterly rejected Emancipation and its works, and the secular-reform-liberal party, which wholly affirmed them. He faced the reality of Emancipation without claiming on its behalf a Messianic valence. Emancipation is here, but coped with; not utterly rejected, as by the Orthodox, nor wholeheartedly affirmed, as by the secular, reform and liberal groups. Zionism therefore demanded that the Jew be accepted as an equal in society because he was a Jew, *not* because his Jewishness was irrelevant. Its suspicion of the liberal stance was based, correctly in my opinion, on the Jews' ambivalence toward Jewishness.

Zionism clearly recognized that the Jewishness of the Jew could never be irrelevant, not to the gentile, not to the Jew. It therefore saw more clearly than the liberals the failures of the European Emancipation and the dangers of American liberalism to Jewish self-respect and Jewish interests. Zionists were quick to perceive the readiness of non-Jewish liberals at their word: We Jews have no special interests, nothing to fight for in our own behalf. Zionists saw Jews had considerable interests, just like other groups, and exposed the self-deceit (or hypocrisy) of those who said otherwise. The liberal Jew wanted to be accepted into the traditions of society without complete assimilation, on the one side, but also without much Jewishness, on the other. The Zionist assessment of the situation differed, as I said, for it saw that Jews could achieve a place in the common life *only* as Jews; and, rightly for Europe, it held this was impossible.

In its gloomy assessment of the European Emancipation, Zionism found itself in a position to cope with the third component in the Jewish problem, the immense, deep-rooted, and wide-ranging self-hatred of Jews. The Zionist affirmation of Jewish peoplehood, of Jewish being, stood in stark contrast to the inability of marginal and liberal Jews to cope with anti-Semitism. Cases too numerous to list demonstrate the therapeutic impact of Zionism on the faltering psychological health of European Jews, particularly of more sensitive and intellectual individuals.

The American situation is different in degree, for here anti-Semitism in recent times has made its impact in more subtle ways, but its presence is best attested by the Jews themselves. Yet if a single factor in the self-respect American Jewry does possess can be isolated, it is its pride in the State of Israel and its achievements. Zionism lies at the foundation of American Jewry's capacity to affirm its Jewishness. Without Zionism, religious conviction, forced to bear the whole burden by itself, would prove a slender reed. To be a Jew 'by religion' and to make much of that fact in an increasingly secular environment would not represent an attractive option to many. The contributions to Jewry's psychological health by the State of Israel and by the Zionist presence in the Diaspora cannot be over-estimated. It is striking, for example, that Kurt Lewin, Milton Steinberg, and other students of the phenomena of Jewish self-hatred invariably reached the single conclusion that only through Zionism would self-hatred be mitigated, even overcome.

The role of Zionism as a therapy for self-hatred cannot be described only in terms of the public opinion of US Jewry. That would tell us much about the impact of mass communications, but little about the specific value of the Zionist idea for healing the Jewish pathology. In my view, the Israelis' claim 'to live a full Jewish life' is a valid one. In Zionist conception and Israeli reality, the Jew is indeed a thoroughly integrated, whole human being. Here, in conception and reality, the Jew who believes in justice, truth and peace, in universal brotherhood and dignity, does so not despite his peculiarity as a Jew, but through it. He makes no distinction between his Jewishness, his humanity, his individuality, his way of living, and his ultimate values. They constitute a single, undivided and fully integrated existential reality.

Part of the reason is the condition of life: the State of Israel is the largest Jewish neighborhood in the world. But part of the reason is ideological, and not merely circumstantial: Zionists always have rejected the possibility of Jews' 'humanity' without Jewishness, nationality and faith. They were not only *not* Germans of the Mosaic persuasion, but also *not* human beings of the Jewish genus. The several sort of bifurcations attempted by non-Zionists to account for their Jewishness, along with other sorts of putatively non-Jewish commitments and loyalties, were rejected by Zionists. It was not that Zionists did not comprehend the dilemmas faced by other sorts of Jews, but rather that they supposed through Zionism they had found the solution. They correctly held that through Zionist ideology and activity they had overcome the disintegrating Jewish identity crisis of others.

At the outset I suggested that, like Judaism, Zionism can be understood from within, from its soul. My claim is that Zionism is to be understood as a solution to Jewish problems that are best perceived by the Jews who face those problems. The 'Jewish problem' imposed by the effects of secularism took the form of a severe and complex crisis of identity, a partial commitment to universalism and cosmopolitan liberalism while claiming the right to be a little different, and a severe psychopathological epidemic of self-hatred. But the way in which Zionism actually solved those problems is more difficult to explain. If, as I suppose, because of Zionism contemporary Jewries have a clearer perception of who they are, what their interests consist of, and of their value as human beings, then Zionism and the State of Israel are in substantial measure the source of the saving knowledge.

But *how* has Zionism worked its salvation on the Jews? Here I think we come to realities that only Jews can understand. They understand them *not* because of rational reflection but because of experience and unreflective, natural response.

Zionism, and Zionism alone, proved capable of interpreting to contemporary Jews the meaning of felt-history, *and* of doing so in terms congruent to what the Jews derived from their tradition. It was Zionism which properly assessed the limitations of the Emancipation and proposed sound and practical programs to cope with those limitations. It was Zionism which gave Jews strength to affirm themselves when faced with the anti-Semitism of European and American life in the first half of the twentieth century. It was Zionism, and that alone, which showed a way forward from the nihilism and despair of the DP camps. It was Zionism, and that alone, which provided a basis for unity in American Jewry in the 1950s and 1960s, a ground for common action among otherwise utterly divided groups.

These achievements of Zionism were based not on their practicality, though Zionism time and again was proved 'right' by history. The Jews were moved by and responded to Zionism before, not after the fact. They were moved because of the capacity of Zionism to resurrect the single most powerful force in the history of Judaism: Messianism. Zionism did so in ways too numerous to list, but the central fact is that it represented, as Hertzberg perceptively showed, not 'secular Messianism' but a profound restatement in new ways of classical Messianism. Zionism recovered the old, still evocative Messianic symbolism and imagery and filled them with new meaning, a meaning that was taken for granted by vast numbers of Jews because it accurately described not what they believed or hoped for – not faith – but rather what they took to be mundane reality. Zionism took within its heuristic framework each and every important event in twentieth-century Jewish history and gave to all a single, comprehensive and sensible interpretation. Events were no longer random or unrelated, but were all part of a single pattern, pointing toward an attainable Messianic result. It was not the random degradation of individuals in Germany and Poland, not the meaningless murder of unfortunates, not the creation of another state in the Middle East. All of these events were related to one another. It was Holocaust and rebirth, and the state was the State of *Israel*.

In so stating the meaning of contemporary events, Zionism made it possible for Jews not only to understand what they witnessed, but to draw meaning from it. Even more, Zionism breathed new life into ancient Scriptures by providing a contemporary interpretation –

subtle and not fundamentalist to be sure – of the prophets. 'Our hope is lost,' Ezekiel denied in the name of God. 'Our hope is not lost,' was the response of Zionism. These things were no accident, still less the result of an exceptionally clever publicist's imagination. They demonstrate the center and core of Zionist spirituality and piety: the old-new myth of peoplehood, land, redemption above all. The astonishing achievements of Zionism are the result of the capacity of Zionism to reintegrate the tradition with contemporary reality, to do so in an entirely factual, matter-of-fact framework, thus to eschew faith and to elicit credence. Zionism speaks in terms of Judaic myth, indeed so profoundly that myth and reality coincide.

# 10 Judaism and the Zionist Problem

*Judaism* 10 (1970), 311–323

The success of Zionism in solving the central Jewish problems of the modern age also creates new dilemmas for the Judaic religious tradition. Since Zionism functions for Jewry in much the same way that religions do for other peoples, the role and function of Judaism – the complex of myths, rituals, social and cultural forms by which classical Jews experienced and interpreted reality – now prove exceptionally ambiguous. Because Zionism appropriates the eschatological language and symbolism of classical Judaism, Judaists face an unwanted alternative: either to repudiate Zionism or to acquiesce in the historicization, the politicization, of what had formerly stood above politics and beyond history. The choice, to be sure, was recognized and faced by small Reform and Orthodox circles, as everyone knows. The classical reformers repudiated Zionism in the name of the mission of Israel, which, they held, required Jewry to take a decisive role in the universal achievement by all men of the Messianic age. Their last, and unworthy, heirs accurately repeat the rhetoric, but do not possess the moral authority of the nineteenth-century reformers. Likewise, Orthodox leadership in Eastern Europe and the USA quite early discerned what they understood to be the heretical tendency of Zionism: the advocacy that Jews save themselves, rather than depend on the Messiah, and return to Zion before the foreordained end of time. Their repulsive continuators present no interesting differences from the anti-Zionist reformers.

For the great mass of American Jews, who take literally the Zionist interpretation of Jewish history and innocently identify Zionism with Judaism, but regard themselves also both as Americans by nationality and Jews by religion, naïve belief substitutes for and precludes close analysis. They have yet to come to grips with the inner contradictions recognized by the extremists of Reform and Orthodox Judaism. Indeed, they exasperate Israeli Zionists as much as Diaspora anti-Zionists. If Zionist, then why American? If the end has come, why not accept the discipline of the eschaton? If the end has not come, how to justify the revision of the Judaic consciousness and its reformation along Zionist lines? Nor has US Jewry taken seriously the demands of logic and intellect for the formation of a credible ideology to explain the status quo and justify it.

'ENLANDISEMENT'

But the problem is not American alone, nor does it face only those who articulately espouse the Zionist idea. Rightly, understood, the problem is not a new one. The tension between ethnicism and religion, between 'enlandisement' and universality, between Jewish nationalism and the mission of Israel, characterizes the history of the Jewish people and of Judaism throughout. Take, for example, the conflict of symbolism represented by Torah and Messiah. One achieves salvation through study of Torah and carrying out its precepts. *Or* one will be saved at the end of days by the Messiah of the House of David. But if Messiah, what need of Torah? And if Torah, why the Messiah? To be sure, the two are harmonized: if all Israel will keep a single Sabbath as the Torah teaches, then the Messiah will come. So the one is made to depend on the other. For the Talmudic rabbis, the Messiah depends upon Torah, and is therefore subordinate. Torah is an essentially particularist means of attaining salvation. Its observance is the obligation of Jews. Of all the commandments therein, only seven apply to non-Jews. The Messiah is primarily a universal figure. His action affects all mankind. Both nature and the nations, as much as Israel and its land, are the objects of his solicitude. Israel first, to be sure, but everyone at last comes to the end of days.

The tension between *holy land* and *holy Torah* as salvific symbols is pointed out by 'Abd al-Tafâhum in a remarkable essay, 'Doctrine' (in A. J. Arberry, ed., *Religion in the Middle East*, Cambridge, 1969, Vol. II, Part 2, *The Three Religions in Concord and Conflict*, pp. 365–412). What is remarkable is that al-Tafâhum (who is, I presume, a Moslem, though he is not identified as such by the editor) writes informedly and sympathetically about all three Middle Eastern religions. He writes (p. 367): 'The whole self-understanding of the Hebrews turns on "enlandisement" and habitation and then, centuries later, on "disen-landisement" and dispersion. Its two poles are Exodus and Exile … The triangular relationship is that of God, people, and territory.'

With the exile, the physical symbol is reinforced, and, in time, moved into the framework of the last things. Internalizing the efforts of historical weakness, the Jews understood the exile as punishment for their sins in the land – 'unrighteous tenancy' – and, as al-Tafâhum says, 'The single theme of "enlandisement" as the sign and pledge of the divine will and the human response' becomes paramount. To this is added a second understanding of exile: 'the nationhood to educate nations, the awareness of election and particularity that embraces a universal parable for all the segments of mankind and all the diversified economic and spiritual tenancies of terrestrial habitation by peoples and races in those interactions that make culture and history'.

The meaning of Jewish history therefore becomes the philosophy of 'experienced Zion', an experience available both in the land and outside of it. The symbolism of Judaic religious experience was ever more shaped by having *and* not having the land. Having the land means standing in a proper relationship with the natural order. Al-Tafâhum refers to A. D. Gordon: 'everything creaturely is material for sanctification ... The land of promise is properly not merely a divine bestowal but human fulfillment'. Love of Zion produces the marriage of Messiahship and kingship, land and nation. Above all, it bears the intense particularities of Jewish existence, the overwhelming love for Israel – land, people, faith – characteristic of Jews through time.

'Disenlandisement', by contrast, produces the universal concern of Israel for all people: the willingness to enter into intimate relationship with each and every civilization. Election stands over against universality, but not wholly so: 'Only you have I known among the families of man, therefore I shall visit on you all your iniquities.' The unresolved tension in the history of Judaism is between privilege and particularity, on the one side, and the privilege of service to men on the other. Unlike Christianity, Judaism never chose to transcend its history, its intimacy with the Jews.

Al-Tafâhum poses the question: 'If Jewry disapproves the universalizing of its human mission which has happened in the Church, how does it continue to reconcile its sense of privilege with the self-transcending obligation, confessed and prized, within that very identity?' Is Israel, the Jewish people, a mere ethnic continuity? Can it equate spiritual vocation with biological persistence? ... 'Can the "seed of Abraham" in any case be, in these times, a physically guaranteed notion? Is destiny identical with heredity and fidelity with birth?' 'Can [Jewry] either delegate its universal duty or realize it merely by the percentage of literal seed?'

In former times, these questions found a response in the allegation that Israel had a mission to carry out among the nations. Israel was a presence within the world, 'absorbing its values, using its languages and participating in its life, while casting off, sometimes almost in embarrassment, the distinctiveness of its own history and cultic life'.

But that response has its limitations, for in discounting the 'historic elements of dogma and sanctity'. Jews also lost all sense of particularity and readily gave up what was unique to themselves to join the commonalities of mankind. The mission ended in assimilation among those to be missionized.

Zionism, al-Tafâhum observes, 'posits in new and more incisive form the old question of universality'. It contains within itself 'an ever sharper ambiguity about the final questions of the universal meaning and obligation of the chosen people ... By its own deepest convictions Judaism is committed to the benediction of all people and without this loyalty its very particularity is disqualified.'

The question therefore stands:

> Has the new 'enlandisement' betrayed the old? Was Diaspora the true symbol or the tragic negation of what vocation means? Are chosen-ness and the law, identity as God's and duty to man, still proper and feasible clues to Jewish existence? Or is the land now no more than the territorial location of a secular nationality apostate from itself?

Al-Tafâhum rightly asserts that these issues are not merely of political interest, for 'they reach most deeply into ... the doctrinal heart'. It would be difficult to improve on this statement of the dilemma raised for modern Judaism by Zionism. If Zionism solves 'the Jewish problem', it also creates interesting problems for Judaism.

### 'EXCEPT THE JEWS'

Jews, too, have recognized this paradoxical quality of Jewish existence, particularly amid a universal, international situation. Writing in the *New Yorker* (21 March 1970, p. 42), I. B. Singer has a character state that:

> The modern Jew can't live without anti-Semitism. If it's not there, he's driven to create it. He has to bleed for humanity – battle the reactionaries, worry about the Chinese, the Manchurians, the Russians, the untouchables in India, the Negroes in America. He preaches revolution and at the same time he wants all the privileges of capitalism for himself. He tries to destroy nationalism in others but prides himself on belonging to the Chosen People. How can a tribe like this exist among strangers ...

One can hardly regard Singer's insight as mere fiction, when the Lakeville studies have shown it is fact. Suburban Jews there, studied by Marshall Sklare and Joseph Greenblum (*Jewish Identity on the Suburban Frontier*, New York, 1967), raise Jewish children in a culture of equalitarianism and send them to colleges where ethnic liberalism predominates. At the same time they expect the children to develop strong Jewish identification. To be a good Jew in Lakeville is to be ethical, kind, helpful. But moral excellence does not derive from the particular ethic of Judaism, though people suppose it does. It is a function of the generalized upper-class liberalism of the community. The authors wonder:

> Will not a secularism which is unsupported ideologically wither away when social conditions change? Will future generations be prepared to live with the dichotomy [with] which the Lakeville Jew abides: a universal humanitarianism as the prime value in combination with the practice of giving priority to Jewish causes? May [future generations] not conclude that their humanitarian aspirations dictate that they place the accent on the general rather than the Jewish?

The paradox expressed by Singer accurately describes Lakeville Jews, who espouse universal values and teach them to their children, while at the same time wanting to preserve their own particular group, to marry their children off only to Jews. If the people is unique, then what is universal about it? If the people wish to preserve its ethnic existence, then why should it claim to stand with, and for, all mankind?

### A HOSTILE VIEW

Zionism solves 'the Jewish problem'. Its success lies only partially in politics. The more profound problems for which it serves as a satisfactory solution are inward, spiritual, and ultimately religious. Just as the Judaic tradition had formerly told Jews what it meant to be Jewish – had supplied them with a considerable definition of their identity – so does Zionism in the modern age. Jews who had lost hold of the mythic structure of the past were given a grasp on a new myth, one composed of the restructured remnants of the old one.

The Jew had formerly been a member of a religious nation, believing in Torah revealed at Sinai, in one God who had chosen Israel, hoping for the Messiah and a return to the land in the end of days.

Jews who gave up that story of where they came from and who they are tell a new story based on the old, but in superficially secular form. To be Jewish means to live in the land and to share in the life of the Jewish nation, which became the State of Israel.

To a hostile observer, things looked like this: the elements of 'Jewishness' and the components of 'Israelism' are to be one and the same – sacrifice, regeneration, resurrection. The sacrifice is no longer in the Temple: no prophets need decry the multitudes of fatted beasts. What must now must be sacrificed is the blood of Israelis and the treasure of the Diaspora. The regeneration is no longer to be the turning of sinners to repentance – *teshuvah* – but rather the reformation of the economic and cultural realities of the Jewish people. No longer 'parasites', but farmers; no longer dependent upon the cultural achievements of the nations, but creators of a Hebrew and 'enlandised' culture, the Jews would be reborn into a new being and a new age. The resurrection is no longer of the dead at the end of time, but of the people at the end of the Holocaust.

The unfriendly witness sees matters this way: the new Zionist identity, like the old Judaic one, supplied a law for the rituals and attitudes of the faith. The old *halakhah* was made irrelevant, the object of party politics. The new was not partisan at all. All believed in, all fulfilled the law, except for sinners and heretics beyond the pale. The new law requires of Jewish man one great commandment: support Israel. Those who do it best, live there. Those who do not, pay a costly atonement in guilt and ransom for the absent body. The ransom is paid through the perpetual mobilization of the community in an unending campaign for funds. The guilt is exorcised through political rituals: letters to Congressmen and – for bourgeois Jews, what would normally be unheard of – mass rallies and street demonstrations. The guilt of Auschwitz and the sin of living in the Diaspora become intertwined: 'On account of our sin do we live today, and in the wrong place at that?' Above all, the guilty and the sinner forever atone by turning to the *qiblah* of the land: there is no land but Israel, and the Jewish people are its product. The development of an American-Jewish, or Judaic, culture is seen as irrelevant to the faith. The philanthropists will not support it, for no funds are left after allocations for Israel and for domestic humanitarian institutions. The rabbis will not speak of it, for the people will not listen. The people will hear of nothing but victories, and victories are won in this world, upon a fleshly battlefield, with weapons of war.

The old self-hatred – the vile anti-Semitism of an Alexander Portnoy – is left behind. No longer weak, one hardly needs to compensate for weakness by pretensions to moral superiority, and then to pay the price of that compensation by hatred of one's own weakness. Jews no longer look down on goyim, for they feel like them. The universal humanism, the cosmopolitanism of the old Jew, are abandoned in the new particularism. The old grandmother who looked for Jewish names in reports of plane crashes has given way to the new grandson who turns off the news after the Middle Eastern reports are done with.

The Jew no longer makes contradictory demands on society. He no longer wants to be accepted into the tradition of society. In the new ethnicism of the hour, he seeks only his share. The liberal dilemma has been resolved. Jews now quite honestly interpret the universe in terms of their particular concerns. Self-hatred, liberalism, the crisis of identity – the three characteristics of the mid-twentieth-century American Jew – all fade into the background. The end of the old myths no longer matters much, for new ones have arisen in their place. The American Jews who did not want to be so Jewish that they could not also be part of the undifferentiated majority have had their wish fulfilled. Some have indeed ceased to be Jewish at all, and no one cares. Many others have found a place in the new, well-differentiated majority – so goes the hostile view.

## AGAINST RELIGIOUS REACTION

In my view, it is reactionary to cavil at these developments. Only an antiquarian cares about the end of the old myths and the solution of the dilemmas that followed. Zionists need make no apologies to those who point out the profound changes that Zionism effects in Jewish existence. They need only ask, is self-hatred better than what we have done? Is a crisis of identity to be preferred over its resolution? Are people better off living among the remnants of disappointed other-worldly hopes, or shaping new aspirations? Surely it is healthier for men to recover a normal life than to lament the end of an abnormal one. Granted that the Jewish situation has radically changed, I contend that it is no worse, and a good deal better, than what has been left behind. All the invidious contrasts in the world change nothing.

Zionism has had a uniformly beneficial effect upon Jewry. Is a crisis of identity to be preferred over its resolution? Are people better off living among the remnants of disappointed other-worldly hopes, or shaping new aspirations? Surely it is healthier for men to recover a normal life than to lament the end of an abnormal one. Granted, the Jewish situation has radically changed. I contend it is no worse, and a good deal better, than what has been left behind. All the invidious contrasts in the world change nothing.

Zionism has had a uniformly beneficial effect upon Jewry. It achieves the reconstruction of Jewish identity by its reaffirmation of the nationhood of Israel in the face of the disintegration of the religious foundations of Jewish peoplehood. Zionism indeed supplies a satisfactory explanation for the continued life of the Jewish group. It reintegrates the realities of Jewish group life with an emotional, intellectual, and mythic explanation for those realities. If Zionism really is a new religion for the Jews, then I think, on that account, it is not obligated to apologize for its success. On the contrary, Zionism works a miracle by making it possible for the Jewish group to renew its life. It redeems the broken lives of the remnants of the Holocaust. But it also breathes new life into the survivors of a different sort of holocaust, the erosion of Jewish self-respect, dignity, and loyalty throughout the western Diaspora. Jews who want more than anything else to become Americans are enabled to reaffirm their Jewishness. Throughout the world, Jews who had lost a religious, Judaic way of viewing reality regain a Jewish understanding of themselves.

Zionism indeed serves as a religion because it does what a religion must do: it supplies the meaning of felt-history; it explains reality, makes sense of chaos, and supplies a worthwhile dream for people who find in Jewishness nothing more than neurotic nightmares. Neither metaphysics nor theology proves necessary, for Zionism explains what the people already know and take for granted as fact. Zionism legitimates what Alexander Portnoy observed but could not accept: that Jews are men of flesh and blood, that (in Portnoy's phrase), *there is an id in Yid*. What is remarkable is that the early Zionists sought to do just that: to normalize the existence of the Jewish people.

THE ZIONIST PROBLEM

In what way, then, does Zionism constitute a problem for Judaism? In my view, it is not its secularity and worldliness, but the mythic insufficiency of Zionism that renders its success a dilemma for contemporary American Jews and for Israeli ones as well.

Let us begin with the obvious. How can American Jews focus their spiritual lives *solely* on a land in which they do not live? It is one thing for that land to be in heaven, at the end of time, or across the Sambatyon for that matter. It is quite another to dream of a faraway place where everything is good – *but* where one may go if one wants to. The realized eschaton is insufficient for a rich and interesting fantasy life, and, moreover, in this-worldly terms it is hypocritical. It means that American Jews live off the capital of Israeli culture. Reliance on the State of Israel furthermore suggests that to satisfy their need for fantasy, American Jews must look forward to ever more romantic adventures reported in the press, rather than to the colorless times of peace. American Jews want to take their vacations among heroes, and then come home to the ordinary workaday world they enjoy and to which Israelis rightly aspire but do not own. The 'enlandisement' of American Judaism – the focusing of its imaginative, inner life upon the land and State of Israel – therefore imposes an ersatz spiritual dimension. We live here *as if* we lived there – but do not choose to migrate.

It furthermore diverts American Judaism from the concrete mythic issues it has yet to solve: Why should anyone be a *Jew* anywhere, in the USA or in Israel? That question is not answered by the recommendation to participate in the spiritual adventures of people in a quite different situation. Since the primary *mitzvoth* of US Judaism concern supplying funds, encouragement, and support for Israel, one wonders whether one must be a Jew at all in order to believe in and practice that form of Judaism. What is 'being Jewish' now supposed to mean?

The underlying problem, which faces both Israeli and American Jews, is understanding what the ambiguous adjective *Jewish* is supposed to mean when the noun *Judaism* has been abandoned. To be sure, for some Israelis and American Jews to be a Jew is to be a citizen of the State of Israel, but that definition hardly serves when Israeli Moslems and Christians are taken into account. If one ignores the exceptions, the rule is still wanting. If to be a Jew is to be – or to dream of being – an Israeli, then the Israeli who chooses to settle in a foreign country ceases to be a Jew when he gives up Israeli citizenship for some other. If all Jews are on the road to Zion, then those who either do not get there or, once there, choose another way, are to be abandoned. That makes Jewishness depend upon quite worldly issues: this one cannot make his living in Tel Aviv, that one does not like the climate of Afula, the other is frustrated by the bureaucracy of Jerusalem. Are they then supposed to give up their share in the 'God of Israel'?

More seriously still, the complete 'enlandisement' of Judaism for the first time since 586 BC forces the Judaic tradition to depend upon the historical fortunes of a single population in a small country. The chances for the survival of the Jewish people have surely been enhanced by the dispersion of the Jews among differing political systems. Until the Second World War, Jews had stood on both sides of every international contest from most remote antiquity. Now, we enter an age in which the fate of Jewry and destiny of Judaism are supposed to depend on the fortunes of one state and one community alone.

That, to be sure, is not a fact, for even now the great Jewish communities in the USSR, Western Europe, Latin America, and North America, as well as smaller ones elsewhere, continue to conform to the historical pattern. But, ideologically, things have vastly changed. With all the Jewish eggs in one basket, the consequence of military actions is supposed to determine the future of the whole of Jewry and Judaism. So the excellence of some 800 pilots and the availability of a few dozen fighter-bombers are what it all comes down to. Instead of the 36 righteous men of classical myth are 72 phantoms – mirages – a curious revision of the old symbolism.

## A JUDAIC ANSWER

Just what is *important* about being Jewish and in Judaism? In my view, the answer must pertain both to the State of Israel and to the *Golah* communities in equal measure. It cannot be right only for American Jewry, for we are not seeking a *Galut* ideology and no one would accept it. Such an ideology – right for here but irrelevant to Israelis – would obviously serve the selfish interests and the peculiar situation of American Jews alone. But the answer cannot pertain only to the situation of the Israeli Jews, for precisely the same reasons.

What is important about being Jewish is the capacity of the Jewish people and its mythic creations to preserve the tension between the intense particularities of their life and the humanity they share with the rest of mankind. That tension, practically unique to Jewry, derives from its exceptional historical experience. Until now, it has been the basis for the Jews' remarkable role in human history.

Others have not felt such a tension. To be human and to be English – or Navaho – were hardly differentiated. Why should they have been, when pretty much everyone one cared for and knew was English, or Navaho? To be a Jew in any civilization was, and is, to share the values held by everyone *but* to stand in some ways apart (not above) from the others. It was, and is, to love one's native land with open arms, to preserve the awareness of other ways of living life and shaping culture.

To be sure, before the destruction of the First Temple, Jewish people may well have been much like others. But from that time forward the land was loved with an uncommon intensity, for it had been lost, then regained, and therefore could never again be taken for granted. And alongside land, the people found, as few have *had* to, that Jews live by truths that could endure outside a single land and culture.

Jewry discovered in itself an international culture, to be created and recreated in every land and in every language. It found in its central moral and ethical convictions something of value for all of civilizations. Its apprehension of God and its peculiar method of receiving and spelling out revelation in the commonplaces of everyday life were divorced from a single place, even the holiest place in the world, where they had begun.

But al-Tafahûm is wrong in supposing that the Jews' 'disenlandisement' was the precondition for the recognition of what was of universal importance about themselves. On the contrary, it was in the land itself that the awareness of ethnic differentiation proved the least vivid. Outside of it the group turned inward, and rightly so, for it became most acutely sensitive to its differences from others. In this respect the gentile students of Judaism do not understand what it is to be a Jew. The Diaspora Jew addresses himself to the nations and in their own language, but in doing so he speaks as a *Jew*. It is the 'enlandised' Jew who sees himself as no different from everyone within his range of vision, therefore as a man among men, rather than a Jew among gentiles. The willingness and necessity to enter into intimate relationship with each and every civilization therefore produced two sorts of encounters: one, between the Jewish man in his land and other men who might come there, or whom he might know elsewhere, men who held in common the knowledge of what it means to belong to some one place; the other, between the world and the always self-aware Jew living in other lands, a Jew sensitive to the language and experience of those lands precisely because he was forever at the margins of the common life.

Jewry did not disapprove of the universalizing of its mission in the Church. It simply did not recognize that the Church ever truly carried out that mission. Jewry perceived no discontinuity requiring reconciliation between its sense of peoplehood (privilege) and its 'self-transcending obligation'. The Jews long ago ceased to be a mere ethnic continuity, and no one, either in the State of Israel or the Diaspora, regards the Jews as merely an ethnic group. One can, after all, become a Jew by other than ethnic and territorial assimilation, through *conversion*. That fact predominates in all discussions of what it is to be a Jew. The issue comes from the other side: *Can* one become a Jew not through conversion, but through mere assimilation? The dogged resistance of Jewry to the reduction of Jewishness to ethnicity alone testifies to the falseness of al-Tafahûm's reading of the Jewish situation.

But his other question is indeed troubling: Is destiny to be equated with heredity and fidelity with birth? The answer to that question can be found only in the working out of the potentialities of both Israeli and Diaspora Jewish life. To be sure, the old Diaspora – the one before 1948 – absorbed the values of the nations and could locate no one center where the distinctiveness, hence the universality, of Jewish history and civilization might be explored. Zionism does indeed posit in new and more incisive form the old question of universality, *but it also answers that question*. In the Jewish State, Jews lose their sense of peculiarity. They re-enter the human situation common to everyone but Jews. In the State of Israel everyone is Jewish, therefore no one is the Jew. This, in my view, opens the way to an interesting development: the reconsideration of Jewish humanity in relationship with the other sorts of humanity in the world. It is now possible for the normal to communicate with the normal.

What the Israelis have to communicate is clear to one and all. They have not divorced themselves from important elements of the Jewish past, but have retained and enhanced them. The possession of the land, after all, represents such an important element. What does it mean to believe that one's moral life is somewhere related to the destiny of the land in which one lives? In times past the question would have seemed nonsensical. But today no people is able to take its land, its environment, for granted. Everyone is required to pay attention to what one does with one's blessing. Today each land is endangered by immoral men who live upon and make use of it. The moral pollution of which the prophets spoke may infect not only a society, but the way a society makes use of its resources. The intimate relationship between Israel and the land is no longer so alien to the existence of other nations, and the ecological-moral answers found in the land and State of Israel are bound to have universal meaning.

I choose this example because it is the least obvious. The record of the State of Israel is, in my view, not ambiguous about 'the final questions of the universal meaning and obligation of the chosen people'. One need not be an Israeli apologist to recognize the numerous ways in which the State of Israel has sought to make war without fanaticism, to wage peace with selflessness. Only indifference to the actual day-to-day record of the State of Israel, with its technical assistance, its thirst for peace, its fundamentally decent society at home, and above all its hatred of what it must do to survive, justifies questions concerning Israel's 'universal duty'. On the contrary, it seems to me that Israeli society has, within the limits of its wisdom and power, committed itself to the benediction of all peoples, and with its loyalty to that very blessing its very particularity is verified and justified. I therefore do not agree that the new 'enlandisement' has betrayed the old. It has fulfilled it.

The other half of the question pertains to the Diaspora. The Diaspora was neither the true symbol nor the tragic negation of Israel's vocation. 'Chosen-ness and law, obligation to God and duty to man' are still proper and feasible clues to Jewish existence *both* at home and abroad. The land never was, and is not now, merely the territorial locus of a secular nationality. The existence of the Diaspora guarantees otherwise. The Diaspora supplies the certainty that men of many languages and civilizations will look to Zion for more than a parochial message, just as the Israelis make certain that Diaspora Jews will hear that message. But, as I said, things are the reverse of what al-Tafahûm supposes. The Diaspora brings an acute consciousness of being different from other men, and therefore turns to the State to discover the ways in which it is like the others. The Diaspora contributes its variety and range of human experience to the consciousness of the State of Israel. But the State offers the Diaspora the datum of normality.

One cannot divide the Jewish people into two parts, the 'enlandised' and the 'disenlandised'. Those in the land look outward. Those outside look toward the land. Those in the land identify with the normal peoples. Those abroad see in the land what it means to be extraordinary. But it is what happens to the whole, altogether, that is decisive for the Judaic tradition. Together, the Diaspora Jew and the Israeli represent a single tradition, a single memory. That memory is of having had a land and lost it, *and* never having repudiated either the memory of the land *or* the experience of living elsewhere. No one in the State of Israel can imagine that to be in the land is for the Jew what being in England is to the Englishman. The Englishman has never lost England and come back. So, one cannot distinguish between the Israeli and the Diaspora Jew. Neither one remembers or looks upon a world in which his particular values and ideals are verified by society. Neither ceases to be cosmopolitan. Both preserve a universal concern for *all* Israel. Both know diversities of culture and recognize therefore the relativity of values, even as they affirm their own.

This forms what is unique in the Jewish experience: the denial of men's need to judge all values by their particular, self-authenticating system of thought. In this regard the Diaspora reinforces the Israeli's view of the world, and the Israeli reciprocates. Both see as transitory and merely useful what others understand to be absolute and perfected. Behind the superficial eschatological self-confidence that Zionism has completed its task or that the world has been perfected, the world is seen by both parts of the Jewish people to be insufficient and incomplete.

The Israelis' very sense of necessity preserves the Jews' neatest insight: without choice, necessity imposes duty, responsibility, unimagined possibilities. The Jews are not so foolish as to have forgotten the ancient eternal cities – theirs and others' – that are no more. They know that it is not the place, but the quality of life within it, that truly matters. No city is holy, not even Jerusalem, but men must live in some one place and assume the responsibilities of the mundane city. But if no city is holy, at least Jerusalem may be made into a paradigm of sanctity. Though all they have for mortar may be slime, Jewish men will indeed build what they must, endure as they have to. The opposite is not to wander, but to die.

But have Diaspora Jews strayed so far from those same truths? In sharing the lives of many civilizations, do they do other than to assume responsibility for place? Do they see the particular city as holy, because they want to sanctify life in it? Or do they, too, know that the quality of life *anywhere* is what must truly matter? Men must live in some one place, and in so far as Jewish men have something to teach of all they have learned in thirty centuries, they should live and learn and teach in whatever place they love. One may err if one underestimates the capacity of the outsider, of the Diaspora Jew, to love.

I therefore see no need either to repudiate Zionism or to give up the other elements that have made *being Jewish* a magnificent mode of humanity. Zionism, on the contrary, supplies Jewry with yet another set of experiences, another set of insights into what it means to be human. Only those who repudiate the unity of Israel, the Jewish people, in favor of either of its segments can see things otherwise. But viscerally American Jews know better, and I think they are right in refusing to resolve the tensions of their several commitments. Zionism creates problems for Judaism only when Zionists think that all that being Jewish means is 'enlandisement' and, thereby, redemption. But Zionists *cannot* think so when they contemplate the range of human needs and experiences they as men must face. Zionism is a part of Judaism. It cannot be made the whole, because Jews are more than people who need either a place to live or a place on which to focus fantasies. The profound existential necessities of Jews – both those they share with every man and those they have to themselves – are not met by Zionism or 'enlandisement' alone. Zionism provides much of the vigor and excitement of contemporary Jewish affairs, but in so far as Jews live and suffer, are born and die, reflect and doubt, raise children and worry over them, love and work – in so far as Jews are human, they require Judaism.

# PART III
## JUDAISM IN THE CONTEXT
## OF THE HOLOCAUST

# 11 A Holocaust Primer

*National Review* 31/31 (1979), 975–979

In January 1945, while the gas chambers were still working, people knew that it was all over for the Jews of Europe. Most were dead, the rest dying. Few would survive until spring. At the annual conference of the Yiddish Scientific Institute held that month, the greatest Judaic theologian of the twentieth century, Abraham Joshua Heschel, a Jew from Poland, said what there was to be said. What lessons there were to be drawn from the death of European Jewry he did not specify; what lessons there were to be learned from its life he proposed to state.

He asked his hearers how one might appraise the historical significance of the world now ended in smoke and ashes. His answer was:

> As Jews, with an old tradition for appraising and judging events and generations, we evaluate history by different criteria, namely, by how much refinement there is in the life of a people, by how much spiritual substance there is in its everyday existence ... We gauge culture by the extent to which a whole people, not only individuals, lives in accordance with the dictates of an eternal doctrine or strives for spiritual integrity; the extent to which inwardness, compassion, justice, and holiness are to be found in the daily life of the masses.

Speaking of the millions of Eastern European Jews, who had borne the brunt of the massacres, he said: 'in this period our people attained the highest degree of inwardness ... it was the golden period in the history of the Jewish soul'. Heschel concluded this oration, which became a book under the significant title, *The Earth Is the Lord's*, as follows: 'Loyal to the presence of the ultimate in the common we may be able to make it clear that man is more than man, that in doing the finite he may perceive the infinite.'

It should not be thought that Heschel addressed the world like a universalist Reform rabbi, speaking 'to all humanity, not *only* to the Jews'. His was a distinctively Judaic message. The penultimate passage of his oration contained that profound sadness, profoundly understated, which expresses the meaning of a long and often trying history:

> Our life is beset with difficulties, yet it is never devoid of mean-
> ing ... Our existence is not in vain. There is a Divine earnestness
> about our life. This is our dignity. To be invested with dignity
> means to represent something more than oneself. The gravest sin
> for a Jew is to forget what he represents. We are God's stake in
> human history ... The time for the kingdom may be far off, but
> the task is plain; to retain our share in God in spite of peril and
> contempt.

But there is a Jewish meaning to the massacre of European Jewry which of itself is also a human meaning. It is that simple affirmation of life in the face of death and that defiance of despair that Heschel expressed, and which he also personally embodied in that cold and terrible January of 1945. For he had been snatched from Warsaw after the Germans had arrived there, and he had lost all of his family. He was the last of them: the witness, the survivor, the brand plucked from the burning, the saving remnant. In his testament is contained the spirituality of Judaism: fully realized, he claimed, in that world which is no more, that world which is only to be mourned. While the dying was still going on, he entitled his testament, 'The Earth Is the Lord's.' There is nothing more to say.

How have we come from the defiance of despair, from that affirmation of God's rule on earth and in heaven, to 'the Holocaust'? For there surely is a contrast between the dignity and hopefulness of Heschel, who had suffered and lost but endured, and the bathos and obsession of those who, 35 years later, want to speak of nothing but transports, gas chambers, a million abandoned teddy bears, and the death of God.

Heschel imputed no enduring guilt to others, whether 'the gentiles', or 'the Christians', or 'the Germans'. Like Leo Baeck, chief rabbi of German Reform Judaism and another survivor of the concentration camps, he may have wondered whether the Germans had forgiven themselves. But he knew that the earth is the Lord's and he affirmed that judgment belongs to God. A man who talked of dignity and who understood that we represent more than ourselves, Heschel spoke with silence. He mourned to the day of his death. But he loved life, accepted all, regretted nothing. Having given his testimony, he went on to other things. The word 'Holocaust' scarcely appears in his vast theological writings. The problem of evil is a problem, but is no more than that. Heschel wrote much more on Job than on 'Auschwitz'. The stench and human degradation, the unspeakable cruelty and inexpressible horror – these he knew full well. But he speaks of dignity and refinement. The epitaph is written not by Hitler, but by Heschel.

But if Heschel spoke the last word in the closing months of the war, whence 'the Holocaust'? We would look in vain in the 1950s for what some call 'Holocaustomania'. The Jews were concerned with other things. There was a return to religion and, among the second and third generations of American Jews, to the synagogue. Indeed, Heschel's theological writings of that period enjoyed a wide and appreciative audience. Describing American Judaism in the mid-1950s, the great sociologist Nathan Glazer managed to write an entire book without making more than passing reference to the destruction of European Jewry.

The contrast with the 1970s is striking. Now there is no way to address the Jewish world without referring to 'the Holocaust'. It is taken for granted that that event, bearing meanings all of us know and note needs to articulate and expiate upon, exhausts the agenda for discussions between Jewry and the world at large.

Now, it should not be thought that in the twenty years following 1945 people failed to notice the absence of more than five million European Jews, who were among more than 20 million European civilians who had perished in the recent war. There was, after all, the State of Israel, created in part as a refuge for those survivors of European Jewry who chose to go there and who supported it in some measure for its role as a phoenix risen from the ashes of the extermi-nated communities of the Continent. Still more important, there were many scholarly works and novels, written both to preserve the events in a factual way and to explore their meaning for the life of the imag-ination. Most important of all, a profound sense of their status as survivors seized world Jewry. American Jews knew that, had their parents or grandparents not left Europe, they too would have been killed. America for them assumed a providential aspect, as did the State of Israel for those Israelis (and they are many) who had lost their families in Poland or Holland or Hungary. So the Jews did not forget. They drew lessons, and taught them. They did not neglect the tasks of mourning and memorialization.

But we do not find in the 1950s what we see today: that obsession with 'the Holocaust' that wants to make the tragedy into the princi-pal subject of public discourse with Jews and about Judaism. The refinement, restraint, and dignity of Heschel and his generation have not been taken as models by his successors. There have even been proposals to set up 'Holocaust centers' in every Jewish community, complete with buildings, professional staffs, exhibitions, programs, and commemorative events. Such 'Holocaust centers' are to function like synagogues. But the faith which brings them into being is not Judaism and its rites, but, rather, one chapter in the history of the Jewish people. One does not have to aim at forgetting the unforgettable in order to judge such 'centers' as nihilistic and obsessive, lacking that dignity and faith of which Heschel spoke.

Now we have the President's Holocaust Commission, which raises the whole business above the level of parochialism and provinciality. Just this spring in the rotunda of the Capitol there was a solemn memorial service, a public event within the context of America's civil religion. So far as America represents itself as a religious nation, with a place for Catholic, Protestant, Jew (and, I hope, Moslem, Buddhist, Russian, and Greek Orthodox, and many more), the Judaic component is now defined by the 'the Holocaust'.

Not a few Jews find the Holocaust Commission puzzling. There has not, after all, been a commission created to memorialize the Armenian massacres of the First World War (the first major act of genocide in the twentieth century), or the political violence and mass murder of Stalinist Russia and Maoist China, let alone the Nazi war against the Poles, Russians, South Slavs, Slovaks, and other people deemed by the racist *Wissenschaft* to be subhuman. Such commissions as these would surely prove equally puzzling to blacks and Indians on our own shores, who would wonder why we commemorate these sorts of acts done abroad, which are forgotten when they occur in our own land.

Since the Armenian people in America shape their distinctive life around their faith and church, and, mourning for the dead, have yet to found Armenian centers of remembrance of Turkish atrocities alongside their institutions of community and church, we must inquire into this aspect of Jewish activity. What role is the 'Holocaust' *as symbol* meant to serve? For it is as evocative symbol, not as historical memory, that 'the Holocaust' wins its capital H and its quotation marks.

If we want to know what important questions 'the Holocaust' answers for American Jews, we have first of all to ask when the sorrow and pain of the European tragedy turned into 'the Holocaust'. Also, we need to discover when 'the Holocaust' became a powerful and evocative symbol. When did it begin to bear its own, unexamined, self-evident meanings, to impose its own unanalyzed significance, so that, without reflection, we all know how we are supposed to feel and think and what we are supposed to do? The answer lies in the career of another distinguished theologian of Judaism, Emil Fackenheim. If Heschel addressed the world that endured the war and personally suffered in it, Fackenheim became the prophet of 'the Holocaust' and one of its powerful ideologists. Tracing the turn in his career helps us to isolate the moment of transition from event to symbol.

Before the 1967 war, Fackenheim was known as a religious existentialist and a scholar of Hegel. Writing on Fackenheim in the late 1960s, his biographer in the *Encyclopaedia Judaica* declared that the theologian's book on Hegel 'contains the substance of his ideas on Jewish thought'. Fackenheim's other books and essays written before 1970 take up established themes of the philosophy of religion and Judaic theology; since that time, however, all of his work has been dominated by the symbol, 'Auschwitz'. To Fackenheim is credited the apophthegm, 'Let's not hand Hitler any more victories.' The practical meaning of that resolution, it is invariably understood, is that Jews should practice Judaism, and Jews and gentiles should support the State of Israel. One of Fackenheim's critics, Michael Wyschogrod, declares that Fackenheim has substituted 'the commanding voice of Auschwitz' for the revelation of Sinai, and Hitler for Moses. While this may be somewhat extreme, it contains a measure of truth.

Clearly, something happened to Fackenheim and his audience between the end of the 1950s and the beginning of the 1970s. This was an experience so fundamental as to impart to the massacre of European Jewry a symbolic meaning, self-evident importance, and mythic quality. Jews had been put to death in unimaginably dreadful circumstances. At the time, Heschel had laid stress on dignity and faith in the earth which is the Lord's; by the 1970s, matters had so changed that dignity, refinement, and faith were no longer acceptable themes. The messages had shifted over the years; now the events were made to speak of other things, and to people other than the original victims and survivors.

What turned an historical event into a powerful symbol of contemporary social action and imagination was a searing shared experience. For millions of Jews, the dreadful weeks before the 1967 war gave a new vitality to the historical record of the years of 1933 to 1945 – the war and its result. Before 5 June 1967 the State of Israel appeared to be doomed: surrounded, penned within its constricted frontiers by vast and well-armed enemies. Worse still, the state was abandoned by all its friends, whose commitments (made after the 1956 war) to open the Suez Canal and to keep open the Gulf of Eilat/Aqaba had proved worthless. One of the critical points in the 'Holocaust' myth (truth told as story) now is that European Jews had

no place to go. The world abandons the Jews in their time of doom –
*and in 1967 it happened again.*

But the story of the extermination of European Jewry could not
serve as the foundation for a usable myth of 'Holocaust' without one
further component. No myth is serviceable if people cannot make it
their own and through it explain their own lives; no story of a life can
end in gruesome death. A corollary of 'Holocaust', therefore, had to
be redemption. The extermination of European Jewry could become
'the Holocaust' only on 19 June when, in the aftermath of a remarkable victory, the State of Israel celebrated the return of the people of
Israel to the ancient wall of the Temple of Jerusalem. On that day the
extermination of European Jewry attained the – if not happy, at least
viable – ending which served to transform events into a myth, and to
endow a symbol with a single, ineluctable meaning.

This is still only part of the story. Once 'the Holocaust' had taken
shape, its suitability for the purpose of the social imagination still had
to be fully exposed. It had to explain more than itself; it had to speak
to more people, about more things, than it had at the outset.
Certainly American Jews and Israeli Jews could not interpret 'the
Holocaust' in the same way and for the same purpose, without doing
violence to the distinctive context in which each group makes its life.

The place of 'the Holocaust' in the civil religion of the State of
Israel is easy to understand. It forms a critical element in the public
explanation of why there must be a State of Israel, why it must have
its present character and not some other, and why every citizen must
be prepared to support the state in peacetime and to fight for it in
war. The state, then, forms the complement of 'the Holocaust', completing and rendering whole that sundered pained consciousness represented by the humiliation and degradation of the event itself. For
Israelis, the myth of 'Holocaust and redemption' provides that core or
common truth on the foundation of which a society can be built. That
it is self-evidently a true myth to Israelis goes without saying.

For American Jews, then, the myth of 'Holocaust and redemption'
must prove puzzling. They have not drawn the parallel conclusion –
that America is that refuge and hope the European Jews should have
had – because America was there in the 1930s and 1940s, yet offered
no refuge and no hope. They could not declare this country to have
contributed a fundamentally new chapter to the history of the Jewish
people, at least not in the way in which Israelis declared the foundation of the State of Israel to have inaugurated a new and wholly fresh
era. So far as the myth of 'Holocaust and redemption' enters into
the self-understanding of American Jewry, it has to answer different

questions from those posed by the creation of a state and the sustenance of a society.

I am inclined to see these questions as two separate and distinct ones: the first addressed to the particular world of the Jews, the second to the world at large. But they are not unrelated, for both of them emerge from the special circumstances of the American of Jewish origin whose grandparents or great-grandparents immigrated to this country. For that sort of American Jew, there is no common and acknowledged core of religious experience by which 'being Jewish' may be explained and interpreted. Because anti-Semitism as a perceived social experience has become less common than it was from the 1920s through the early 1950s, there is also no common core of social alienation to account for the distinctive character of the group and to explain why it continues, and must continue, to endure. Indeed, many American Jews, though they continue to affirm their Jewishness, have no clear notion of how they are Jewish, or what their Jewish heritage demands of them. Judaism, for this critical part of the American Jewish population, is merely a reference point, one fact among many. For ideologists of the Jewish community, the most certain answer to the question of the third generation must be, 'There is no real choice.' 'The Holocaust' provides that answer: '*Hitler* knew you were Jewish.'

The formative experiences of 'the Holocaust' are now accessible, alas, without learning and without commitment. No person can encounter the events of 1933 to 1945 without entering into them in imagination. It is better to understate the matter. The experience of 'the Holocaust' is not something that ended in 1945; it ends when I wake up in the morning, and it is renewed when I go to sleep. So it is for all of us. These 'Judaizing experiences', then, do serve the role that Fackenheim had found in them: as Wyschogrod complained, they do take the place of Sinai in nurturing an inner and distinctive consciousness of 'being Jewish'.

The first of the two questions before us, the inner one, is therefore the question of who we are, and why we are what we are and not something else. 'The Holocaust' is made to answer that question. The second is a social question: Who are we in relationship to everybody else? The utility of 'the Holocaust' in this context is not difficult to see, once we realize that the TV counterpart to *The Holocaust* is *Roots*. It follows that, for American Jews, 'the Holocaust' is that ethnic identity which is available to a group of people so far removed from culturally and socially distinctive characteristics as to be otherwise wholly 'assimilated'. 'The Holocaust' is the Jews' special thing: it is what sets them apart from others while giving them a claim upon those others. That is why Jews insist on 'the uniqueness of the Holocaust'. If on campus the blacks have soul food, the Jews will have kosher meals, even if they do not keep the dietary laws under ordinary circumstances. Unstated in this simple equation, *Roots = The Holocaust*, is the idea that being Jewish is an ethnic, and not primarily a religious, category. For nearly a century American Jews have persuaded themselves and their neighbors that they fall into the religious – and therefore acceptable – category of being 'different', and not into the ethnic – and therefore crippling and unwanted – category of being 'different'. Now that they have no Jewish accent, they are willing to be ethnic.

Thus a profound inner dilemma and a difficult matter of social differentiation and identification work themselves out within the myth of 'Holocaust'. As to the 'redemption' chapter of the story, the State of Israel tells the same truths to American Jews as to Israeli Jews. But since American Jews do not, and cannot, infer the same consequences from that story of redemption that Israeli Jews must infer, a certain incongruence has arisen between the two versions. After all, it is difficult to speak much about a redemption that we do not really wish to experience. A salvation which works for others and not for oneself is, in the end, not of much value. The 'Holocaust' part of the myth therefore tends to play a larger part in this country than it does in the State of Israel.

With these facts in mind, we can readily understand why, in appealing for the support of Jewish voters, the White House should turn naturally to the formation of a President's Commission on the Holocaust. I should guess that, if the Armenians were sufficiently numerous and vocal to warrant a President's Commission on something of interest to them, it might well take some form other than a commemoration of the tragedy of 1915 (though I do not know what that might be). Clearly, the blacks want something other than a memorialization of centuries of slavery. They want something for themselves, for today – as well they should: a completely equal share, at the very least, in all that America has to offer.

As Richard L. Rubenstein, a brilliant Judaic theologian of whose thought 'the Holocaust' forms the critical center, says in this context, 'The most appropriate American memorial to the victims of the Holocaust ought to be a national effort for the understanding of large-scale political injustice and violence.' For the issue, properly phrased, of the destruction of European Jewry is the human issue of our unhappy century: how to nurture, in an age of disintegration and destruction, that inwardness, compassion, injustice, and holiness in which we perceive whatever is infinite in ourselves.

# 12 The Implications of the Holocaust

*Journal of Religion* 54/3 (1973), 293–308

### EFFECT ON JEWISH PSYCHOLOGY

The events of 1933–48 constitute one of the decisive moments in the history of Judaism, to be compared in their far-reaching effects with the destruction of the First and Second Temples, 586 BC and AD 70; the massacre of Rhineland Jewries, 1096; the aftermath of the Black Plague, 1349; the expulsion of the Jews from Spain, 1492; or the Ukrainian massacres of 1648–49. But while after the former disasters the Jews responded in essentially religious ways, the response to the Holocaust and the creation of the State of Israel on the surface has not been religious. That is to say, while in the past people explained disaster as a result of sin and therefore sought means of reconciliation with God and atonement for sin, in the twentieth century the Jews superficially did not do this. Instead, they have done what seem to be secular, not religious, deeds: they raised money, engaged in political action, and did all the other things that modern, secular men, confident they can cope with anything, normally do. They did not write new prayers or holy books, create new theologies, develop new religious ideas and institutions.

Yet I should argue that the response to the Holocaust and the creation of the State of Israel differs in form, but not in substance, from earlier responses to disaster. The form now is secular. The substance is deeply religious. For the effect of the Holocaust and the creation of the State of Israel on the Jews has been to produce a new myth – by which I mean a transcendent perspective on events, a story lending meaning and imparting sanctity to ordinary, everyday actions – and a new religious affirmation. Let me recount the salvific story as it is nearly universally perceived by the senior generation of American Jews, those who came to maturity before 1945:

Once upon a time, when I was a young man, I felt helpless before the world. I was a Jew, when being Jewish was a bad thing. As a child, I saw my old Jewish parents, speaking a foreign language and alien in countless ways, isolated from America. And I saw America, dimly perceived to be sure, exciting and promising, but hostile to me as a Jew. I could not get into a good college. I could not aspire to medical school. I could not become an architect or an engineer. I could not even work for an electric utility.

When I took my vacation, I could not go just anywhere, but had to ask whether Jews would be welcome, tolerated, embarrassed, or thrown out. Being Jewish was uncomfortable. Yet I could not give it up. My mother and my father had made me what I was. I could hide, but could not wholly deny, to myself if not to others, that I was a Jew. And I could not afford the price in diminished self-esteem, of opportunity denied, aspiration deferred, and insult endured. Above all, I saw myself as weak and pitiful. I could not do anything about being a Jew nor could I do much to improve my lot as a Jew.

Then came Hitler and I saw that what was my private lot was the dismal fate of every Jew. Everywhere Jew hatred was raised from the gutter to the heights. Not from Germany alone, but from people I might meet at work or in the streets, I learned that being Jewish was a metaphysical evil. 'The Jews' were not accepted, but debated. Friends would claim we were not all bad. Enemies said we were. And we had nothing to say at all.

As I approached maturity, a still more frightening fact confronted me. People guilty of no crime but Jewish birth were forced to flee their homeland, and no one would accept them. Ships filled with ordinary men, women, and children searched the oceans for a safe harbor. And I and they had nothing in common but one fact, and that fact made all else inconsequential. Had I been there, I should have been among them. I, too, should not have been saved at the sea.

Then came the war and, in its aftermath, the revelation of the shame and horror of holocaust, the decay and corrosive hopelessness of the DP camps, the contempt of the nations, who would neither accept nor help the saved remnants of hell. At the darkest hour came the dawn. The State of Israel saved the remnant and gave meaning and significance to the inferno. After the dawn, the great light: Jews no longer helpless, weak, unable to decide their own fate, but strong, confident, decisive.

Then came the corrupting doubt. If I were there, I should have died in hell. But now has come redemption and I am here, not there. How much security there is in knowing that if it should happen again I shall not be lost. But how great a debt has been paid in guilt for being where I am and who I am!

This constitutes the myth that gives meaning and transcendence to the petty lives of ordinary people – the myth of darkness followed by light, of passage through the nether world and past the gates of hell, then, purified by suffering and blood, into the new age. The naturalist myth of American Jewry – that it is not the leaders' alone – conforms to the supernatural structure of the classic myths of salvific religions from time immemorial. Well it might, for a salvific myth has to tell the story of sin and redemption, disaster and salvation, the old being and the new, the vanquishing of death and mourning, crying and pain, the passing away of former things. The vision of the new Jerusalem, complete in 1967, beckoned not tourists, but pilgrims to the new heaven and the new earth. This, as I said, is the myth that shapes the mind and imagination of American Jewry, supplies the correct interpretation and denotes the true significance of everyday events, and turns workaday people into saints. This is the myth that transforms commonplace affairs into history, makes writing a check into a sacred act.

It is not faith, theology, ideology, for none of these offers reasons for its soundness, or needs to. It is myth in that it so closely corresponds to, and yet so magically transforms and elevates, a reality in which people take vision and interpretation for fact. They do not need to believe in or affirm the myth, for they know it to be true. In that they are confident of the exact correspondence between reality and the story that explains reality, they are the saved, the saints, the witnesses to the end of days. We know this is how things really were and what they really meant. We know it because the myth of suffering and redemption corresponds to our perceptions of reality, evokes immediate recognition and assent. It not only bears meaning, it imparts meaning precisely because it explains experience and derives from what we know to be true.

But one must ask whether experience is so stable, the world so unchanging, that we may continue to explain today's reality in terms of what happened yesterday. The answer is that much as we might want to, we cannot. The world has moved on. We can remember, but we cannot re-enact what happened. We cannot replicate the experiences that required explanation according to a profound account of the human and of the Jewish condition. We cannot, because our children will not allow it. They experience a different world – perhaps not better, perhaps not so simple, but certainly different. They know about events, but have not experienced them, and what they know they perceive through their experience of a very different world. The story that gives meaning and imparts transcendence to the everyday experiences of being Jewish simply does not correspond to the reality of the generations born since 1945. They did not know the frightful insecurity, did not face the meaninglessness of Jewish suffering, therefore cannot appreciate the salvation that dawned with the creation of the State of Israel.

Theirs is a more complicated world. Not for them the simple choice of death or life, the simple encounter with uncomplicated evil. For them Jewishness also is more complicated, because the world of the 1930s and 1940s imparted a 'Jewish education', and a 'Jewish consciousness' was elicited by reading a newspaper or simply encountering a hostile society, while today's world does not constitute a school without walls for the education of the Jews. That is, I think, a good thing. Being Jewish is no longer imposed by negative experiences, but is now called forth by affirmative ones. For the younger generation the State of Israel stands not as the end of despair, but as the beginning of hope. It enriches the choices facing the young Jew and expands his consciousness of the potentialities of Jewishness. Not its existence, but its complexity is important. Not its perfection, but its imperfection is compelling. It is important as the object, not of fantasy, but of perceived reality.

The effect of the Holocaust on Jewish psychology today has to be regarded as ambiguous and equivocal, because we deal with two quite separate generations. The first is the one that lived through the frightening, sickening events of the decade and a half of Hitler. The second is the one that has not. In my view the new generations – those born since 1945 – have to be understood in entirely different terms from the old generations. The major difference is that the new generations are considerably healthier and, if they choose to be Jewish at all, their Jewishness is substantially more affirmative. That is not to suggest they are less involved with the Holocaust and with the State of Israel. The contrary is the case.

The reality of the State of Israel turns out to fascinate the younger generation still more than the fantasy mesmerized the fathers. If the 1950s and 1960s were times in which the State of Israel rose to the top of the agendum of American Jewry, in the 1970s it seems to constitute the whole of that agendum. No other Jewish issue has the power to engage the younger generations of Jews as does the issue of the State of Israel. Anti-Zionism and anti-Israelism are virtually non-existent among the new generation of Jews. (Those on the fringes are not interesting in the present context.) That is to say, whether or not there should be a State of Israel, why there should be such a state, how one must justify the existence of a Jewish state in terms of a higher morality or claim in its behalf that it is a light to the nations – these modes of thought are simply alien. The State of Israel *is*. The issue for the younger generation is not: Is it a good thing or a bad thing? The issue is: Since we know no other world but one in which the State of Israel is present, how shall we relate to that important part of the world in which we live?

The younger generation exhibits a healthier relationship to the State of Israel than did its fathers, not because it is more virtuous (despite its fantasies), but because it has not had to live through the frightening, sickening experiences of those fathers. If the myth of the fathers is irrelevant to the children, and if the fantasy-ridden relationships of the fathers are not replicated by the children, the reason is that the young people have grown up in a healthier world. It is a world not without its nightmares, but with different, less terrifying nightmares for the Jews in particular. In days gone by, the 'Jewish problem' belonged to Jews alone. Whether we lived or died was our problem. But now the problem of life or death faces all mankind; we are no longer singled out for extermination. The terror is everyone's. If there is a just God, a mark of his justice is that those who did not share our anguish must now share our nightmares – an exact, if slow, measure of justice. We who saw ourselves all alone in the death camps have been joined by the rest of the world. Next time fire instead of gas, perhaps. But meanwhile it is an easier life.

Nor should we ignore the fact that for the younger generation being Jewish has conferred the practical advantages of a group capable of mutual protection in a generally undifferentiated society. It has been a positive advantage in the recent past. Add to this the devotion of the Jewish parent to the Jewish child. Jewish children are treated in Jewish homes as very special beings. This makes young Jews strive to excel in the rest of society as they did at home. To be sure, this produces a large crop of Jewish adults who blame their Jewishness for the fact that the rest of society does not treat them as did their parents. These are people who need evidence to explain what they see as their own failure, which is actually explicable by their own impossible demands on themselves and on society. Being Jewish in the recent past has, on balance, been an advantage rather than a disability. The younger generation is better off on that account.

To summarize, the generations that lived through disaster and triumph, darkness and light, understand the world in terms of a salvific myth. The generations that have merely heard about the darkness, but have daily lived in the light, take for granted the very redemption that lies at the heart of the salvific myth. The psychological consequences for the one should be different from those for the other. In theory, at least, the effects of the Holocaust on those who went through it, either in the flesh or in the spirit, have been sickening. The survivors will have a survivor mentality; they will see the world as essentially hostile and will distrust, rather than trust, the outsider. They will exhibit the traits of citizens of a city under siege, feeling always threatened, always alone, always on the defensive. The new generation, which has not lived under siege, should develop greater trust in the world. It should regard the world as essentially neutral, if not friendly, and should have the capacity to trust the outsider. Yet, though the psychological experiences differ, the end result is much the same. The new generation is just as Israel-oriented as the old; if anything, it identifies even more intensely than before with the Jewish people.

### EFFECT ON JEWISH THEOLOGY

The theological impact of the Holocaust and the rise of the State of Israel is normally assessed in terms of two significant names, Richard L. Rubenstein and Emil Fackenheim. Rubenstein's response to the Holocaust has been searching and courageous. He has raised the difficult questions and responded with painful honesty. The consequence has been an unprecedented torrent of personal abuse, so that he has nearly been driven out of Jewish public life. He has been called a Nazi and compared with Hitler! The abuse to which he has been subjected seems to me the highest possible tribute on the part of his enemies to the compelling importance of his contribution. Since what he has proposed is evidently seen to be unanswerable, the theology has been ignored, but the theologian has been abused. Consequently, Rubenstein has taken the view that anyone who does not agree with his position is an 'Establishment' theologian – as though American Judaism has anything like a theological Establishment. To Rubenstein's credit, he argues with his opposition by name and in a respectful way. His most prominent critic, Emil Fackenheim, by contrast, writes about a (nameless) 'radical' (his quotation marks – I do not know what they are supposed to mean here) Jewish theologian, but in much of his writing rarely alludes to Rubenstein by name, and when he does, it is to compare Rubenstein with Nazis, for instance, Ulrich Heidegger. This sort of onomastic homicide not only does no credit to the magician, it also does not work. It surely is not a dignified way in which to carry on theological discourse. But perhaps dignity and autonomy are the wrong categories of criticism; in the presence of emotions bordering on hysteria, even rational criticism itself is probably too rational an expectation.

What is Rubenstein's message? It has been eloquently stated in various places. I believe the most cogent expression of his viewpoint on the centrality of the Holocaust is in his contribution to *Commentary's* 'Symposium on Jewish Belief', reprinted in his *After Auschwitz* as follows:

> I believe the greatest single challenge to modern Judaism arises out of the question of God and the death camps. I am amazed at the silence of contemporary Jewish theologians on this most crucial and agonizing of all Jewish issues. How can Jews believe in an omnipotent, beneficent God after Auschwitz? Traditional Jewish theology maintains that God is the ultimate, omnipotent actor in the historical drama. It has interpreted every major catastrophe in Jewish history as God's punishment of a sinful Israel. I fail to see how this position can be maintained without regarding Hitler and the SS as instruments of God's will. The agony of European Jewry cannot be likened to the testing of Job. To see any purpose in the death camps, the traditional believer is forced to regard the most demonic, antihuman explosion in all history as a meaningful expression of God's purposes. The idea is simply too obscene for me to accept. I do not think that the full impact of Auschwitz has yet been felt in Jewish theology or Jewish life. Great religious revolutions have their own period of gestation. No man knows the hour when the full impact of Auschwitz will be felt, but no religious community can endure so hideous a wounding without undergoing vast inner disorders.
>
> Though I believe that a void stands where once we experienced God's presence, I do not think Judaism has lost its meaning or its power. I do not believe that a theistic God is necessary for Jewish religious life. Dietrich Bonhoeffer has written that our problem is how to speak of God in an age of no religion. I believe that our problem is how to speak of religion in an age of no God. I have suggested that Judaism is the way in which we share the decisive times and crises of life through the traditions of our inherited community. The need for that sharing is not diminished in the time of the death of God. We no longer believe in the God who has the power to annul the tragic necessities of existence; the need religiously to share that existence remains.*

---

*Richard L. Rubenstein, *After Auschwitz: Essays in Contemporary Judaism*, Indianapolis, 1966, pp. 153–54.

It should not be supposed that Rubenstein's is an essentially destructive conclusion. On the contrary, he draws from the Holocaust a constructive, if astringent message:

> Death and rebirth are the great moments of religious experience. In the twentieth century the Jewish phoenix has known both: in Germany and eastern Europe, we Jews have tasted the bitterest and the most degrading of deaths. Yet death was not the last word. We do not pity ourselves. Death in Europe was followed by resurrection in our ancestral home. We are free as no men before us have ever been. Having lost everything, we have nothing further to lose and no further fear of loss. Our existence has in truth been a being-unto-death. We have passed beyond all illusion and hope. We have learned in the crisis that we were totally and nakedly alone, that we could expect neither support nor succor from God or from our fellow creatures. No men have known as we have how truly God in His holiness slays those to whom He gives life. This has been an liberating knowledge, at least for the survivors, and all Jews everywhere regard themselves as having escaped by the skin of their teeth, whether they were born in Europe or elsewhere. We have lost all hope and faith. We have also lost all possibility of disappointment. Expecting absolutely nothing from God or man, we rejoice in whatever we receive. We have learned the nakedness of every human pretense. No people has come to know as we have how deeply man is an insubstantial nothingness before the awesome and terrible majesty of the Lord. We accept our nothingness – nay, we even rejoice in it – for in finding our nothingness we have found both ourselves and the God who alone is true substance. We did not ask to be born; we did not ask for our absurd existence in the world; nor have we asked for the fated destiny which has hung about us as Jews. Yet we would not exchange it, nor would we deny it, for when nothing is asked for, nothing is hoped for, nothing is expected; all that we receive is truly grace.*

Fackenheim's contrary view is that 'Auschwitz' produces a new commandment to the Jewish people: to preserve the Jewish people and the Jewish religion. Michael Wyschogrod summarizes Fackenheim's viewpoint as follows:

What then, is adequate? Only obedience to the Voice of

*Ibid., pp. 128–29.

Auschwitz. This voice, as heard by Fackenheim, commands the survival of Jews and Judaism. Because Hitler was bent upon the destruction of both, it is the duty of those Jews who survived Hitler to make sure that they do not do his work, that they do not, by assimilation, bring about the disappearance of what Hitler attempted but ultimately failed to destroy. For the religious Jew, this means that he must go on being religious, however inadequate Auschwitz has shown his frame of reference to be. And for the secular Jew, the Voice of Auschwitz commands not faith, which even the Voice of Auschwitz cannot command, but preservation of Jews and Judaism. Speaking of the significance of the Voice of Auschwitz for the secular Jew, Fackenheim writes: 'No less inescapable is this Power for the secularist Jew who has all along been outside the Midrashic framework and this despite the fact that the Voice of Auschwitz does not enable him to return into this framework. He cannot return; but neither may he turn the Voice of Auschwitz against that of Sinai. For he may not cut off his secular present from the religious past: The Voice of Auschwitz commands Jewish unity. The sin of Rubenstein is, therefore, that he permits Auschwitz further to divide the Jewish people at a time when survival is paramount if Hitler is not to be handed a posthumous victory, and survival demands unity. Because this is so, Rubenstein should presumably soft-pedal his doubts so as not to threaten the Jewish people at a time when everything must be secondary to the issue of survival.*

What may be said on behalf of Fackenheim's argument? He has the merit of placing the Holocaust at the head of Judaic theological discourse, and of doing so in such a way that the central problem is not theodicy. Rubenstein's stress on the issue of how a just God could have permitted so formidable an injustice – an understatement of the issue to be sure – leads him to the position just now outlined. Fackenheim's formulation of the issue of the Holocaust in terms of its meaning to the secular, not to the religious, Jew sidesteps the surely insoluble issue of theology and so opens a constructive and forward-looking discourse on the primary issue facing contemporary Judaism – the issue of secularity and unbelief.

Rubenstein tends, therefore, to center his interest on the tragic events themselves, while Fackenheim prefers to make those events speak to the contemporary situation of Jewry. One may compare

*Michael Wyschogrod, 'Faith and the Holocaust,' *Judaism* 20 (Summer 1971), 286–94.

Rubenstein's mode of thought with that of the first-century apocalyptic visionaries; Fackenheim's with that of the rabbis of the same period. After 70 AD the issue of the destruction of the Second Temple predominated and could not be avoided. No religious discourse, indeed, no religious life, would then have been possible without attention to the meaning of that awesome event. The message of the apocalyptics was that the all-powerful God who had punished the people for their sins very soon would bring them consolation, punish their enemies, rebuild the Temple, and bring on the Messianic age. People who heard this message fixed their gaze upon the future and eagerly awaited the Messianic denouement. When confronted by the Messianic claim of Bar Kokhba, they responded vigorously, undertaking a catastrophic and hopeless holy war. The rabbis after 70 AD had a different message. It was not different from that of the apocalyptics in its stress upon the righteousness of God, who had punished the sin of Israel, but the conclusion drawn from that was not to focus attention on the future and on what would soon come to compensate for the catastrophe. The rabbis sought to devise a program for the survival and reconstruction of the saving remnant. The message was that just as God was faithful to punish sin, so He may be relied upon to respond to Israel's regeneration. The task of the hour therefore is to study Torah, to carry out the commandments and to do deeds of lovingkindness. Therefore, from the stubborn consideration of the present and immediate difficulties came a healthy and practical plan by which Israel might, in truth, hold on to what could be salvaged from disaster. Redemption will come. In the meantime there are things to do. Just as the Jews awaited a redemptive act of compassion from God, so they must now act compassionately in order to make themselves worthy of it. The tragedy thus produced two responses, the one obsessed with the disaster, the other concerned for what is to happen afterward, here and now.

It seems to me that Rubenstein carries forward the apocalyptic, Fackenheim the classical and rabbinical, mode of thinking. The difference between them is not in the contrast between a negative and destructive approach, on the one side, and an affirmative and constructive one on the other. Rubenstein is not a nihilist, as I have shown. Fackenheim's 'commanding voice of Auschwitz' speaks to people beyond despair, demands commitment from the nihilist himself. The difference is in perspective and focus. In Fackenheim's behalf one must, as I said, point to the remarkable pertinence of his message to the issues of the 1970s. He has, in a way, transcended the tragic events themselves, just as did the first-century rabbis.

Fackenheim does not say only the obvious, which is that one must believe *despite* disaster. He holds that the disaster itself is evidence on behalf of belief, a brilliant return to the rabbinic mode of response to catastrophe. In this regard Rubenstein and Fackenheim, representative of the two extreme positions, cannot be reconciled, except within the events of which they speak. Confronting those events, both theologians perceive something 'radically' new and without precedent in the history of Judaism. With that shared claim, the two extremes come together. What is to be said in response to the claim of both Rubenstein and Fackenheim that 'after Auschwitz' things are 'radically' different from before?

First, it must be stressed, other theologians have not been silent. A. J. Heschel, for example, responded to the Holocaust with an immortal Kaddish, *The Earth Is the Lord's*. Milton Steinberg, Mordecai M. Kaplan, and Arthur A. Cohen, among others, take account of the Holocaust without admitting the central contention of the recent 'Auschwitz theologians'. They take seriously the problem of evil, but regard the problem as posed effectively by any sort of misfortune or by the whole history of the Jewish people, for they find themselves equally disturbed by the suffering of one person as of one million. One indeed may argue that 'after Auschwitz' became an effective slogan, along with 'never again' and similar allusions to the Holocaust, too long after the liberation of Europe to constitute merely a response to the events of those far-off days and distant places.

But the central allegation is contained in the word 'radical', by which is meant that the Holocaust is unprecedented and changes everything. This viewpoint is not shared by Kaplan, Heschel and others. The most important critique comes in Wyschogrod's review of Fackenheim. There he meets head-on the issue of 'radical evil' and, in my opinion, demolishes the constructions of the whole 'after Auschwitz' school. Because of the importance of his critique, I quote his exact words at some length:

> I have already termed Fackenheim's enterprise 'negative natural theology,' a phrase which deserves brief explanation. Traditionally, natural theology has been the enterprise whereby the existence of God is demonstrated on the basis of some rational evidence, without recourse to faith or revelation. Most commonly, the point of departure for such an attempt was some 'positive' feature of the world as it appears to man: its order, its beauty, or its harmony. It was then argued that such characteristics could not be the result of pure chance and that it was, therefore, necessary to posit some

all-powerful and rational being as the author or creator of a universe possessing the respective positive characteristics ... Fackenheim's point of departure is, of course, the opposite of the 'positive.' Instead of being the order, beauty, harmony or justice of the universe, it is a totally unique crime, unparalleled in human history. But once we get over this initial difference, similarities appear. In the positive version, a positive characteristic of the universe is noted and it is argued that no natural explanation for it is adequate. In negative natural theology, an evil is pointed out for which also, it is alleged, no natural explanation is possible. Of course, the conclusion in negative natural theology cannot be identical with that of positive natural theology, inasmuch as the problem of theodicy cannot here easily be ignored. Nevertheless, the conclusion which Fackenheim draws, the sacred duty to preserve the Jewish people, is the functional equivalent of the existence of Judaism, a foundation as fully serviceable to the secularist as to the believer. One is almost driven to the conclusion that in the absence of the Holocaust, given Fackenheim's profound understanding of the irreversibility of the secular stance, no justification for the further survival of Judaism could have been found. With the Holocaust, amazing as this may appear, Judaism has gotten a new lease on life.

Wyschogrod, finally, reaffirms the classical position of Judaic theology on the suffering of the Jewish people:

Israel's faith has always centered about the saving acts of God: the election, the Exodus, the Temple and the Messiah. However more prevalent destruction was in the history of Israel, the acts of destruction were enshrined in minor fast days while those of redemption became the joyous proclamations of the Passover and Tabernacles, of Hannukah and Purim. The God of Israel is a redeeming God; this is the only message we are authorized to proclaim, however much it may not seem so to the eyes of nonbelief. Should the Holocaust cease to be peripheral to the faith of Israel, should it enter the Holy of Holies and become the dominant voice that Israel hears, it could not but be a demonic voice that it would be hearing. If there is no salvation to be extracted from the Holocaust, it is because to those who believe, the voices of the Prophets speak more loudly than did Hitler, and because the divine promise sweeps over the crematoria and silences the voice of Auschwitz.

This seems to me all that needs to be said in response both to the 'commanding Voice of Auschwitz' and to the joy of 'nothingness' alike.

## EFFECT ON CONTEMPORARY JEWISH AFFAIRS

Various unrelated social, cultural and political phenomena have been interpreted as a response to the Holocaust. I do not allude to the creation of the State of Israel or to the great 'return to religion' of the 1950s, an event much criticized at that time but sorely missed today. I refer to the reaffirmation of Jewish self-interest in times of political crisis, to the recognition that the Jews do have serious interests in political, social and economic life, and that sometimes these interests come into conflict with those of other groups. I refer to the electrifying popular response to the Six-Day War and to the generally favorable reaction to the slogans of the Jewish Defense League, if not to its mindless activities. I refer to the publicity about 'freeing Soviet Jewry' and to the obvious sense that in making such efforts people are doing today what they wished they (or someone) had done in the 1930s. I refer to the non-academic thrust toward 'Jewish ethnic studies' in the universities and the students' manifest claim to want to learn something – anything – Jewish. I refer, finally, to the serious efforts of younger Jews to participate, in their own idiom, in the Judaic tradition, to the creation of Jewish newspapers by the university students, and to the success of *Response* and similar (if not so excellent) magazines, to the creation of Jewish communes and communities, according to an ideology with (alleged) roots in the ancient *havurot*. These have been exciting events; possibly, some may prove important. None could have been predicted a generation ago, let alone in the 1930s. Then it seemed the way ahead lay downward and outward, for the future looked bleak. Today, say what one will in criticism of details of the 'ethnic assertion' of young Jews in its several forms, one cannot take a negative view of their devotion to the Judaic tradition and their loyalty to the Jewish people.

But the question is: Is the current ferment in Jewish community affairs the result of the Holocaust; is it one of the implications of the Holocaust? In my opinion, the answer is negative. The 'after Auschwitz' syndrome in Jewish theology and the appeal of 'never again' in Jewish community affairs both constitute creations of the late 1960s and early 1970s.

From 1945 to about 1965, the Holocaust was subsumed under the 'problem of evil'. The dominant theological voices of that time did not address themselves to 'radical evil' and did not claim that something had happened to change the classical theological perspective of Judaism. The theologians of the day wrote not as if nothing had happened, but as if nothing had happened to impose a new perspective on the whole past of Jewish religious experience. To be sure, the liberal, world-affirming optimism of the old theological left was shaken; Kierkegaard and Niebuhr, through Will Herberg and others, found a sympathetic Jewish audience. But the Holocaust – 'Auschwitz' – was part, not the whole, of the problem.

What happened, I think, was the assassination of President Kennedy, the disheartening war in south-east Asia and a renewed questioning of the foundations of religious and social polity. 'Auschwitz' became a Jewish code-word for all the things everyone was talking about, a kind of Judaic key word for the common malaise. That – and nothing more. The Jewish theologians who claim that from Holocaust events one must draw conclusions essentially different from those reached after the destruction of the Second Temple or other tragic moments, posit that our sorrow is unlike any other, our memories more searing. But they say so in response not to the events of which they speak, but, through those events, to a quite different situation. They also necessarily select some events, and not others, for the purpose of their theological enterprise. They speak of 'Auschwitz', and 'radical evil', but not of Jerusalem rebuilt and the dawn of redemption. If the former is a more than merely a this-worldly event, why not the latter? But *if* the latter be taken seriously, then why no place for redemption in the response to the former?

Alongside 'Auschwitz' comes Fackenheim's emotional claim that 'we should not hand Hitler any posthumous victories'. The appeal – one can hardly dignify it as an 'argument' – is meant to buttress any form of traditional belief or practice that comes to mind. Hitler hated Judaism, therefore we must be religious Jews – an ironic revision of the Talmudic dictum: God is merciful and holy, therefore we must be merciful and holy. 'Auschwitz' replaces Sinai.

The argument might enjoy a measure of historical pertinence if Hitler had distinguished among the Jews those who were religious or kept kosher or wore *tzitzit*. But since Nazism ignored the lifestyle of the Jews and sought only to end all Jewish life, the sole necessary consequence one can draw is that having Jewish babies – however one raises them thereafter – is a defeat for Hitler. The rest is either mere sentimentality or meretricious. It is an argument that cannot be examined, let alone criticized; it is not open to rational inquiry, and it has unlimited consequences. Since Hitler liked Wagner and sauerkraut and did not like to see animals mistreated, are we to give up *The Flying Dutchman* and cabbage and beat our dogs? If so, why in 1972 and not in 1946?

Classic Judaic theology was not struck dumb by evil, and neither changed its apprehension of the divinity nor claimed on its own behalf a renewed demand on the Jews on account of disaster. To be sure, important theological issues require careful, indeed meticulous attention. But to debate those issues outside of the classic tradition and under the impact of grief can produce few lasting or even interesting results.

In my view, Jewish public discourse has been ill-served by 'Auschwitz' without the eternity of Israel, misled by setting the response against Hitler in place of the answer to a God who commands, and corrupted by sentimentality, emotionalism and bathos. These have produced in people less sophisticated, less responsible than either Rubenstein or Fackenheim, vacuous mysticism on the one side and mindless sloganeering on the other. As Elie Wiesel writes in *Legends of Our Time* (New York, 1986): 'No cocktail party can really be called a success unless Auschwitz, sooner or later, figures in the discussion.' In such a setting, 'Auschwitz' profanes Auschwitz; the dead are forcibly resurrected to dance in a circus, the survivors made into freaks. It is enough. Let the dead lie in peace and the living honor them in silent reverence. Again Wiesel: 'Leave them there where they must forever be ...; wounds, immeasurable pain at the very depth of our being.' Why should they serve the living as a pretext for either belief or unbelief, for a naturalist God or a supernatural God? The truth is there is no meaning in it all, at least none discerned for mortal man. The fact is that the living live. The choice is about the future, not the past. Theologians and politicians alike should let the dead rest in peace. We are not well-served by the appeal to the Holocaust, either as the rationalization for our Judaism or as the source of slogans for our Jewish activism and self-assertion.

What, then, are the implications of the Holocaust? In one sense, I claim that there is *no* implication – none for Judaic theology, none for Jewish community life – which was not present before 1933. Judaic theologians ill-serve the faithful when they claim that 'Auschwitz' marks a turning, as in Rubenstein's case, or a 'new beginning', as in Fackenheim's. In fact, Judaic piety has all along known how to respond to disaster. For those for whom the classic Judaic symbolic structure remains intact, the wisdom of the classic piety remains sound. For those to whom classical Judaism offers no viable option, the Holocaust changes nothing. One who did not believe in God before he knew about the Holocaust is not going to be persuaded to believe in Him on its account. One who believed in the classical perception of God presented by Judaic theologians is not going to be forced to change his perception on its account. The currently fashionable 'Jewish assertion' draws on the Holocaust, to be sure, as a source of evocative slogans, but it is rooted in America and in the 1970s, not in Poland and in the 1940s. It has come about in response to the evolving conditions of American society, not to the disasters of European civilization. Proof of its shallowness and rootlessness derives from its mindless appropriation of the horrors of another time and place as a rationale for 'Jewish assertion' – that, and its incapacity to say more, in the end, than, 'Woe, woe.' 'Jewish assertion' based on the Holocaust cannot create a constructive, affirmative and rational way of being Jewish for more than ten minutes at a time. Jews find in the Holocaust no new definition of Jewish identity because we need none. Nothing has changed. The tradition endures.

# PART IV
## SECULARISM, SELF-HATRED, AND JEWISH HOPE

# 13 Jewish Secularism in Retreat

*Jewish Spectator* 59/3 (1994–95), 25–29

A social entity – a group of people who identify with one another through time – takes many forms, large and small, and takes shape for many diverse reasons, from sentiment to shared interest. Among the varieties of social entities that the world has known, none competes with the religious entity in what is deemed to define the stakes for the entity's existence. For while the nation-state appeals to senses of loyalty on grounds of common genealogy of language or culture, and while the working class appeals to common economic interest, only the religious group explains itself by calling upon God, Creator of heaven and earth and all of life, to account for the group.

That is why religion defines the foundation and cohesion of large and enduring groups in humanity, whether vast and transnational, such as Islam or the Catholic Church, or modest in numbers and geographically parochial, such as the Armenian National Church or the Bahai. It also explains why, however many associations and identifications members of a religious group may possess, the religious one imparts its character to all the others, so that there will be Jewish War Veterans and Catholic Physicians. Religion explains more traits of the social order than other variables of the social order explain religion. Religion allows us to predict the attitudes and actions that will characterize a group, even when all other variables appear to be neutralized.

During the nineteenth and twentieth centuries, secularization formed the wave of the future. Religion, it was maintained, eroded, and vast realms of social activity were deemed inaccessible to religious conviction and action. The intellectual classes – book readers, book writers – in particular persuaded themselves that religious belief formed a vast iceberg in a warm ocean, melting away in the balmy tropic sea of reason, science, philosophy, social science, nationalism and diverse other dominant currents of the day. Accordingly, none can have predicted what has taken place, which is the ascendancy of religion on the stage of world history.

Communism pronounced God dead, but when Communism fell, the churches filled up, and synagogues reopened that had been closed three generations earlier. Nazism exploited religious sentiments, attracting to its cause the leading German theologians of its time. But in the end, religion stood in judgment of Nazism, and only those who placed God before the political leader emerged from the catastrophe possessed of moral authority. In the Moslem world nationalism gives way to Islam; in the world of Judaism in the State of Israel, the institutions of religion thrive, those of Zionism separated from Judaism decay. Christianity in its uncompromising forms flourishes throughout the West and particularly in the USA, while those Christianities that made their peace with secularism atrophy. A generation ago a sensational theological pronouncement, 'God is dead', captured peoples' imaginations. Looking back, we realize that 'God is dead' stated what a waning secularism wanted, not what was or was to be.

In the earliest stages of the post-secular age that now takes shape we must ask ourselves, how fares the state of Judaism within Israel, the holy people? By Judaism I mean the religion, or the set of religious systems, that appeals to the revelation by God to Moses of the Torah, oral and written, at Sinai. The answer is, among Jews who practice Judaism – that is, Judaist Jews – the faith prospers, as it always has, as it always will. But Judaist Jews form only one sector of the Jews as a group – that is, of all the people in the world who call themselves Jews and who are regarded by others as Jews. In some places they are numerous, in others, modest. Judaist Jews keep the faith and live by it; define the rhythm of their days and of their lives in accord with its heartbeat; explain to themselves who they are and what they must do by appeal to the Torah as expounded by those who study its texts; and form the Israel that is sanctified, set apart for God's purpose, of which the Torah speaks. Whether the particular Judaic system calls itself Reform or Orthodox or Conservative or Reconstructionist (to use American categories), or Lubovitch or Satmar, Agudah or Misrachi (to use the Israeli and European ones), whether the system is integrationist (as most of the American Judaisms are) or segregationist (as many of the European and Israeli and a small segment of the American ones are), all Judaisms have in common a single conviction: that they form an 'Israel' that belongs to God and has made its way through time and toward eternity as God's first love.

In the beginning of the 200 years of militant secularization and ideological secularism, Judaism encompassed all of the Jews and met no competition anywhere. Today, as for much of the twentieth century, Judaism competes with other definitions of Israel besides the religious one. The first is political Israel, the State of Israel. But competition with Israeli statism scarcely exercises much attention among the

Judaisms where the two systems meet in confrontation, that is, in the State of Israel itself. For statist Israelism, lacking the markings of Judaism in a formal sense, time is measured by Judaism, the life cycle is counted out by Judaism, the resources of intellect are handed on by Judaism, for example, so that statist Israelism wins slight, if any, attention. Israeli nationalism is infused with Judaism and subverted by Judaism. The competition that Judaism faces in the State of Israel comes from materialism or statism or from nihilism, just as is the case with Catholic Christianity in Italy and Poland, or with Islam in Algeria and Egypt.

By contrast, in the Diaspora, and especially in the vast and imperial American Jewish community that in competition with Israeli nationalism defines the social patterns of the Diaspora, the religious systems that together form Judaism do struggle with a powerful secularism. That is to say, outside of segregationist Orthodoxy, which makes up less than 10 percent of American Jewry (a smaller proportion of American Jews than those who celebrate Christmas by going to church), the regnant ideas that animate American Jews and explain to them who they are and what they must do in no way exhibit the traits common among religious ideas and attitudes.

Most American Jews do not do the things that Judaism says Judaist Jews should do. If Orthodox, the pattern of compromise formed within a consensus of the non-observant integrationist Orthodox competes with the observant one; if Conservative and Reform and Reconstructionist – the differences matter only to the religious virtuosi, such as rabbis – proportions of those who identify with Judaism and actually practice the faith prove negligible, except on a few distinctive occasions. Beyond argument, when Jews explain to themselves who they are and what they must do, they do not appeal to God's will and do not look into the Torah. In place of God they use embarrassed euphemisms, and then only if they have to. In place of the Torah they speak of tradition or culture. In place of holy Israel, God's first love, they find themselves a position within the ethnic mosaic of American society.

The Jews' own ethnicization of Judaism takes two principal forms, which fit together well. The first involves the definition of what matters about the Jews by appeal to the Holocaust, which, over the past quarter-century, has become a dominant source of explanation to Jews of why they should be Jewish. The second identifies the point of coherence that draws Jews together in the State of Israel. Jews have defined their group identity around blood and iron, the blood of the Holocaust, the iron of the nation-state surviving through its own might. Evidence that these two foci form the parameters of Jewish existence – the place where the Jewish group makes its life – hardly requires much searching. The dominant form of the making of buildings in American Jewry is the building of Holocaust memorials. The one thing that unites Jews in any locale is a broad, if shallow, interest in Israeli affairs. For two generations, American Jews outside of a negligible proportion of genuinely religious folk have built their collective existence around those two overseas events, the murder of Jews in Europe and the building of the State of Israel.

The Holocaust memorials bear the message, first, that gentiles are not to be trusted, most of them having stood idly by, while many of them murdered Jews, and only a pitiful minority did anything to save lives. Therefore Jews should remain Jewish. Second, that the State of Israel, where Jews bear arms to defend themselves, offers the last, best, hope of survival. The organized Jewish community has spent a quarter-century, from the Six-Day War of June 1967 to today's triumphant conclusion, to deliver the message to itself.

When asked who are the Jews, the Jewishness of Holocaust and Israelism therefore answers: 'We are the survivors of the Holocaust, and our task is to survive; we help those people over there build the ancestral homeland into a viable state, and our task is to contribute.' Neither component of the secular Jewish ideology of survival, no detail of the explanation of who the Jews are and why they should continue to be, has appealed to the supernatural, none to transcendent aspirations of sinful humanity. Every important element of the Jewishness of Holocaust and Israelism conformed to the this-worldly framework of those for whom groups take shape around shared, secular traits: a common history, a common fate, for instance. Jews were then supposed to be Jewish and to stay Jewish because all of them came from one place, if not a single family then a shared genealogy of horror. They had work to do together, and that too accounted for their present and made them accountable to a long future: be together, stay together, to survive; to help the Jewish state survive.

What is wrong with the Jewishness of Holocaust and Israelism depends upon one's convictions concerning what is right about Judaism. Neither the Holocaust as an ideology of Jewishness nor Israelism as a policy for everyday conduct has ever appealed for context, let alone intellectual validation, to the Torah, that is, to what the world calls Judaism. The Holocaust is represented in wholly this-worldly terms, forming for militant secularism an unanswerable argument against the conception that God rules the world. Israelism appeals for Israel's redemption to activities in this world, by Israel, the

Jewish people, and by Israel, the Jewish state; no place is left for that Israel, the holy people, God's stake in humanity, of which the Torah speaks.

The secular theory of Israel, in our time taking the form of the Holocaust-and-Israelist position, has maintained that the Jewish group can adequately sustain itself on the foundations of that position. That is why vast resources have flowed into the institutions and programs of the secular position. Money flows along the paths laid out by vision, and if you want to know what people really think, see where they spend their money. It follows that Jews who want the Jewish group to continue, in the USA and overseas as well, consider the secular option to serve quite well. Are they right?

The answer can only derive from whether or not the two generations educated in Holocaust and Israelist Jewishness have found themselves persuaded to remain Jewish by reason of that secular ideology. The facts are now in hand. Holocaust and Israelist Jewishness coalesced in 1967. Now, 25 years later, an entire generation of Jews has grown up with the ethnic Jewishness of Holocaust and Redemption – don't trust the gentiles, do depend for psychic security on the State of Israel. Living as a minority of about 2 percent in the USA, where gentiles have elected a Senate that is 10 percent Jewish, and the federal budget dependably provides the State of Israel with billions from year to year, rarely even visiting its supposed 'spiritual center' (scarcely 20 percent of American Jews have set foot in Jerusalem, even for a day), Jews have defined for themselves a life that is lived somewhere else than where they are located.

Appealing to the 'self-evident' meaning of events that they have not experienced, in places where they do not live, an entire generation has explained to its children the reason they are Jewish. How have the children responded to this Judaism consisting only of memory? The same years that mark the triumph in American Jewry's civil religion of the Judaism of Holocaust and Redemption have also witnessed an unprecedented wave of intermarriage between Jews and unconverted gentiles. In the past eight years alone, more than half of all Jews entering marriage did so with gentiles. That proves two things. First, gentiles want to marry Jews. So America is not Germany, where they didn't. And second, Jews vote not only with their feet – choosing not to live in the State of Israel – but also with their heart – choosing not to raise another generation of Jews. Holocaust-and-redemption Judaism has simply failed in its chosen mission to keep Jews Jewish.

Does that mean that the religion Judaism may not make its way onto the stage and take over the leading role in the drama of contemporary Jewish life? If, as I maintain, secularism has receded throughout the world and even in the Jewish community, and has shown itself implausible, then is religiosity – Judaism or the Torah – the inevitable next stage?

For two reasons, I cannot offer an unqualified and positive answer. First, within the realm of Judaic religiosity, in the synagogues themselves, Judaism does not today govern. To explain why I think so, I point to what I observed in a synagogue in Finland, in the town of Abö (Turku in Finnish). There, in a synagogue with separate seating, with a completely Orthodox davening, I noted on the Sabbath after Passover a quite remarkable 'reform' in an otherwise unimpeachable Orthodoxy. These Orthodox Jews came to the synagogue and the Sabbath and *simply omitted the Torah reading.* Here, in a synagogue of Orthodox Jews, most of them of Polish or Russian origin, native Finns, three or four generations in Turku, men come to the synagogue on the Sabbath out of a deep sense of Jewish loyalty, but omit from their worship the reason that Judaism specifies for coming to the synagogue at all.

To reach such a decision, these Orthodox Jews had to possess enormous resources of pure ignorance. The Talmud is explicit that people may say their prayers at home, not in a quorum, except for the requirement of hearing the Torah declaimed. For that, they must come to the synagogue (or form a quorum of their own, which is the same thing). When we say our prayers, we speak to God; when the Torah is read, as everyone knows, God speaks to us, holy Israel, that is, Jews made holy by the sanctifying act of accepting the Torah – in that place, at that time.

The forms of Orthodoxy endured; the substance – Torah study – did not. Judaism does not thrive, and it also does not die for merely demographic reasons. Whether there are more Jews or less Jews hardly matters, since in the end we cannot compete in any numbers game. I was present for the death of Judaism in Abö, but, in the nature of things, I was also the only mourner. To mourn, you have to know a death has taken place. A religion is like a language. It does not matter how many people speak the language. But once people no longer speak the language, even though they may think they are emitting its natural sounds, the language has come to an end. The case in point explains why I am not at all certain that Judaism, even within Orthodoxy in Europe, survives at all.

The second reason that the demise of secularism does not carry in its wake the renewal of religiosity within Holy Israel derives not from the sociology of Orthodox synagogue life, but from the theology of the Torah. So far as the Jews wish to make use of the Torah ('Judaism') as the medium for maintaining the Jewish group, the Torah cannot help them accomplish their goals. The reason is that, for Judaism as for all other religions, religion is not a means to an end but an end in itself. It is not a dependent variable, a contributory factor. Religion is an independent variable, one that explains other things but is not explained by other things. If people do not find self-evidently compelling the requirements of faith, then faith cannot come to realization for those people. If we have learned anything through 200 years of militant secularization of the Jews, it is that, when originally religious attitudes and actions are taken over for worldly purposes, they lose their power. Commandments presented as customs and ceremonies no longer compel. Truths set forth as preferences, convictions transformed into merely secular facts (as in 'Jewish history proves' in place of 'the Torah says' and 'God spoke to Moses saying, speak to the children of Israel and say unto them') lose all power of persuasion. What compels when believed does not even influence when not believed. Kosher when applied to food means, this is how God wants us to eat, or what God wants us not to eat. Kosher when used to indicate a style of cooking on a menu that lists French or Italian or Chinese or Mexican dishes as well, is why kosher-style sells mainly pickles.

It follows that if people appeal to Judaism as the foundation for 'Jewish community', as the self-styled 'organized Jewish community' in the form of united Jewish charities contends should be the ideology of the hour, none will respond to that appeal for very long. Such an appeal – our 'ideology' for being Jewish is now to be Judaism, as it has been Holocaust and Israelism – asks that the religion, Judaism, or as I prefer, the Torah, accomplishes not the transformation of the Jews into Holy Israel, but merely the transposition of the Jewish ethnic group from one mode of ethnicity to some other form of the same secular ethnicity. But Judaism defies the Jews' ethnicity. The Passover Seder without divine intervention celebrates not God's power to redeem, but merely Israel's power to survive, and the meal becomes a secular banquet with a quaint ritual. That is not religion. The Day of Atonement speaks of sin and atonement, humanity's contrition and God's mercy. Turned into an occasion for the gathering of the clans, the rite is ritualized and loses its power to transform and to enchant. Having sat in a Conservative synagogue in Tampa, Florida behind a couple who were engaged in caressing ordinarily appropriate in a bedroom, but not in a place of worship, I know that the widespread synagogue observance of the New Year signifies togetherness, but not a shared quest for God on the occasion of remembrance.

The broadly based American-Jewish conception that, if we build programs of 'continuity', we assure the future of the ethnic group, represents a profound misunderstanding of the nature of religion. That is because 200 years of militant secularism have left a huge proportion of the Jews completely uncomprehending concerning religion, religiosity, and the character of what the world calls 'Judaism' and what is called, in its native category, 'the Torah'. The upshot is that what people do not believe, they cannot utilize, and that which they do believe to be truth stands beyond all secular utility. The retreat of Jewish secularism, the failure of ideologies resting on a this-worldly explanation of who the Jews are and why they should be what they are – these palpable events of the day do not open the way to a renewal of Judaism and a rebirth of Judaic religiosity, on the one side, and active piety, on the other. The alternative to secularism is not religion, it is nihilism.

So secular a view of religion as the one that asks religion to carry out an essentially this-worldly social task profoundly misunderstands religion. A religious group is formed and sustained by people, whom God has marked, to whom God has been made manifest; a religion records what that group knows about God. Religions represent what happens when people believed that, in what happens, God speaks to them, meets them, sets forth what God wants them to do together. To be sure, those are convictions that can be manipulated for secular purposes, but they are not affirmations that can be fabricated for the occasion. All religious people know that to be self-evident, and no secular people understand that at all.

The matter is to be compared to the relationship of the dance to music. Martha Graham once said to me, 'the dance is the physicalization of music'. When she heard music, it would be in movement and gesture that she embodied what she heard. When in Chicago she saw for the first time the painting of the girl with the scarlet sash, she wanted immediately to dance the painting, and she knew just what she would do. Her limbs told her. In the context of religion, Judaism identifies God's revelation with words written down in a book. For the kindred religions that identify book writing as a principal medium for conveying knowledge of God, Islam and Christianity, a book is the writing down of religion. That is to say, the encounter with God in time and in the present moment. Holy books in the view of those who made, valued and later preserved them as authoritative and true, preserve what it means to know God, as much as the dance preserves what it means to embody music. The metaphor then compares 'know' to 'embody'. Encounter with God is not philosophical. Encounter with God is religious, that is, meeting with the living and very particular God who creates, commands and is concerned with Israel. But the knowledge of the encounter, recorded in words and in writing, makes possible our encounter afresh (so Judaism maintains concerning the Torah).

True, the sages did not confuse map with territory, encounter through learning with the actuality of encounter itself, any more than Martha Graham conceived that the physicalization of music took the place of the music. The ballet would always begin with the notes of the orchestra (or the silent beat before the sound began), and the study of the Torah would always commence with the prior knowledge of the God present in the Torah.

These are remarkable and noteworthy writings, not to be reduced to trivial dimensions of whether or not a particular ethnic group, in the perspective of history, survives another day or not. Ahad HaAm stated the secular perspective, its profound incomprehension of what is at stake in the religion Judaism, when he said, 'More than Israel kept the Sabbath, the Sabbath kept Israel.' From his perspective, he explained why the Sabbath matters. But that is not the perspective of God, who said, 'I am the Lord your God who brought you out of the land of Egypt, out of the house of bondage: Honor the Sabbath day to keep it holy.' If people keep the Sabbath so that the Jews will survive, they will not have kept the Sabbath, whether or not the Jews survive. For Judaism, the retreat of secularism marks not the advance of religiosity, only the demise of the old gods. To the God who is made manifest in the Torah that event is simply not relevant.

# 14 Assimilation and Self-Hatred in Modern Jewish Life

*Conservative Judaism* 26 (1971), 50–60

Assimilation denotes the reception of aliens by a host society and the aliens' gradual acceptance of the traits of that host culture. The history of the Jewish people is the story of how the Jews entered into one culture after another, and came to regard their cultural acquisitions as essentially Jewish. Eastern European cuisine among American Jewry is one obvious example; Greek philosophy among Spanish Jewry is another; Roman methods of legal codification among Palestinian Jewry is a third. In all three instances Jews took over and Judaized cultural traits derived from other cultures, and thereafter defended and cherished them as quintessentially Jewish. So we have stuffed derma, Maimonides, and the Mishnah, to name three examples of the assimilation through Judaization of originally alien traits or creations.

The extent of the Jews' assimilation of the various cultures encountered in their history cannot be overestimated. We may not take for granted that we may find peculiarly 'Jewish' approaches to intellectual life, for example. Some people suppose that Talmudic dialectic is uniquely Jewish. The dialectic, however, is formed of Roman principles of legal codification and Greek principles of rhetoric. Perhaps one might find parallels among contemporary Syriac, late Babylonian and Hellenistic traditions, if these were sufficiently well-known to us. The Jewish academies of late antiquity certainly are similar in important ways to the Christian monasteries of the same time and place. Although a discipline may be peculiar to a tradition of learning and still be derivative, I doubt that Jewish learning can be associated over a long period of time with any particular discipline. The Jews can lay no persuasive claim to exclusive possession of subtlety or cleverness, devotion to the intellectual life, dedication to matters of the spirit or any of the other traits, pejorative or complimentary, claimed for them by their religious and secular enemies or apologists.

In the early days of Reform Judaism, it was thought that if we could uncover the 'origin' of a practice or belief, we could then decide whether it is 'essential' or peripheral. Nowadays we see less interest in questions of origin. The exposure of the genetic fallacy may have been part of the reason for this shift. We recognize that determination of origin does not exhaust the meanings of beliefs or practices. Yet there is another source for this dwindling of interest: it has become progressively more difficult, with the advance of scholarship, to discover any deeply 'Jewish' or 'Judaic' practice which was not in some degree the creation of another culture or civilization.

The Jewish calendar, that 'unique' construction of Judaism, derives mostly from the Canaanites. One may argue that the festivals were 'monotheized' or 'Judaized'. But, in fact, different verbal explanations have been imposed on the same festivals celebrating the same natural phenomena of the same Palestinian agricultural year. The Jews, over long centuries, have assumed as their own what was produced originally by others. Their infinite adaptability has been made possible by short memories and by tenacious insistence on the Jewish origins of purely gentile or pagan customs. Whatever was or was not Jewish, a great many things have *become* so. Jewishness thus is not static, but dynamic, and assimilation is the source of the dynamism.

## ASSIMILATION AS CHALLENGE

It is clear, therefore, that the history of Judaism is also the history of the assimilation by the Jews of the cultural, social, and religious traits characteristic of their neighbors. How shall we evaluate that phenomenon? Here I advance the view of my former teacher, Professor Gerson D. Cohen:

> A frank appraisal of the periods of great Jewish creativity will indicate that not only did a certain amount of assimilation and acculturation *not* impede Jewish continuity and creativity, but that, in a profound sense, this assimilation or acculturation was even a stimulus to original thinking and expression and, consequently, a source of renewed vitality. To a considerable degree the Jews survived as a vital group ... because they changed their names, their language, their clothing, and with them, some of their patterns of thought and expression. This ability to translate, to readapt and reorient themselves to new situations, while retaining a basic inner core of continuity, was largely responsible, if not for their survival, at least for their vitality.*

* 'The Blessing of Assimilation in Jewish History,' *Commencement Address*, June 1966, Hebrew Teachers College, Boston.

Cohen points out, to be sure that people on the fringe preferred to identify with the majority group. This occasionally happened. But, he stresses:

> We Jews have always been and will doubtless continue to be a minority group. Now a minority that does not wish to ghettoize itself, one that refuses to become fossilized, will inevitably have to acculturate itself, i.e. to assimilate at least to some extent.

Assimilation is a fact of Jewish life and, on the whole, it is a fact Jews may accept with optimism. As Cohen stresses, Jews confront the problem of assimilation in two ways. One is to withdraw. The other is to utilize assimilation for a new source of vitality. Cohen cites Ahad HaAm, who distinguished between *hiqqui shel hitharut* and *hiqqui shel hitbolelut* – imitation stimulated by the challenge of new ideas and imitation motivated by the desire to be absorbed. Cohen advances the notion:

> I would ... rather speak of the healthy appropriation of new forms and ideas for the sake of our *own* growth and enrichment. Assimilation ... can become a kind of blessing, for assimilation bears within it a certain seminal power which serves as a challenge and a goad to renewed creativity. The great ages of Jewish creativity ... have always been products of the challenge of assimilation and of the response of leaders, who were to a certain extent assimilated themselves.

Following Cohen, Jews need not regard the assimilation of Jewry into Western civilization as disheartening or threatening. They ought, rather, to see it as an invigorating and challenging situation. Nor should one suppose that the state of Israel is exempt from the assimilative situation of Diaspora Jewry. Israel uses Hebrew to farm in the modern mode, to manufacture for the world market, to think in a wholly contemporary fashion about the great issues facing modern man, to make war according to the requirements of modern technology. Israeli Jews do not differ from western Jews; both have adopted the international culture – music, art, literature, philosophy – of Western Europe and North America. There is no place to hide from the transistor radio. No one wants to 'escape' form modern medicine. No ghetto is immune from the healthy virus of modernity.

## LIVING AMONG – OR WITH – GENTILES

Let us now turn to one of the unwanted consequences of the movement of Jewry from an isolated culture into international civilization. In the past, the Jews lived well-insulated from the opinions of gentiles. Their social setting tended to separate them, and their theological conviction rendered them indifferent to what the gentiles had to say about them. Jews not only knew they were different from others, but regarded those differences as a matter of destiny. The statement in the *Alenu* prayer, 'Who has not made us like the gentiles', was a matter of thanksgiving, pride and joy, a self-conscious articulation of Israel's unique peoplehood. The myth of peoplehood transformed difference into destiny.

In modern times, however, assimilation, formerly unconscious and unplanned, became both a public program and a personal policy. The Jews determined that they should live not only among gentiles, but with them. They would share their way of living, their cultural, social and economic life and values. In one respect only would they differ: in matters of religion, meaning chiefly questions of faith – and these were not important. Thus reversal of traditional attitudes was espoused not only by Reform Judaism in Germany, but also by modern Orthodox leaders such as Samson R. Hirsch, who taught that Jews could be both good Germans and strictly traditional Jews, read both Goethe and Talmud. Orthodoxy differed from Reform in its order of priorities: the Torah would stand as the criterion of modernity, and not the reverse.

But before Jews, whether Reform or Orthodox, could conceive of themselves in such a new situation, they had to affirm modern culture in a way in which they had never accepted or affirmed the cultures of ancient and medieval times. The assimilation of ancient and medieval cultures had come about naturally and quietly. It had not challenged the beliefs and practices that Jews regarded as eternal and unchanging, but had allowed those beliefs and practices to continue with renewed vigor. Modern assimilation, however, held as a deliberate and positive goal the dejudaization of the Jews.

## PATHOLOGICAL SELF-HATRED

Now, for the first time in centuries, Jews took to heart what gentiles said about them. And since the European Jews lived in an age of virulent anti-Semitism, most of what gentiles had to say was derogatory. The 'right' regarded Jews as agents of change and thereafter hated them; the 'left' differed – it hated only what was *Jewish* about the Jews. Liberals argued that allowing Jews to enter into the common life of European politics and culture would hasten their dejudaization. So the Jewish problem resolved itself into a debate on how to rid Europe of Jews and Judaism.

One result was the Zionist movement, which accepted the premises of European anti-Semitism, and held that the only solution to the Jewish problem was the creation of a Jewish state, which would 'normalize' the character of the Jewish people. That is to say, Zionism proposed to make the Jews like the gentiles. Another result was Reform Judaism, which also accepted the premises of European anti-Semitism, and held that the only solution was to limit the differences between Jews and gentiles to matters of religious belief. Reforming Jewish tradition would permit Jews to become more like their neighbors. Individual Jews reacted in still a third way – and it was profoundly tragic. They responded to the hatred of gentiles by hating themselves as Jews, by hating those traits that the gentiles thought of as peculiarly Jewish.

European Jewish self-hatred was pathological, producing psychosis and occasionally leading to suicide. But by and large this sickness remained outside of Jewish institutions and leadership strata, for those infected by self-hatred fled the Jewish community. The most profound analysis of European Jewry's self-hatred is found in Theodor Lessing's *Der jüdische Selbsthass* (Berlin, 1930). Lessing stresses that the Jews of Europe wonder, 'Why does no one love us?' And they answer, 'Because we are at fault.' Lessing sees this as a contemporary psychological counterpart of the traditional theology of disaster: 'Because of our sins, we have been exiled from our land.'*

Lessing tells the story of six European Jewish intellectuals, most of whom ended as suicides. One wrote as follows:

> I force myself not to think about it. But what does it help? – It thinks within me, it thinks of itself, it does not ask about my wish and will and the natural urge to flee from what is painful, ugly, deadly. It is there, all the time, it is within me: this knowledge about my descent. Just as a leper or a person sick with cancer carries his repulsive disease hidden under his dress and yet knows about it himself every moment, so I carry the shame and disgrace, the metaphysical guilt of my being a Jew.
>
> What are all the sufferings and disappointments and inhibitions

* Lessing himself was murdered on 31 August 1933 in Marienbad, by three Sudeten German-Czech Nazis who were paid 80,000 marks for the deed by Goering (*Der Spiegel*, 22 June 1970, pp. 150–2).

which come from outside in comparison with this hell within? To have to be what one despises! ... Because here all rationalizations, all attempts to cover up, all desire to lie to oneself, all this is useless here. It is quite clear to me, ruthlessly clear: Jewishness lies in existence. You cannot shake it off. Just as little as a dog or a pig can shake off its being a dog or a pig, just so little do I tear myself, my own self, away from the eternal ties of existence, which hold me on that step between man and animal: the Jews.

The closing passage is without parallel even in the pathological literature of Jewish self-hatred:

There exists today hardly a more tragic fate than that of those few who have truly fought themselves free from their Jewish ancestry and who now discovered that people do not believe them, do not want to believe them. Where, where can we go? Behind us lie revulsion and disgust, in front of us yawns an abyss ... Nameless, rootless. Mercilessly exiled into a circle of hatred rigid with death ... And I feel as if I had to carry on my shoulders the entire accumulated guilt of that cursed breed of men whose poisonous elf-blood is becoming my virus. I feel as if I, I alone, had to do penance for every crime those people are committing against German-ness ... And to the Germans I should like to shout: Remain hard! Remain hard! Have no mercy! Not even with me!

Germans, your walls must remain secure against penetration. They must not have any secret little door in the rear which could be opened for single persons. Because, surely, some day through this little door treason would creep in ... Close your hearts and your ears to all those who from out there still beg for admission. Everything is at stake! You last little fortress of Aryanism, remain strong and faithful!

No, no, no – it was not just that God wanted to spare Sodom and Gomorra because of one righteous man! Not even for the sake of ten, not for the sake of a hundred righteous men.

Away with this pestilential poor! Burn out this nest of wasps! Even though along with the unrighteous a hundred righteous ones are destroyed. What do they matter? What do I matter? No! Have no mercy! I beg of you.

(Translated by Horst R. Moehring)

Self-hatred is not unique to the Jews. It is an element in every human personality. All men fight the conflict between self-esteem and self-hatred. Self-esteem begins in earliest childhood. Eric Erikson writes, 'through the coincidence of physical mastery and cultural meaning, of functional pleasure and social recognition, one achieves a realistic self-esteem' (*Childhood and Society*, New York, 1963). The child naturally begins with self-love, but it must be corroborated by experience that gives the child the feeling that he fulfills his own ego-ideal. Erikson stresses that there must be tangible social recognition, 'a feeling of continued communal meaning', in order for the adolescent to develop a mature sense of self-esteem.

But the Jewish child in Europe and in North America faces discontinuity between what he learns in childhood and at home, on the one side, and continued communal meaning, on the other. At home he learns that he is a Jew. What he learns about the meaning of that fact will vary. In some few homes, being Jewish is a source of joy and endless pleasures; in many others, it is merely a social datum. But the fact of Jewishness contains within itself no pleasures or joys, no larger meaning, nothing of communal or theological significance.

It also contradicts a communal fact that the child perceives quite early: not everyone is Jewish. Most people are something else. The child rapidly senses that being Jewish is 'different'. Being Jewish, therefore, stands as an obstacle to the child's growth. The cultural meaning of the home conflicts with the social recognition achieved outside of the home. The Jewish child's self-love is *not* corroborated by experience – for the child cannot expect an opportunity to employ what he learns in the Jewish experiences of childhood and to acquire thereby a feeling of continued communal meaning.

Now add to the fact that the Jewish child finds himself different, the fact that the gentile world openly or insidiously tells him the 'Jewish difference' is a bad one. The majority is not only different, but better – for, after all, the world celebrates Christmas, but only some Jews celebrate Hanukkah. The psychological consequences, in terms of Erikson's analysis, will be obvious. The Jewish child will sense a deep discontinuity, and will see himself as inferior, different, and bad because of the difference. If the Jewish child attends a public school, this awareness cannot be postponed beyond the second or third grade, a period in which the earliest psychological conflicts are by and large dormant. At that age the child may continue to compare himself with his father; this comparison may arouse a sense of guilt and of inferiority (Erikson, p. 124). Now the religion of the father enters the picture: The family is Jewish. Being Jewish is being different. Being

Jewish is not as good as being gentile. The father, towards whom guilt is already present, is Jewish and made the child. The normal guilt of the earliest school years may thus turn into hatred of the father, or it may produce hatred of the self as a surrogate for hatred of the father.

Let us bring together the two approaches to the problem of Jewish self-hatred. Lessing tells us that the culture and religion of the Jews taught them over the centuries to blame themselves for their own misfortunes. Erikson tells us that the personality development of each child is apt to produce severe psychological problems if self-esteem cannot be fully established in the earliest years through communal as well as familial support. Jewish children in the Western communities experience being a minority and being different from people one admires. The response is cultural and historical, on the one side, and psychological and personal on the other. The inevitable union of history and culture with psychology and personality development cannot be postponed; the one supplies explanations for the experiences produced by the other.

If we look for pathological cases of Jewish self-hatred among North American Jewry, we should easily find them. On the whole, self-hatred takes a different form here. It is merely neurotic, but it is not limited to individuals. It characterizes the community as a whole, and is reflected in the Jewish community's commitment to non-sectarianism, and in its niggardly support for the cultural, scholarly and religious programs and institutions that make Jews Jewish.

How to account for the difference? I think the obvious answer is that on the whole Jews in the United States and Canada enjoy an enviable status in economic, social, cultural and political life. Anti-Semitism does not take the virulent and destructive forms it did in Western Europe before the Second World War. We have no anti-Semitic political parties; universities are, on the whole, open to Jews; most professions accept Jews; discrimination in the executive suite and in upper-class social clubs by and large constitutes a form of social snobbery, not an ideology of race and culture. American and Canadian societies in the balance are not racist. But the facts cannot change the situation of the *Galut*: The Jews are still a minority, still correctly see themselves as different from the majority. Those differences still add up to abnormality.

### THE DILEMMA OF THE JEWISH 'LIBERAL'

Why are Jews in the United States and Canada in the forefront of universal causes, to the exclusion of their own interest and identity? Charles Liebman, writing in *The Religious Situation 1969*, examines

the reasons often given for this phenomenon. He rejects the notion
that Jewish liberalism, cosmopolitanism and intellectualism rest on
'traditional' Jewish values, for, he points out, it is the secular not the
religious Jew who espouses cosmopolitanism. Jewish religious values,
in fact, are folk-oriented rather than universalistic. He likewise rejects
the view that the Jews' social status, which is not commensurate with
their economic attainments, accounts for their attraction to the
fringes of politics. This theory accounts, Liebman says, for Jewish radicalism rather than Jewish liberalism. Further, Jewish radicals, a small
element of the community, normally abandon Jewish community life,
while the liberals dominate it.

A third explanation derives from the facts of history: liberal parties
supported the emancipation of the Jews; conservative parties opposed
it. But this was not the case in the United States. Indeed, until the
New Deal, Jews tended to be Republican, not Democrats or Socialists.

Liebman posits that the appeal of liberalism is strongest among
Jews estranged from the religious tradition. This appeal, he says, 'lies
in the search for a universalistic ethic to which a Jew can adhere *but*
which is seemingly irrelevant to specific Jewish concerns and, unlike
radical socialism, does not demand total commitment at the expense
of all other values'. Since the Emancipation, Jews have constantly
driven to free themselves from the condition which Judaism thrusts
on them. Liebman writes:

> The impetus for intellectual and religious reform among Jews,
> the adoption of new ideologies and life styles, but above all else
> the changing self-perception by the Jew of himself and his con-
> dition was not simply a desire to find amelioration from the
> physical oppression of the ghetto. It was rather a desire for
> emancipation from the very essence of the Jewish condition.

Jews brought the ideals of universal humanism and cosmopolitanism home to the community so that Jewish difference was played
down. Look, for example, at the *Union Prayerbook*, and count the
number of times the congregation prays for 'all mankind'. The *New
Liberal Prayerbook* in England so emphasizes the universal to the
exclusion of the particular that one might write to the English Liberal
rabbi responsible for the liturgy: 'Warm and affectionate regards to
your wife and children, and to all mankind.'

Liebman concludes, 'The Jew wished to be accepted as an equal
in society *not* because he was a Jew, but because his Jewishness was *irrelevant*. Yet at the same time, the Jew refused to make his own Jewishness

irrelevant ... He made ... contradictory demands on society. He wants to be accepted into the tradition of society without adapting to the society's dominant tradition.' Minorities feel themselves 'particular,' view their traditions as 'ritual,' and distinguish between the private, unique, and personal and the public, universal and commonplace. Majorities do not; they accept the given. This constitutes the liberal dilemma: how to affirm universalism and remain particular.

WHY BE JEWISH?

The 'Jewish problem' is most commonly phrased by young Jews as: Why should I be Jewish? I believe in universal ideals; who needs particular ones as well? Jews who ask, 'Why be Jewish?', testify that 'being Jewish' separates a person from the things he wants. Men who are different from the majority frequently affirm that difference, but the affirmation may contain such excessive protest that it is not much different from denial. The quintessential datum of Jewish existence is anti-Semitism, along with the uncertainty of status, denial of normalcy and self-doubt.

Kurt Lewin pointed out 'every underprivileged minority group is kept together not only by cohesive forces among its members but also by the boundary which the majority erects against the crossing of an individual from the minority to the majority group'.* A member of an underprivileged group will try to gain in social status by joining the majority – to pass, to assimilate. The basic fact of life is this wish to cross the boundary, and hence, as Lewin says, 'he [the minority-group member] lives almost perpetually in a state of conflict and tension. He dislikes ... his own group because it is nothing but a burden to him ... A Jew of this type will dislike everything specifically Jewish, for he will see in it that which keeps him away from the majority for which he is longing.' Such a Jew is the one who constantly asks, 'Why be Jewish?', who fantasizes about a common religion of humanity and universal values that transcend, and incidentally obliterate, denominational and sectarian boundaries. It is no accident that the universal social movement – Communism – and the universal psychology – Freudianism – were in large measure attractive to marginal Jews.

When Jews assimilate and try to blot out the marks of their particularity, they become another type of Jew, but they do not cease being Jewish. The real issue is never 'to be or not to be a Jew' any more than it is, to be or not to be my father's son. Lewin makes this

* *Resolving Social Conflicts. Selected Papers on Group Dynamics*, New York, 1948, p. 164.

wholly clear: 'It is not similarity or dissimilarity of individuals that constitutes a group, but interdependence of fate.' Jews brought up to think that being Jewish is chiefly, or only, a matter of religion, soon discover that disbelieving in God does not make them non-Jews. They still are Jews; they still are obsessed by that fact and compelled to confront it, whether within the society of Jews or outside it.

Indeed, outside of that society, Jewish consciousness becomes more intense. Among Jews one is a human being, with peculiarities and virtues of one's own. Among gentiles one is a Jew, with traits common to the group one seeks to reject. That is probably why Jews still live in mostly Jewish neighborhoods and associate, outside of business hours, mostly with other Jews. And when crisis comes, as it frequently does, then no one doubts that he shares a common cause, a common fate, with other Jews.

### LEADERS FROM THE PERIPHERY

Kurt Lewin says:

> In a minority group, individual members who are economically successful ... usually gain a higher degree of acceptance by the majority group. This places them culturally on the periphery of the underprivileged group and makes them more likely to be 'marginal' persons ... Nevertheless, they are frequently called for leadership by the underprivileged group because of their status and power. They themselves are usually eager to accept the leading role in the minority, partly as a substitute for gaining status in the majority. As a result, we find the rather paradoxical phenomenon ... Instead of having a group led by people who are proud of the group ... we see minority leaders who are lukewarm toward the group.

This, I think, is very much true of United States Jewry. American Jews want to be Jewish, *but not too much*, not so much that they cannot be part of the imaginary undifferentiated majority. Herein lies their pathology. A human being does not begin as part of an undifferentiated mass. Once he leaves the maternity ward, he goes to a home of real people with a history.

What does this mean for the community life of the Jews? Howard Singer calls the Jewish 'Uncle Tom' – Cousin Merwyn.* Who is this

---

* *Bring Forth the Mighty Men*, New York, 1969.

Cousin Merwyn? He honors all religions – but his own. 'He averts his eyes in embarrassment when he sees a Jew carrying a *lulav* on Sukkot, but he is touched and respectful when he sees Christians carrying palms on Palm Sunday.' A Jewish Bar Mitzvah is loud and vulgar, but an Italian street festival is picturesque. But, Singer reports, there are two kinds of Merwyns. Merwyn Outside and Merwyn Inside. Merwyn Outside 'will have nothing to do with anything Jewish … Liberalism will have to serve as his kinship and culture group, his ethnic and religious orientation, his hope of heaven and his social milieu … Merwyn Outside yearns to transcend his parochial origins.' But Merwyn Inside is the more characteristic self-hating Jew:

> Merwyn Inside suffers from the same malady, but in another form. He too, will flee his Jewishness, but his flight is disguised. His technique is to take the Jews with him, to make Jewish life less recognizably Jewish. He will join a synagogue, but suggest innovations in the religious service that make it untraditional in spirit. When they are made he will not attend anyway. He will send his child to Sunday school, and perhaps join the religious school board, but he will oppose raising the educational standards on the grounds that the children are overburdened with Public School work … With a sparkling conscience, and always in the name of 'progress' or good fellowship, he will vulgarize and corrode the institutions of Jewish life.
>
> Merwyn Outside is merely a dead loss to the Jewish group, but Merwyn Inside is a galloping disaster. For Merwyn Inside is often wealthy, energetic, and willing to work. These qualities soon bring him into positions of influence and authority. And if American Jewish organizations have lost touch with Jewish needs, it is because Merwyn Inside dominates those organizations.

What then is to be done? In my view, nothing at all. Once a person has explained a problem and persuaded people of its importance, he is supposed to announce the solution, found an organization and ask people to write out checks. Everyone feels better. People have *done something*. But organizations administer no cure for self-hatred. It is part of the Jewish condition; it is the Jewish part of the human condition of self-devaluation. Yet I contend that rational perception itself is therapeutic: to know, to understand, to accept; these lead to healing and, in turn, to the transformation of neuroses into creative and redemptive forces. Let us recognize that ambivalence about being Jewish exists – with honesty, with compassion and with dignity.

# 15  The Life of the Ever-Dying People

*Moment* 3/10 (1978), 62–64

We are a people obsessed, and it is our own death that obsesses us. The great Jewish philosopher Simon Rawidowicz, who died just two decades ago, gives us an important insight into ourselves when he says, 'The world makes many images of Israel, but Israel makes only one image of itself, that of being constantly on the verge of ceasing to be, of disappearing.' This he says in his essay, 'Israel, the Ever-Dying People.'* Our task, therefore, is to find a way of living with our own mortality, of accepting what cannot be changed and of living out our destiny with dignity and maturity.

Rawidowicz spells this out:

> He who studies Jewish history will readily discover that there was hardly a generation in the Diaspora period which did not consider itself the final link in Israel's chain. Each always saw before it the abyss ready to swallow it up ... Each generation grieved not only for itself but also for the great past which was going to disappear for ever, as well as for the future of unborn generations who would never see the light of day.

It is not hard to see how such a gloomy perspective has gripped our people. In our own time, for example, we need only look at the small Jewish communities to understand its development. In my own community, as in so many others, the Jews grow old, their children have moved to the larger cities, there is no vision, no leadership, no sense of possibility, and no energy to build. There is a sense of ending, of death. Not long ago, I lectured in Bloemfontein, in the Orange Free State of the Republic of South Africa, where within five years a community of 300 families has become one of 195. It is clear that five years from now, there will not be 100. A few have gone to the State of Israel, a few to this country and many to Johannesburg and Cape Town. There, too, the evidence is plain – and depressing.

Nor is the decline of populations restricted to the smaller communities. We have to take into account as well the demographic facts

* *Israel, the Ever-Dying People, and other essays* (Rutherford, NJ, 1986).

facing American Jewry at large, the State of Israel's loss of one out of every ten of its population to other countries (over 300,000 out of three million Israelis live outside the state) and equivalent figures for assimilation, marriage out of Jewry, a low birth rate and similar disheartening phenomena all over the Jewish world.

But the real problem, of course, is not so much numbers, and everyone knows it. Numbers hide something more difficult to face. The Jews can go forward as a group, and Judaism as a religion, even if we are not so numerous as we currently are. So long as a demographic point of no return has not been crossed, the community may endure. The thing that troubles is the absence, within Jewry, of sizable numbers of people who derive any personal joy and meaning from being Jewish. There is a sad routineness to being Jewish, a passivity and dependence upon others. These traits, more than declining numbers, are deeply disturbing, for they mean that Judaism will soon lose the vitality it still enjoys, that a larger number of Jews will lose even the tenuous relationship they currently maintain.

To be very blunt: in this country, most Jews get little personal satisfaction either out of being Jewish or out of Judaism. Most Jews pay their Jewish dues, both social and psychological, and their philanthropic taxes as well. But if you ask people: 'What is it about being Jewish that you genuinely enjoy?', the answers are not encouraging. When you ask graduating college students: "What is your best and your worst Jewish experience?', many report that they have never had a 'best' or a really 'good' Jewish experience. All name 'Hebrew school' as their worst.

Where is Judaism to find the inner strength, the substance rooted in the lives of people, for the coming generations? I frankly do not know, because the Jews I see find little to sustain their Jewish daily lives; they do not live Jewish daily lives. But if being Jewish is not an everyday thing, then being Jewish is no longer a way of living. If that is the case – if Judaism is deprived of its centrality as a way of life, so that the simplest Jewish rites are totally alien – then what is left? I do not mean what is left for the living. I mean what is left for those to come?

If, therefore, we look at the Jewish world around us, it is difficult not to engage in that classic and characteristic exercise of seeing ourselves as disappearing, and perhaps to feel that our generation is more genuinely entitled to the premonition of death than any that came before. Indeed, none of the propositions I have laid out is particularly startling. Some I first spoke of as long as 20 years ago. Rawidowicz was correct in describing our generation. As much as any prior generation in all of Jewish history, more, perhaps, than most, we believe about ourselves that 'with us the great tradition ends'. We believe it in our small communities and in our large ones, in Africa, in Europe and in Latin America, in Australia, here in the United States, and, in some ways, even in the State of Israel.

No. No, no, not only because it ought not to be, because it is not. Our 'ever-dying' community is also a living community, and before we wrap ourselves in a smothering shroud, there are fundamental criticisms of the melancholy perspective that need to be heard. Hearing them, we learn that the luxury of melancholy and the habit of self-pity do not withstand examination.

While it is true that there will likely be no Jewish community at all in Bloemfontein in the year 2000, and none in Kimberly by 1990, and perhaps none in a half-dozen or so American cities where communities now exist, that obviously does not mean that there will be no communities anywhere. We have lived in many places, and none is holier than the next. Kimberly in its day, Providence in its day, Afula in its day, no less, no more than the great centers of our past; each comes to the fore, each passes on. What matters is not that there are Jews in this place or in that, but that there are Jews. What matters even more is that there be Jews of quality and of character. What matters is not whether there is, or will one day be a final resting place. What matters is that in the meanwhile, the people endures, wherever it may be.

Do we endure? For all the talk of death, there are important signs of life to notice. Let me return to Rawidowicz, for he stated this point very well:

> One often gets the impression that many ... of the spiritual leaders and spokesmen of traditional Israel in the last centuries saw before them the imminent disappearance of the Sabbath, the end of tefillin, piety, *yirat shamayim* (fear of heaven) and faith in general. These centuries are today considered by us as a kind of flowering of Jewish thought and life. Those great Jews, whom we regard as important inaugurators of Jewish values and ideas ... saw themselves as the last guardians of a treasure that would soon disappear forever.

A leading poet of the Haskalah (cited also by Rawidowicz) wrote: 'For whom do I labor? Who will tell me the future, will tell me that I am not the last poet of Zion, and you my last readers?' But during the very time of Y. L. Gordon, who penned these lines, Haim Nahman

Bialik was growing up. So Gordon despaired, when Bialik, also Tchernichovsky, and yet others were coming to the fore. He despaired, because he could not see. It is a sin for a Jew to despair. Bialik for his part also saw himself as the end of the end, and a convention in the Hebrew writing of the first half of this century – the century that saw the creation of the State of Israel and the renaissance of the Hebrew language – is that these are the last Jewish writers, writing for the last Jews.

Now, when we contemplate the American Jewish community, we follow this same convention, this ritualistic melancholy. We count too few: we are not happy with the caliber of leadership; we find nothing but decay. Is there not something to place on the other side of the balance?

I think there is a great deal, though we shall not appreciate our accomplishments and gain strength from them if we wish to luxuriate in self-pity. For one thing, American Jews have shaped that mode of Jewishness which is found useful throughout the Jewish world of the *Golah*. It has its faults, but it is surely not a negligible achievement that we have found a way. For another, there is, at this very time, an extraordinary renaissance of Jewish intellectual life, Jewish thought, Jewish scholarship, Jewish learning and Jewish teaching, and it is happening in America and Canada. Today, apart from a few European-trained scholars who survive, the State of Israel is second in Jewish scholarship of the creative kind to American Jewry, in most, though not all, of the fields of Jewish learning. When you consider that learning to us is the object of labor, that we are not raised in Jewish texts and in the Hebrew language, you realize that even for us to be competitive with the Israelis is an achievement. But we turn out to be more than competitive, as proved by the numerous appointments of American Jews, and American-trained Jews, in the fields of Jewish learning in Israeli universities.

Yet another achievement of American Jewry is its present political alertness. Things we could not do 30 years ago we can do today. American Jews have achieved a capacity to make their wishes known and to persuade the larger political community to take these wishes seriously. This is an achievement. It did not come from Heaven. It was something people did for themselves. These are the achievements of the elite, of the people in scholarship and in Jewish studies, in political life, in business. What shall we say of us all?

Here I think we have to point to an achievement so obvious that we cannot reckon with its worth: we have learned how to form and to transmit some form of a Jewish pattern of life in this country.

Obviously, none of us is satisfied with that pattern, nor can we even be proud of it. But when you consider that the fathers and mothers and grandparents of the present generation were entirely unable to transmit their mode of being Jewish to their children, you realize what has been accomplished. That is, the immigrant generation was a success in the shaping of a generation at home in America, and that was the immigrant generation's highest aspiration, and naturally so. But the immigrant generation transmitted nothing, beyond personal example, of a Jewish way of life, and a Jewish way of life reduced to aspects of ethnic culture is hopeless.

The immigrants, to name one thing, used Yiddish, but their children did not. So Yiddish died out. They may have come from a very strict way of life, but their children rarely took up that way of life. What the children got from the parents, by way of a Jewish way of life, was a folk culture of a rather unimpressive character. When you consider the demands that being Jewish makes upon us, the demands to be different from the majority, to marry other Jews, to eat different food and live a different sort of life, you must wonder whether it is worth doing all these things just to participate in a folk culture that cannot yield decent cooking. Why be Jewish in order to get a bellyache? Who needs it? The point is that the way of being Jewish that we know today is our own way; it was not bequeathed to us by the immigrant generation.

It was in part the second, and in part the third generation of American Jews who found their way to a mode of Judaism and an expression of Jewishness such as we now know. I do not mean to praise it, but I also do not think it is time to bury it. One thing is clear: that this mode of Judaism and this expression of Jewishness are something we can transmit to our children. Our forefathers and mothers, on the other hand, did not create a mode of Judaism and an expression of Jewishness that they could transmit to their children. This generally accepted pattern, for all its faults, is something which has endured in America and does endure today. I wonder how many people realize that, two or three generations ago, most people were fairly sure there would be no Jews in America by the end of the twentieth century. Now, we may be reasonable certain that there will be Jews in America at that time and for some time thereafter.

If it is true that we are not dying, and I do not think we are, even though, in this place or in that, there will be drastic changes, then what is happening to us? Why is it that we witness this dread, this foreboding, this sense of impending doom? It is an important question, because so long as our thoughts are melancholy, we shall be paralyzed and find ourselves too tired to do the work of the day. What we fear will happen, we shall make happen.

Why is it that we see ourselves as a dying people, we who look back upon the longest continuous history among all the peoples of the world? Rawidowicz has this to say:

> I am often tempted to think that this fear of cessation in Israel was fundamentally a kind of protective individual and collective emotion. Israel has indulged so much in the fear of its end, that its constant vision of the end helped it to overcome every crisis, to emerge from every threatening end as a living unit, though much wounded and reduced. In anticipating the end, it became its master. Thus no catastrophe could ever take this end-fearing people by surprise, so as to put it off its balance, still less to obliterate it – as if Israel's incessant preparation for the end made this very end absolutely impossible.

This is yet another insight we owe to Professor Rawidowicz, that the self-understanding of the Jewish people is part of its protection. For if we fear we are dying, we take those protective measures that will secure our future.

This may be natural, but I think there is a price to be paid, and it should be specified. It is not wise to dwell too much upon the future, as though it were more than what, in substantial measure, we make of it. If we become persuaded that we are doomed, we shall cease those healthy efforts at self-criticism and those successful efforts at self-improvement which already have made so much difference. The luxurious melancholy will paralyze us and make us think we have a power over the future independent of what we do in the present. What we have to learn from our fears for our own future is to look deeply into an unsatisfactory, but not hopeless, present.

Rawidowicz says: 'A nation dying for thousands of years means a living nation. Our incessant dying means uninterrupted living, rising, standing up, beginning anew.' If we may go back to the premonitions of Jewish dissolution of the 1920s, we gain hope and not discouragement at the achievements even of the 1930s and 1940s. If we remember the fears of the nineteenth-century rabbis and scholars, we shall be pleasantly surprised at the disproof of those fears.

We have to regard everything Jewish and enduring as remarkable. Then we shall appreciate what we have and so understand how much better we can be. Perhaps to be surprised by what we have, we have to fear for the future, so that we may deem remarkable and amazing the small attainments of the hour. That is the only value I can see in the obsession with 'the end of the Jewish people' and with annihilation from within.

From the moment of birth we are destined to death. But what a glorious interval, what a splendid in-between! The Jewish people, too, is dying, but it has taken a long time and will take a long time to do it. It seems to me that while there will be changes, even changes we may not understand or approve of, still, in the end, we shall be very long in dying, whatever happens in this place or that place, however much it means to us in particular, where we happen to be at some one moment. We have to learn how to do a good job of living.

# PART V
## TRAVELS IN JUDAISM

# 16 A Stranger at Home: An American Jew Visits in Israel

*Judaism* 11 (1962), 27–31

I have visited the State of Israel three times: during the summer of 1954 on the Jewish Agency's Summer Institute; during the academic year 1957–58 as a Fulbright Scholar at the Hebrew University; and this past summer on the Jewish Agency's Seminar for Educators. I have traveled the length and breadth of the country, from Eilat to Metullah, from Jerusalem to Safed, from Haifa to the Dead Sea. I have been obsessed with the land and the state, both as a believing Jew and as an American Zionist.

The more I know about Israel, the less I feel I understand. The more I meet Israelis, the less I comprehend them. The reality of the state and its people overwhelms me, perplexes me, troubles and disturbs me. The astonishing fact about Israel is that it is what it claims to be, a Jewish State built by Jewish people on Jewish soil and by Jewish labor; a state in which the Hebrew language and the Jewish creative genius form the foundation of national culture; a state in which the Jew is at home, no longer challenged by the Gentile to explain who he is and why he persists in history, no longer faced with the task of mediating between his Jewishness and another culture. These are facts, no longer hopes, and hence are easy to forget. Perhaps the only time one really faces them is in the first few days in Israel. Afterward, the reality of Israel fades away, because it is commonplace, and one pays more attention to the superficialities of daily life. Each visit to Israel I have faced these facts, and asked myself the question too many Israelis ask, Why do I not settle here? Too much troubled by the question, I seek, and find, the answers in daily life, both at home and in Israel.

At home, one is most aware that one is a Jew, because that is how one is distinguished from the other Americans, with whom one has so much in common. In Israel, one is mostly an American, or, less appropriately, an 'Anglo-Saxon' (I think certain exclusive hotels and country clubs would find that interesting). Even though I want to feel at home, more often than not I am treated as a foreigner and a tourist: I am an American. In the end, I find myself affirming just that: I am an American, both sentimentally and culturally, and my deepest loyalties are to America.

How then may I, as a Jew, take into account the astonishing facts that the State of Israel realizes? If it is all true, as it is, then how am I to respond? Anyone might find numerous answers, in the superficialities of daily life there and in the profundities of civilization here. Here I find much that I like, admire, accept, and want to transmit to the future. I do not believe any society has been so open or free, so fundamentally decent, as American society. I do not believe daily life anywhere else can be so easy and relaxed. I do not find any national culture developing with such vigor, variety, or soundness, the proof of which is the eagerness of other nations to appropriate elements of American culture. Here, furthermore, I find an ideal, a 'way of life', unique in human affairs today, and I want to share in the defense of that ideal, which is, quite simply, democracy in political, cultural, social, and religious life. Just as the Israeli easily forgets the astonishing facts represented by Israel, so we regard the unique achievements of American democracy as commonplace, and are more aware of contradictions of the democratic ideal within American society than of its realizations.

Israelis do not understand the nationalism and patriotism of Jewish Americans, for in no European country was a Jew able to feel that he was part of the 'majority' culture; the exceptions, in Western Europe, were few in number, and generally entered the majority by relinquishing ties to their own religious and cultural minority. Israelis generally regard the loyalty of American Jews to America as similar to the loyalty of 'Egyptian' Jews to the fleshpots of Pharaoh, and similarly reprehensible. It is difficult for the Israelis I met to refrain from warning me of historical facts I know full well, that no other Diaspora community was ever entirely spared, at some points in its history, the rigors of anti-Semitism. I often replied that security is not available to a people that persists too long in history. No matter where one lives, if one stays there for long enough, times are likely to change, and earlier certainties vanish. I ask only the uninterrupted and generally happy tenure of the Jews in Babylon, longer, in fact, than that of the Jews in Palestine. The Jews in Palestine trace a history, during the First Commonwealth, of about six hundred years, and during the second, of about eight hundred years (measuring from the return under Cyrus to the beginning of the fourth century AD), while (so far as we can tell) the Jews in Babylon lived under reasonably secure conditions, by comparison to those affecting other peoples in Mesopotamia, from the time of Jeremiah at least until the decline of the Sassanian empire in the sixth century AD, 1,100 years, or even further, until 1948. In truth, security could hardly be the criterion to measure the value of settling among forty million hostile Arabs. Finally, the experience of German Jewry, which felt analogously toward Germany, is hardly decisive, first, because America is not Germany, and has no such black hatred of Jews as part of its nationalism, and second, because if Rommel had won at El Alamein in 1942, Palestinian Jewry would, alas, have had no better fate than Dutch, German, or Italian Jewries. In fact, history proves nothing about the truth of ideas, but renders them, without reference to their rightness, either real or tragic.

Daily life in Israel seemed to me unnecessarily difficult, not only because of the difficulty of making a living, but because of different attitudes toward the conduct of life and standards of right action. It would be discourteous of a visitor to become specific, but on more than one occasion, I felt 'Israel for the Israelis'.

At times I felt that the xenophobia of Israelis, and, in particular, their disdain for American Jewry, expresses less a considered judgment than a response to the question, What are *we* doing here? One well educated young Israeli told me that he would find a certain satisfaction in forced emigration of American Jewry, and, in general I can see *shelilat hagolah* as little more than a very specific form of xenophobia, expressed also in ridicule of the pronounced American accent in speaking Hebrew, of American ways of dress, of Americans' insistence even on clean kitchens and sanitary facilities. We, for our part, ought not to feel we must criticize the conditions of Israeli life and social intercourse in order to justify our 'remaining' in America. I do not think we need to exalt the situation of *Golah*, its cultural and social benefits, in order to defend our status quo. I was born in America, as a part of the third generation of American Jews and an educator of the fourth; I do not feel the necessity to affirm reality, or to promise, even, to write a Babylonian Talmud in order to justify life in our modern Babylon. 'Blessed is he who inspires the inhabitants of a place with love for it.' I neither affirm nor deny destiny, but only accept it.

I think that a far more significant problem than American *aliyah* or Israeli *yerida* (since 1948, more Israelis have settled in the western hemisphere than Americans both north and sough of the border, have immigrated to Israel) is the problem of future relationships between the state and the Disapora, particularly the American Diaspora. The tragic necessities of the past decades, of saving a remnant and helping them to build a homeland, have demanded an awful price in blood. They have, however, only begun to manifest the price to be paid by the living. The American Jewish community has generously responded to

Israel's legitimate financial requirements, and will, I hope, continue to do so for decades. It has received in exchange a great and welcome return: the state itself, its extraordinary achievements, its successful refutation of any and every anti-Semitic canard against the Jewish people. In truth, whatever factual basis anti-Semitism ever had in economic, social, political, or cultural life has been swept away. The Jew can no longer be accused of economic parasitism, for he has recovered and enhanced his own heritage; of political impotence, for he has reentered the drama of history. All this has been achieved by the State of Israel.

The state has, moreover, ended the corroding fear of Jewish home-lessness, and however secure the Jew is in America, he has shared that fear if he has read either history or the daily newspaper. Israel owes absolutely nothing to American Jewry, and can never be properly repaid for the blood and iron it has lavished to create and sustain itself. I think a great part of American Jewish consensus has to do with the pride and affirmation of American Jewry toward the state and the Zionist cause. In this sense, Israel has served to unify American Jewry, to give its disparate elements a common cause and a common purpose. Finally, the cultural benefits of the state have only begun to reach and fructify our community life.

Israelis, on the other hand, have too little awareness of how much they have given American Jews, and have a sense of obligation that is neither appropriate nor affirmative. They see themselves as takers, not givers, and such a self-image does not lead to pride or love. I think another part of Israeli xenophobia may be therefore explained by the Israeli's need to show his independence of his 'rich American' guests. 'We may be dependent on your money,' I was told, 'but we will not therefore kowtow to you.' (Alas, not a few tourists expect just that.) Nonetheless, the interest most Israelis seem to have in the *Golah* communities is apparently limited by Israeli needs for money and manpower. 'Be kind to tourists, they bring hard currency', a poster for children reads; and another, 'Every tourist is a potential immi-grant'. I found very little curiosity about the development of American-Jewish life, except as related to Israeli affairs; very little interest in non-Zionist activities in general; and none whatever in our hopes for American Jewry's future. Furthermore, I regretted to find that Israelis are far less prepared to support voluntary communal activities than American Jews are.

When a perfectly legitimate social welfare institution or cultural activity requires support, the first and primary source of financial support is either the government – or the *Golah*. It is certainly true that Israelis have much, much less to give. Giving, however, is measured not only by the size of the gift, but by the benefit to the giver. For example, a certain synagogue in Jerusalem was built mainly by American Jews. When two women who had shared in the project asked the president of the congregation why no landscaping had been done for the building (now standing for more than a decade on one of Jerusalem's main streets), he replied that they ought to ask their husbands to raise the funds. (Indeed, the synagogues pay their rabbis abysmal salaries, most of which come from government funds.)

Seeing themselves, however inaccurately, as takers and not givers, Israelis apparently see the need to defend whatever they do against moderate and intelligent criticism. They appeal all too often to clichés in order to explain deficiencies. An old story, out of the 1930s, tells about an American who is shown through the new subway in Moscow. He is impressed by the marbled halls, the immaculate floors, the displays of fine art on the walls, and asks, 'This is all very lovely, but where are the subway trains themselves?' 'And what about the Negroes in the South?' his guide exclaimed. In Israel, I found 2,000 years of *Golah*', or alternatively, to 'the first Jewish State after 2,000 years', or, secondly, to the relative youth of the country, and its obviously formidable achievements in so few years. Israel is, however, not a great deal younger than the organized American Jewish community, which for all practical purposes may be dated at about 1880 (Reform and Conservative institutions). In any case, how long does it take to clean the garbage that litters the streets in so many cities? I once asked why the newest and most modern apartment houses invariably have obvious and malodorous garbage cans in the front entry, instead of at the back door, and was accused of being a Jewish anti-Semite or an assimilationist. Indeed, one of the costliest charges of building the state has been paid by the Jew's ancient, resourceful capacity to laugh at himself.

As I said, the problem that troubles me most is the future relationship between the state and the American *Golah*. It is fashionable in Israel to ridicule the Jewish Agency, but what I know of its work impresses me. It is actively interested in bringing *Golah* Jews to Israel, and I think its interest is not only *aliyah* or potential leadership in pro-Israeli activity, but also in a cultural and national renaissance, based on the foundation of Israeli realities and Hebrew culture, throughout the Jewish world. I heard a speech by an Agency official, on the importance of Jewish education everywhere, in which the attraction of Castro for South American Jewish youth was described as a great calamity. That official, and his colleagues, voiced concern for the future of South American Jewry not on account of specific Israeli interest, but on the account of the interest of the Jewish nation everywhere. The Agency's work has only just begun. If, as I believe, a Jew who has visited Israel for any substantial period is fundamentally changed in his attitude toward himself as a Jew and toward the potentialities of Jewishness and Judaism, then the importance of the Jewish Agency's program is greatly enhanced. A Jew who has seen the state, the land, and the people must be utterly different from a Jew who has not. The Agency, for all its imperfections, is one effective means of bringing Israel and its benefits into the lives of Jews everywhere.

I do not understand the State of Israel yet, but I understand the fact of its existence, and find myself compelled to rethink the meaning of the Jewish faith and of Jewish destiny because of that fact. That is why I shall return, I hope, to Israel many times, perhaps to stay, not because of what I could ever hope to give to the Jewish state, but because of what the Jewish state has already given me.

# 17

# With the Jews of South Africa

*Moment* 2/2 (1976), 18–22

I went to South Africa to speak to Jews about Jewish things, to give the keynote address at the National Congress of the South African Jewish Board of Deputies. I went determined not to talk about what I came to call 'The Subject' – race, apartheid – and not to 'tell people how to solve their problems'. After three weeks and 30 or more public appearances, in Jewish community meetings, student gatherings and university lecture rooms, I discovered that Jewish things and The Subject cannot be kept apart. And I found no fewer than a dozen scenarios for the future of that beautiful, tormented country and its weak, inconsequential, but truly worthy Jewry. I went to South Africa to learn about the potentialities of Judaism on the moral frontier of humanity. I left ashamed to be a human being but ineffably proud to be a Jew.

Johannesburg and Pretoria, Bloemfontein and Potchefstroom, Cape Town, Simonstown, Stellenbosch, Paarl, Port Elizabeth, Durban, East London – Swaziland, Lesotho, Zululand – once merely place names, now, for me, people: proud, intense, beleaguered. The white minority, not five million out of more than twenty, speaks two languages; the Indians, coloreds, several more; and the blacks more still. Jews speak English but have studied Afrikaans and Hebrew, and of course there are, as everywhere, the Yiddishists.

What does it mean to live among people of different speech, to know that what is intimate and particular to you is unknown to the other? To wonder, what is he thinking, he who speaks words you scarcely grasp, he who thinks words and remembers history which are not yours?

It means that the other is the alien. There is no bridge of shared experience, contained in language, from the one to the next. What does it mean to know that the mass of your countrymen lives in utter human degradation, unable to dwell in the same nice neighborhood you live in, educate children in decent schools, make use of the same toilet facilities and buses, enjoy the same salary for the same work, take for granted the same fundamental rights of citizenship and permanent residence, benefit from equal protection of the law, remember a past of dignity and hope for a future of comfortable death? How does a person live with the knowledge that the comfort of one is built on the deprivation of the other? What do you call a country which is called by at least three names by its own people – South Africa to the English speaker, Suid Afrika to the Afrikaans speaker, and Azania to the blacks?

How, in other words, do Jews live in South Africa? More interesting: What happens to Judaism there? The Jews live very well indeed. But despite that fact and against it, Judaism as a tradition of moral imperative and commitment to one Torah for the whole human condition is not yet extinguished.

In diverse ways, the Jews are South African. I met none who was not a white supremacist in the simplest terms. In a country in which censorship and secret police enforce laws against free expression of opinion, the Jews enforce on themselves censorship which requires acute circumlocutions for the expression of the simplest truths. In a land of abundant, untrained labor, Jews – like other whites – employ an unlimited number of household servants, paying the usual R50 or R60 ($60–$72) monthly. In a land in which physical work is degraded and demeaning, associated as it is with 'inferior' races, Jews – like other whites – have contempt for work and the worker. In a land in which to be a liberal means to concede that blacks are human, Jews – along with other liberals – play the role of Lady Bountiful. In a truly Christian country, whose Christianity requires the closing of movies on Sundays, Jews work out an equally ritualistic and formalized mode of Judaism. Orthodox Judaism exercises a veto on all speakers brought to the Republic by the organized Jewish community. (A case in point is Samuel Sandmel's course on Biblical Thought, introduced through the Academy Without Walls of Haifa University, under the sponsorship of the Board of Deputies. At the Congress, an Orthodox rabbi condemned the use of a 'heretical' course by a Reform rabbi, albeit conceding that he had not even seen the course.) In a country far from the centers of Western culture, accomplished in science and technology but out of touch with the life of the humanities, the Jews scarcely acknowledge that being Jewish takes shape in the life of the intellect. Among the handful of rabbis and scholars serving the small community I met only a few who might, on any terms, be employable anywhere else in the Jewish world.

I asked the Congress: 'In all the Jewish world, who reads a book written on a Jewish subject by a South African Jew? Who consults a work of scholarship in Jewish learning done by a South African-trained and educated Jew? What Jewish ideas come to illuminate our common condition and to inform our minds, from South African

Jewry? Why is it that among the Jewish communities in all the world, your reputation does not include praise for your devotion to the intellect of the Jewish people, to the heart and mind and soul of Jewry?' The answer, of course, is that the sorts of people who think and write cannot make their lives where the state watches their words. Great Jewish writing does come from South Africans – but not, in the main, from those resident in South Africa.

But art is the expression of life already lived. The heritage of Judaism shapes the perceptions of Jews, and South African Jews include Judaists. That is the other half of the matter. How does Judaism endure in that racist and oppressive society? We know about the émigrés, including 9,000 *olim* in the State of Israel from a community that numbers about 120,000, the highest rate of *aliyah* from any country that permits free emigration. Constituencies with sizable Jewish populations send to the Volksraad (parliament) Progressive-Reform representatives, of whom Mrs Helen Suzman is best known abroad. Serving long prison sentences are Jews who have passed out leaflets or joined organizations deemed subversive. True, they work hard at finding language capable both of expressing what is to be said and of being heard and understood by a closed-minded ruling minority. But the resolutions do pass. Mrs Suzman's brother-in-law, Mr Arthur Suzman, has for 16 years given an address to the National Congress of the Board of Deputies on 'public relations', in which he links events in the world to the life of the community. This year he emphasized that 'events in the north' (meaning Angola) 'have imposed new urgency upon the quest for racial justice' – perhaps mild words for us, but in context, no small matter – and his words met with general approval.

Yet not what we say but what we do matters. What the Jews of South Africa do is full of contradiction The Jewish community includes major industrialists who pay equal wages for equal work to white and black workers – and some who do not. The Union of Jewish Women, one of the strongest Jewish organizations, is devoted to social work in the African townships, bringing food to the hungry and medicine to the sick. But in Port Elizabeth my (Jewish) hostess laughed at her servants for trying to enter the elevator with us. 'You don't honestly think you can ride with us, do you? Go down the stairs!'

Yet I also saw Jews – and they are not a few – who talked with blacks with genuine respect, who had taken the trouble even to learn the music of the Africans' language and to sing out the words in the same timbre and rhythm. True, in some Jewish homes servants serve the food while wearing white gloves; in one, the serving lady wore a large red sash over her white uniform. But it was also in Jewish homes that I saw genuine camaraderie and love, human appreciation clearly shared among equals, even affection expressed, on both sides, in human physical contact – a pat on the back – which in the context is not to be ignored. If within South African Israel there are those who trample the head of the poor into the dust of the earth, cows of Bashan in the Rand who oppress the poor, who crush the needy, there are also those, and they are not few, who hate evil and love good and try to establish justice in the gate.

It is in South Africa that the Christian religion lives in its old Calvinist form. The Afrikaners are very pious, very Christian. They come through as decent and kindly people, very certain of their right-eousness in a sinful world. Not a few times I was asked whether I did not agree that Israel (by which they mean the state) and South Africa must unite against the conspiracy of atheism and Communism which threatens the world. I do not know how the Afrikaner divines, devot-ed to the Bible as they are, read the literature of the *nevi'im*. But during my three weeks in the country I found myself obsessed with the simple verities of Amos and Isaiah. I could not put out of mind the noble aspiration of the Talmudic rabbis to create an orderly and just society. I never saw a black but that I thought of myself with a yellow star. But his star is his skin, and his Holocaust is for centuries and slow.

The Jews of South Africa are professedly Orthodox. What being Orthodox means is difficult to say. Most of the community leaders whom I met do not keep kosher outside of their homes and do not keep the Sabbath. The major service comes on Friday evenings, as in the old Reform liturgical week. But, then, the Jews are professedly Zionist. Being Zionist means giving vast sums to the State of Israel. It also means to listen with very great care lest something out of con-formity with the party line (mainly Revisionist) be said, crouching for the attack on the most innocent thought. My own blunder in this regard came when I said that I thought that Zionism must mean a focus on *aliyah*, and I suggested that Zionists see to it that *all* young people of university age spend a year of study or work in the State of Israel (as I think should be the case in American and Canadian Jewry) as a kind of *aliyah lesha'ah*. I had stepped on a toe: 'You don't seem to realize that we presently send several hundred students every year.' The students are of high school age, not likely to make an immediate commitment to remain in the country. The programs of bringing young adults to the State of Israel reach a couple of hundred, not thousands by any means. In the main, they are the work of the Jewish

Agency, not primarily the local community part of the Zionist agenda, even in a community where almost every family has children or close relatives in Israel.

The 'proud record of philanthropy' is, of course, enviable. There are no income tax deductions for the South African equivalent of UJA. Yet people give. On the other hand, if the per capita rate of giving is the highest in the Jewish world, as I was told, the per capita rate of wealth may well also be the highest. A fund-raiser showed me cards on which the estimate of the donor's capacity to give is listed alongside what the donor actually does give. Among several dozen, the figures did not coincide, any more than they do here in the US; none gave so much as, let alone more than, what peer communities estimated he should. The Jews are very certain of their righteousness, taking delight in their solemn assemblies and their rich, fat offerings to the State of Israel. Yet there are also those who search out springs of justice and give their lives – in prisons, as exiles, but also in universities and in industry – to make righteousness roll down like an ever-flowing stream.

Are these last the same Jews who comprise 'the organized Jewish community'? The students whom I met perceive the community as staid, cautious, self-satisfied, as indeed I did. But are the decent others not Jews too? Do they not come out of the same families, the same tradition of prophecy and law? In South Africa I learned that the issues of Judaism are drawn starkly and in all their simplicity. South Africa is a land of simple truths. In my last lecture, in Johannesburg the day before I left, I spoke about the indivisibility of freedom, the slavery of the master, the degradation of the superior race. In order to be heard, I said this with as much tact as I could muster. But it slipped out that I thought authentic Judaism is expressed by the prisoners and the exiles, the Jewish whites who give their lives to alleviate the condition of the blacks (only the blacks can change that condition, by rejecting it, as they may now have begun to do), the businessmen and lawyers and industrialists who concretely and in practical ways do what they can (and it is a great deal) to establish for blacks the chances for a life of human dignity. A critic said, 'But many of the people to whom you refer are not observant Jews and have nothing to do with the Jewish community.' I replied, '[years ago] I would have agreed with you. But then life seemed more subtle and complicated than it does now, than it does here or at home. In my understanding Judaism has always taught that what God wants of human creatures is to do justice, love mercy, walk humbly with God. Jewish people who, to do justice, go to prison or into exile, who, to love mercy, spend their lives and fortunes for others, who have the humility to see the Creator in the face of all creatures – such people testify that Judaism endures, even triumphantly, in this time and place.'

Yet there is not only Judaism to consider, there is also the Jewish group. What of them and their country? The Jews are weak and unimportant, about one half of 1 percent of the population of the Republic of South Africa, not much more than 2 percent of the white minority of the population. They are socially and psychologically isolated from the other and much larger components of the white minority. Old-fashioned anti-Semitism flourishes. South African television (SABC) wanted to delete the episode on genocide from *The World at War* series of Jeremy Isaacs. It televises anti-Semitic preachers, who quote from the *Protocols of the Elders of Zion*. Jewish community officials sometimes compare their own work to that of members of the Judenrat. Letters sent to high government officials reach the hands of anti-Semitic leaders, meetings with officers of the Bureau of State Security on organized anti-Semitic movements in the country are made known forthwith to those same movements. At least 2,500 Nazis and other anti-Semites are known to Jewish agencies. The white population is utterly uninformed about Judaism. An SABC official told a Jewish community officer that the reason SABC will not televise programs dealing with the Jews is that there is no reason: 'Jews are not really part of South Africa and are aliens (after three or four generations!) anyhow.' And no one is interested. Serious and sane Jewish leaders expressed to me their recurrent nightmare: seeing 120,000 South African Jews in transit camps in the State of Israel, coming only with a suitcase of clothing, because of white, not black, action. For their part, Jews live in small enclaves, primarily among other Jews.

What to do? In effect, it has to begin to wind down the affairs of the community. But if that is not an acceptable alternative, the Board of Deputies, which stands for the continuity and legitimacy of Jewish life in South Africa, should engage in a vast program of public relations (in the American sense), to reach out to all populations in the country and to teach the facts of the devotion and contribution of South African Jewry to the life of the Republic, on the one side, and of Judaism as a living religion, on the other. The Jews, for their part, would reach out to these same groups, learn the other languages. Afrikaans would become a language of daily use within Jewry, and the history and culture of the Afrikaans people would be known and shared among Jews, just as Jews in Quebec know and live with French language and culture. Positions in Jewish Studies would be created in the universities of the Afrikaans, Indian, colored and black populations wherever they are accepted. To provide faculty for such positions, native South Africans, of all language groups and races, would be recruited for study in the relevant fields of Jewish learning and sent abroad – to the State of Israel, Europe and North America – for doctorates. In this way Jewish culture would be better known, and the Jews perceived as they are: another variety of South African. A council of Jews, Christians, and (in Natal and the Cape) Moslems should be organized, for projects of mutual understanding and cooperation. Much could be done to persuade others that Jews belong in and to the Republic, have contributed and now contribute to its culture and prosperity, and above all share in its future.

Either, or. But what can be done to persuade Jews of these same facts? For the ordinary folk are neither Zionists (since they remain and evidently plan to remain in South Africa) nor diasporists (since, while remaining, they talk incessantly of emigrating. To me, two things symbolize the ordinary folk, not the students or industrialists, the prisoners of conscience or the exiles. One is the buying of diamonds, while remaining comfortably in the rich suburbs of Johannesburg and Cape Town. The other is the little bells. As I said, certain kinds of work are for the blacks; 'kaffirwork', I believe, is the word. ('Kaffir' is not used in liberal society.) One sort is the serving of food. When families eat, the lady of the house has a little bell. This she rings when there is work to be done, and the black man and lady come in, white-gloved, bringing the food and taking away the plates. I do not live in a level of American society in which people have servants or want them. Among many things that made three weeks in the Republic a personal trial, the hearing of the little bells, the pretense of a life of leisured wealth by rather ordinary folk living on ordinary incomes, stand out. There is nothing degrading about serving food or helping people to raise their families. But the notion of waiters and waitresses – servants who call their employers 'master' – gliding in and out in response to a bell, is grotesque and contemptible.

For three weeks I abided by the rules, carefully reading the signs on public toilets to find one for white males, employing porters to carry my attaché case, because that was expected, trying to concentrate on the requirements of a rather strange and highly formal system of social relations. Only when, about to depart from Johannesburg to London, I came to Smuts International Airport for the last time, did I rebel. I got a dolly, put my own luggage on it, pushed it myself to the check-in line, and loaded it myself onto the scale – not to deprive the porter of his wages, but to give myself, for the first time in three weeks, the pleasure of raising a hand in labor, however slight. It was no one's business but mine, and I meant only to use my own arms and muscles in my own service. It was my modest way of asserting my humanity, a gesture that could have meaning only in that utterly freaked-out country of Calvinist Christianity, white supremacy, Jewish time-serving and enjoyment of life's comforts, that loved land of Jewish, Christian, Moslem, white, brown, yellow, and black anguish, suffering, self-sacrifice, and despite all things, hope. I came to Suid Afrika/South Africa. I left Azania.

# 18 Journey to the Interior: Min-ne-so-ta, Hats off to thee!

*Response* 12 (1979), 57–63

In the fall of 1978 I traveled. And I traveled and traveled and traveled, mainly in Minnesota. The reason was that I like to travel, see things, meet people, and do so at every chance. Many chances came last fall, and I took them all. What did I learn about America and, especially, about universities and Jews – my two favorite subjects?

Let me explain, first of all, which universities and which Jews. I had been invited to serve as Hill Foundation Visiting Professor at the University of Minnesota for the fall quarter. Since I could not bring my four children and wife for a brief period of ten weeks, it was agreed that I should commute from Providence Rhode Island to Minneapolis-St Paul Minnesota every other week. So, to begin with, there were five round trips to the Twin Cities, out on Monday, home on Thursday night. Then there was (supposed to be) a trip to a temple in Duluth, and a lecture at Carleton College, Northfield, Minnesota. And, as chairman of the History of Judaism section of the American Academy of Religion, there was a three-day trip to New Orleans. There were yet more lectures at a synagogue in New York City, and at the University of Chicago. But the main thing was the University of Minnesota.

Professors at Ivy League universities are not supposed to know about 'the real world'. I went to Minnesota to find out. Our students, after all, survive a highly competitive process of selection. We do not have to go searching for books; our university libraries are excellent. We teach humane and easy assignments. Our administrations are accessible and friendly. They are ourselves. But 'out there' where the real world is, there are supposed to be sullen students, churlish deans, no books, and life is hard, so nothing we suggest about the shape of a curriculum and the purpose of university education in the liberal arts need be taken seriously. We don't know how things really are.

When I got to Minnesota, the professors warned me that 'Minnesota students won't read.' They told me about the 'Minnesota poker-face', that is, the student who sits through lectures with no facial expression whatever, no visible response to anything, any question, even any joke. My peculiar mode of teaching, which is to insist that the students discover the points I want to make through their response to questions of mine and through their discussion (even) with one another, would not be possible in Minnesota. It was lecture to whom it may concern or die. We Ivy League professors should not expect to transfer to a mass institution what we can do with elite students.

Before I go on with the narrative, let me tell about how I dealt with the alleged 'Minnesota poker-face.' As I said, I teach by asking questions. So, after appropriate beginnings, I asked my first important question.

'Does everyone understand it?' A ritual nodding of the heads.

'Does everyone know why it is an important question, and why it is the first that has to be asked, before we can do anything else?' More ritual nodding.

Then I: 'Fine, so what's the answer?'

Silence.

Not a half a minute of silence, and not a minute.

I timed the silence. I come from stubborn folk. I was not going to say another word until someone attempted an answer. So I sat on the top of the desk, and the students sat in their chairs. I looked out of the window, on an early fall day, in the bright, clear Minnesota air, over the handsome brick buildings of the University of Minnesota. I know they're brick. I counted the bricks. The students stared at the ceiling, or at me.

After 20 minutes of silence, someone spoke.

The answer was not relevant.

I said so.

Another 20 minutes of silence.

Then things got started.

In other words, I dealt with the poker-face by making clear that I was serious. I asked a question because I wanted an answer to that question. Once we all agreed it was a right question and in what seemed to be the right time and place, then it was the students' task to deal with it. From that point onward, they did. Not all of them, not very happily, and not often with real success. But they tried their best. This meant doing the reading on time, so that they would have facts and ideas with which to shape their answers and their questions.

At the end, I am sorry to report, the whole thing collapsed. After steadfastly preparing with some care and even critical acumen for most of the course, for the final session, which to me was the crucial point in the unfolding interpretive scheme I had worked so hard to present, the students, it turned out, were too busy to master the assigned reading (some claim they did it, but none made any sense of it, except one middle-aged lady, of whom more below).

So I went back to the first day. This time, instead of waiting out an answer, I walked out. People don't do that every day – and professors had better not. But once in a while, it may have an educational result. I don't know whether it did. I do know that one *can* teach in a vast, 'big-ten' university. One can teach in much the same way that teaching is done in a small school such as Brown; expect the students to learn on their own and work reasonably carefully; and in all ways give of oneself and demand the students do the same. My fundamental faith in the worth of mass education was shaken in Minnesota, but it came out strengthened as well as tempered by reality.

I came to Minnesota because I believe in mass institutions, in open admission (somewhere, if not everywhere), and above all in a nation that has full and ready access to its institutions of learning and of culture. That is for the sake of the vitality and inner power of universities, as well as of the social and cultural vitality of the nation that pays for them. I wanted to have the experience of teaching at the largest of the great state universities. Minnesota is one which, I think, succeeds in joining class to mass, in a way that my own university would not attempt, and in a way in which most mass institutions do not attempt either. Minnesota is excellent *and* has 65,000 students.

The students mainly are commuters, a great many of them work more than 20 hours a week. In general the university is not the center of their lives, as it is at Brown. It is something which has to compete – not always successfully – for their attention. It was my conception that after an encounter with the biggest and the best of the biggest (or, at least, one of the best), I could hold my head up in conversations with professors who do not teach within 50 miles of the Atlantic or the Pacific coasts. These are the colleagues who do not teach the one student out of five or eight or ten who has survived an admissions competition. They do not teach students who mostly live in university residential halls, eat together, have long days to spend in the library, if they want, or anywhere else they want, and in general live a privileged and remarkably expensive life. I could say, 'Yes, I too have been there.' Now I have. What did I learn?

The first thing I learned is that the professors were not entirely wrong (though I think they have been discouraged by too little success) in thinking that their students are not used to using their minds and had best be told what to think. In a university as large as Minnesota, as in any public school and college, the class room is a

cross-section of the city. My students were as young as 16 or 17, and
as old as 60 or 70. Indeed, the novelty I most noticed in Minnesota
was the older women and men who came to my course and did the
work. Most of them, to be sure, seem to me uneducable, because they
can not follow a logical argument for more than two steps, and never
have a clear notion of what is relevant and what is not. By far the
most perceptive student, and the one who learned by far the most,
was a Jewish woman in her early fifties.

Still, the variety of capacities in a public university classroom is its
single most striking trait. A few students had good muzzle-velocity,
some were inarticulate. A few of them could follow an argument
through its stages and even reverse its course. Many could not follow
any sort of discussion. Some of them could be relied upon to read and
understand what they read. Many could not be expected to read.
What I learned, which I did not expect to learn, was that elite
universities really are better than mass universities, in that the educational achievements of the students are markedly greater. Perhaps this
is not so in the natural sciences and mathematics, but in the humanities, I think it is clear that a selected student body is easier to teach,
enjoys challenge and stimulation from its own midst, and can be
relied upon to provide its own motivation for hard work and clear
thought.

That is not to suggest that public universities do not have good
students. On the contrary, I have always believed that there is not a
single college and university in this country without its share, however
small, of first-class young people. I am more than ever convinced that
that is the case. But I also have to concede that, while cultures should
be diffused, some universities really do have a greater opportunity for
serious and solid educational work than others. The work of those
others is all the more important on that account. For a university like
Minnesota has a profound impact on the everyday culture of its
region. Ivy League universities have a profound impact, at best, on the
high culture of a small class of people widely scattered across
the major cities of the country. It is not the same thing. They make a
difference. We don't.

Another conviction, which, happily, I now may affirm on the basis
of the sample of my experience, is that there is not a faculty in
this country entirely lacking in teachers of vitality, intelligence, and
intellectual power. Minnesota, if I may boast, is exceptionally rich in
interesting scholars. I learned much from people there, in history, art
and art history, humanities, classics, and other fields. I met a good
number of colleagues whom I should have been glad to bring with me

to Brown, and many whom I miss. The administration, for its part, seemed to me less boastful than it should be of its faculty and of the achievements of the university in both education and scholarship. I think that administrations of state universities tend to be cowed and discouraged because of public hostility to government spending. It is difficult to find fault with the discouragement. But I think a better case can be made for the public university than has been made. More is to be said about why this, above all, is where we should be glad and proud to spend our money. To generalize, I found the faculty far better than the students (which is not the case at some of the 'ivy-type' small colleges, where the students are brighter and more interesting than the faculty), and the administration somewhere in-between.

Minneapolis and St Paul are separate cities. They say that the east ends at Saint Paul, and the west begins at Minneapolis. The two Jewish communities are separate as well, each with its own Jewish federation, for example. Both cities justifiably take pride in the excellence of daily life in them, their cleanliness, their natural beauty. I do not think there is a prettier drive in America than the one down the St Paul side of the Mississippi River, from the University of Minnesota to the airport. I took it five times. I cannot forget it. Apart from the vicious Siberian climate in the winter, I think the people in the Twin Cities who maintain it is the nicest place in the world to live cannot be far from right.

But I always wondered, with so much on their side, why people in the Twin Cities – and throughout the middle west, wherever I went – find it necessary to ask visitors what they think of their town. I cannot remember ever asking a visitor to Providence what he thought of Providence. The first evening I was in the Twin Cities, at a supper party, I was asked, 'What do you think of the Twin Cities?' I said I thought things were pretty nice, from what little I'd seen. 'Well, what do you really think?' 'I really think things are pretty nice.' 'But tell me the truth, what do you really, really think?' 'Well,' I replied, 'the woman at the hotel desk was pretty rude when I registered.' The answer, 'Well, I've been to New York, and they were ruder there.' It's a no-win situation.

The Jewish communities are what they are: full of marvelously talented people, pursuing splendid careers of every kind. That is why I do not believe the Jewish businessmen who run the 'community' would tolerate in the running of their businesses the incompetence and indifference to sheer quality of 'product' that they think all right in Jewish organizational life. I am struck at the disparity, among the various communities I visited, between private excellence and Jewish public slovenliness. I can list no fewer than five encounters which made me think that, when it comes to Jewish things, people really just don't care.

Little things, big things: I was supposed to lecture in Duluth. One week before the lecture, someone called to ask me to come, instead, next spring. 'But I want to come now.' 'But if you come now, there will be only 20 or 30 people to hear you.' 'But I don't mind talking to 20 or 30 people, if they want to listen to me. I've talked to five or to a thousand – it never mattered much.' 'But to us it matters. Don't come.' So much for Duluth. What had happened I never quite found out. But the fact that I had an invitation which was a contract, approved by the board of the Temple which had invited me, never meant a thing. A business man would think twice – perhaps even that particular business man would think twice – about unilaterally canceling a contract over the protest of the other party. But not when the Jewish community is involved.

Slightly bigger: I wrote to a federation director, offering to teach, at no fee whatsoever, adult study groups for the federation through the length of my stay in the Twin Cities. For a very long time, there was no reply. Then came a reply which indicated that I was thought to be looking for a job. I made it clear that I wanted to *serve, for free*, because I wanted to learn what the Jews are like, what's on their minds. About two months later, I gave up on that project – there having been no reply. Shortly thereafter came a letter explaining that we in Minnesota don't always answer letters right away. So much for my aspiration to serve.

Bigger yet: A different federation planned a major educational program with me. I was asked to attend a committee meeting 'to discuss the topics for the program'. That was the first time in my career that such an invitation had come to me. The usual practice has been to settle the matter with the federation director, rabbi, or other responsible executive. Aha! I thought, a new experience. I went. I proposed a topic. It was shot down. I proposed four more. All duds. Finally, I said, 'Well, I want to talk about such-and-so.' Woman across the table: 'I suppose you have a lecture in your file on that subject which you wrote three years ago.' I'm not very good at group-work techniques. I left and (with mutual agreement) cancelled my commitment, because I did not think I could be very useful to that sort of person, and her colleagues.

Along different lines: the Hill professor gives a public lecture. Mine was on 'The Talmud as History'. The November date was chosen in June and put on the community calendar at that time. Two weeks before the lecture a synagogue announced that Elie Wiesel would lecture on that same night. Minneapolis-Saint Paul are not New York or Boston. There are not public lectures every night, and there is no tradition of going to them. I reckoned our program was dead; who can compete with Wiesel for a Jewish audience, or should even want to? But my job was to give the lecture.

What bothered many of us at the university was the suspicion that the Jewish community just didn't care about Jews out there. How such a conflict of programs of a similar sort could have come about is very simple. Someone did not bother to check the community calendar – or someone didn't care. I never found out. I didn't want to know. As it happened, about five hundred people came to my lecture, twelve hundred to his, so from that viewpoint everyone was happy. I would guess people left the other lecture somewhat more satisfied than mine. But the faculty who were at mine, as well as some of the students, seemed to me to have listened carefully and the questions, in the main, showed attentiveness. I also thought I had said something worth knowing.

So there was one occasion on which two major lectures were planned for the same, fairly small community, on the same night, because people just don't care to check. Ten days later I flew to New Orleans, to attend the American Academy of Religion meeting there. A former student of mine, a Methodist minister, is Protestant chaplain at Louisiana State University, Baton Rouge. He asked me to come to Baton Rouge when I went to New Orleans and to speak to the Sunday night program there.

I said, 'Well, I don't reckon I have much to say, in a religious context, to Christian students, and I'm not much of a believer in conferences of Christians and Jews.' He: 'But we'll have the Hillel students, and they'll be the majority.' I: 'My lecture will be either to Jews as a Jew or to students as a teacher, but I can't do both.' He: 'Talk to Jews as a Jew. The rest will listen in and learn.' He meant well, and I meant well, but we didn't reckon with the Jewish community. When I got to the New Orleans airport, I was told that the Jewish community had scheduled a lecture that same night by Ellis Rivkin. It would be at a local temple. Baton Rouge Jewry could not sustain two lectures a month. It was quite clear to me that no one would come to two lectures in one night. They were not at the same hour, and I doubted that the Jewish community would come to mine, at the university, in preference to his, at a temple. (In fact no one did.) Still, we drove on, through the bayous and by Lake Pontchartrain, on up to Baton Rouge, a very depressing ride that gray night.

I saw my host: 'Did the Jewish community know about my lecture?' He: 'Yes, it had been publicized for months. The people just didn't care.'

I can't take it personally. At my lecture were about seventy-five people, a vast majority of them Catholic or Protestant – no Jewish faculty, perhaps ten or fifteen Jewish students, for a lecture on, of all things, 'The Ever-Dying People.' I suppose I chose a better topic than I had realized, but it was the (third and) last time I could imagine giving that lecture. The reason is that it is too painfully right.

That is not to suggest things are different when you travel. When we travel, we take not only our suitcases and ourselves, but also our world. Providence is no different from Duluth, Baton Rouge, Saint Paul, or Minneapolis. Once, when I was very critical of the low standards of lay peoples' sermons at the conservative congregation I attended, an acquaintance who is a psychiatrist criticized me:

> You expect too much. People don't share your striving for excellence, your wanting to improve or do better. They're happy just as they are, and they don't want to be bothered. They don't care. This one gets up and talks, and everyone says, 'It was a great talk,' and next time, that one gets up and talks, and everyone says, 'It was a great talk,' and so it goes, and everybody is happy. Why should you mix in? Why all this criticism, why all this striving for excellence?

Well, I do care. I know others care too. I do not think the Jewish community is well served by (so-called) 'professionals' who are sloppy and indifferent to the way in which they do their work, let alone by (so-called) 'leaders' – presidents, board members and the like – who really do not think they have a right to criticize the way in which 'their' organizations conduct business. The 'professionals' are not very professional, and the 'leaders' do not lead.

All of us have difficulty in joining our Jewish to our 'ordinary' lives. For me it is hard to move from the Jewish community, with its standards and its conceptions of achievement, to the university, with its different, higher standards and different – far more rigorous – definitions of achievement. For Jewish lawyers, physicians, engineers, government officials, people in all of the infinite variety of businesses and professions, it is equally difficult to move from that one world into that unique, Jewish world. None knows how to bridge these two worlds.

In the university world I see diversity and want to encourage it. In the University of Minnesota, I know people who strive to do good teaching and to make good articles and books, people who travel to India to study old buildings and come back and tell us things worth knowing about them, people who do law or humanities and help construct this country's legal system or define its humanistic scholarship and shape its expression. Just because an institution is big, it does not have to be mediocre, and just because it is diverse, it does not have to adhere to the standards of the least able or the least caring, or the most brazen and coarse. The power is diversity. The strength is access. The hope is the engagement of as many as will share and join. That is so in universities.

It also is so in the Jewish community – or should be so. Why should we be in the hands of people who do not really criticize themselves and try to improve, from year to year, upon the conduct of their office (except [of course] in the budget raised and spent)? Why should our leaders decline to take an interest in the organizations they are chosen to head? Why should there be so little caring, except in the raising and the spending of money, by people who in that other half – or far more than half – of their existence strive to improve and seek after excellence? If I am critical of my work as a teacher and as a scholar, always trying to do better than I have ever done, should I not be critical of my work within Jewry and in its organizations? *And I am everyone.*

This, then, is my journey to the interior, to the middle west and south, from an east Coast, Ivy League university to a middle-west, big ten university, from an old, small, moribund and staid Jewish community to a large, proud, vigorous and ambitious one – my trip from home to home. I learned about the Jewish community that the Jews are better than their community, more talented, more caring, more ambitious for excellence, more committed to solid achievement – and much, much less satisfied with themselves than their organizations, and the people who make their living from their organizations, would like to think.

Oh, by the way, if I have not mentioned any rabbis, it is because I never met any. At least the federations undertook and suffered an encounter. The 'pulpit' rabbis were not heard from. So from them I learned nothing. About them? I prefer not to say. I am inclined to think the talent of Jewry flows in different directions from Jewry, which is why, as I said, the Jews are better than their community.

# 19 Jubilee in Tübingen

Moment 3/2 (1977), 61–62

In October 1977 the Eberhart-Karl University of Tübingen celebrated the semi-millennial anniversary of one of the two important events of 1477. The other was not even mentioned. The anniversary was of the founding of the University of Tübingen. The forgotten event was the expulsion of the Jews from Tübingen. The two are not unrelated. The count of Württemberg in 1477 had made a trade-off: the citizens of the town of Tübingen – located about twenty miles south-west of Stuttgart, in south Germany – agreed to accept the university. The count agreed to remove the Jews.

It was an odd and curious experience for me to join in the university's jubilee, for, like any Jew, I have a double vision of Germany. Words that for others call up one set of thoughts bring to the surface quite another for me. Then there is the music. On the day of the *festakt*, the ceremony of celebration, the medieval streets of the old town of Tübingen filled with several dozen village bands. Most were made up of children. As soon as I saw those quaint costumed bands playing their not-very-quaint Prussian military marches, I found myself transported to the east. I stood on the platform of the Auschwitz railway station and heard the bands playing to welcome the trainloads of victims. Especially to welcome the children.

Why not think of Auschwitz, when, a few minutes before, I had heard a great ceremonial sermon on the theme, *Die Wahrheit macht frei*, truth will make you free. To the words *macht frei* I supplied the Jewish protasis: *Arbeit*. Over the gate of the hell of Auschwitz were the words, *Arbeit macht frei*, work will make you free. To hear first this talk and then that music brought pain beyond bearing.

But what is worth reporting is that the pain was mine alone. I could not express it to my German hosts, not because they would have been offended (that would not have bothered me) but because they would not have heard nor understood at all. To them the expulsion of the Jews from Tübingen took place a long time ago; there is nothing worth remembering. The founding of the university that same season – that is something else again. The impact of today's

Germany on the Jew of today is something Germans simply cannot grasp; they have known no Jews. The bad memories of their country's history are not to be mentioned.

Had the students been present, they would have had their say. But the jubilee celebration was so timed that there would be no students at all. It came toward the end of the vacation, before classes would call back the university's 18,000 young people. Still, more than 1,500 made a celebration of their own, way out of town in a field. Between them and the official, civic celebration stood 1,000 policemen, carrying sub-machine guns. But the students had set up an exhibition, and in it were pictures of Tübingen in another age. It was not the age of the great Tübingen school – the school that created New Testament scholarship as we now know it, the school that stands behind the massive theological contribution of the Germany of humanism and philosophy. It was the age of Tübingen as the most brown of the brown, the Nazi, universities. Even the students did not present a picture of the Nazi Kittel, who made a fine edition of the Hebrew text of the Hebrew Bible while the Jews were being removed and burned.

In truth, the history that cannot be mentioned means that no history can be brought to speech. The ceremonial addresses all focused on current political events – the terrorists for this was the week of the Lufthansa hijacking – and the overproduction of university graduates, no longer to be absorbed into the economy. There were the high-sounding speeches on truth and freedom, and exceptionally pompous and vacuous hours of greetings by the foreign delegates. (Only three greeted the university in the name of their faculties *and students* – Brown, Colorado and Wyoming. All the others spoke of faculties or presidents or senates.) No one referred to the brown days of Tübingen, and therefore, none to the golden days of the Tübingen school of the nineteenth century either. You cannot have the one without the other. so there will be no history at all on the occasion of the university's 500th anniversary.

My own lectures, delivered for the Protestant theological faculty, dealt with Judaism in ancient times, in the early centuries before and after the beginning of the Common Era. Tübingen today is the center of that approach to the New Testament which draws richly upon the Judaic evidences of the period of the founding of Christianity. Among its scholars, both young and old, are distinguished masters of the study of Hellenistic Judaism and its sources, the Dead Sea Scrolls, and other Jewish writings of the period. These lectures were the theological faculty's contribution to the celebration, part of the official program. There can be no doubt that the prominent inclusion of Judaic studies was meant as a powerful statement of rejection of one past and affirmation of another. Tübingen, after all, also was the home of Adolph Schlatter, one of the earliest New Testament scholars of rabbinic sources. One of his principal monographs dealt with Yohanan ben Zakkai. To be sure, the monograph was only marginally competent; its clearly theological bias was evident. It is not history but a curiosity of history. Still, there was Schlatter, and today there are others with a keen interest in Judaic sources and a desire to hear about them.

But even to those who approach Judaic learning with the best will in the world, Judaism is a dead religion, and Jews are a people of some other place. Germany provides virtually no encounter between a vigorous and self-respecting Judaism, on the one side, and an equally vigorous Christianity, on the other. The stray Israelis who come by do not much change the picture; some of them are perceived, even by the Germans, to whom a Jew can do no wrong, as charlatans. Christianity, for its part, is established, a state-supported religion.

To be sure, it is not one religion. The Reformation is still alive. The Catholics in the Theologicum, the building housing the theological faculty, occupy one floor, the Protestants another. Since I was invited by the Protestants, I began to think of myself as one of them. In a celebration of the Catholic faculty of the same jubilee, I looked around the room and remarked to the dean of the Protestant faculty, 'You know, you and I are the only Protestants here.' At the moment, it did not seem funny. Because the two Christianities have long memories there is yet another past one cannot mention. In the cathedral of Münster, I am told, the cages in which Free Church dissenters were suspended in mid-air while they starved to death are still displayed. The display seemed in poor taste to my informant, a Free Church dissenter from America.

So many histories we cannot confront! While I was in Germany, the abduction of Schleyer had not yet led to his murder. I remarked rather casually that I would not be heartbroken if that leader of the Hitler youth and member of the SS were to die; Germany would have one Nazi less on its hands. Again, in Berlin, at an art museum which, in New York or Boston, would have been filled with young Jewish people, I felt again the pain of Holocaust, the utter absence of Jews. I remarked on it to my host: I see no Jewish faces, except in the pictures (works of the 1920s). Again, in Tübingen, when I did observe that there was, after all, a double celebration, one happy, the other sad, once more I found the same response. In these three, and in other instances, it was an absence of response. Nothing was said, no emotion indicated even in the face, in a gesture. If I had said something one does not say, even that was not communicated in a way in which I might perceive it.

But, of course, I knew I *had*, just as I knew I had to. This became clear when, in Berlin, my host's wife returned from a vacation on the island of Rhodes, and I remarked, when looking at the pictures she brought back, that before the Second World War there had been quite an interesting Jewish community there. But the people had all been shipped north, and most died even before reaching the death camps, having frozen to death. This seemed to me something important and memorable, something worth saying when speaking of Rhodes. There was no comment.

Once more in Berlin, where I also gave a lecture, this time for the Free University and the Evangelische Hochschule (Protestant divinity school) – I stood with my host looking east, across the wall, at the other side. He remarked that some of the great cultural institutions are being built near the wall so that, if Germany is reunited, they will serve the east as conveniently as the west. I said, 'True, but they will meld, since there can be no reunification of Germany without an atomic war. In any case, it is in the interest neither of the USSR nor the USA, nor indeed of Europe, for such a reunification to take place. After all, from 1870 to 1945 we did have a single Germany and it did not make for the stabilization of Europe, did it?'

These long, long thoughts of world historical forces and powers did not win the attention of my host. Nor did the apocalyptic sense toward the Brandenburg Gate, a long mall with parks on both sides, presently used, I was told, mainly by roving prostitutes. That is where the West comes to an end: no history, no human connection, no commitment, no emotion, at the empty spaces on the edges of a beleaguered city, filled in by the denizens of hell.

There really was a Holocaust.

# PART VI
## PERSONAL POSTSCRIPT

# 20 Interview by William Novak

*New Traditions* 2 (1985), 10–31

*Jacob Neusner's resume fills fourteen pages, so we won't even try to summarize his career in a single paragraph. He is University Professor and Ungerleider Distinguished Scholar of Judaic Studies at Brown University. He is a prolific scholar of ancient Judaism, whose many books in the field include* A History of the Jews in Babylonia *(5 volumes),* A History of the Mishnaic Law of Purities *(22 volumes), and numerous other scholarly works, anthologies, and textbooks. He has written hundreds of articles and reviews for a wide variety of Jewish and general publications. As we go to press, his most recent book,* How to Grade Your Professors and Other Unexpected Advice, *has just been published by Beacon Press.*

*What follows is an edited version of our conversation at Neusner's home in Providence, Rhode Island, on May 7, 1984. W.N.*

### THE NATURE OF THE ENTERPRISE

*What are you working on these days?*
I'm involved in a big project on the Babylonian Talmud. I'm trying to examine the text to see whether it's possible to describe the mentality of its authors. What I want to know is, What can we learn about the worldview of the people who made these statements?

*Is this what you mean when you speak of moving from text to context?*

Yes. I want to know why people say things in a certain way and not in some other way. It's really a question of style, because the Talmud is an enormously stylized document. How do you translate aesthetics and rhetoric – rituals of language – into cultural data? When you're dealing with questions of word choice and the arrangements of words, the Talmud lets you know that this stuff is vital. The speakers are always asking: 'Why does he say it this way and not that way?' The assumption, which is absolutely valid, is that the speakers were vitally concerned with issues of aesthetics and rhetoric.

*And what about the meaning of words?*

That's something I don't work on. That's been done for a hundred years or more, and for most texts what we have is sufficient. Instead, I work on questions that have been ignored, questions of aesthetics and rhetoric, problems of description and interpretation of the whole document. Look: you and I express ourselves through sentences with a certain cogency. We argue propositions based on a shared logic that is basic to our culture. That's how we communicate. These people did too. Those are the aspects of a document that lead you into the worldview of the people who wrote it.

*It almost sounds as though you don't want to get too close to the text.*

You have to strike a balance. If you're too close to the text, you become an authority not *about* the text but *of* the text. You end up repeating what the text says, but in your own words.

So there has to be perspective and critical autonomy. On the other hand, you can have too much of a good thing. If you're too far from the text, it all dissolves into generalities. If you're standing up on a mountain, everything below looks pretty much the same.

I see the humanistic study of religious texts as a three-part process. First, we translate the text. Second, we determine its context: When was it written? How is it argued? Who was it written for? What is the system of logic it uses? Finally, we make generalizations about the text: we compare that world to other worlds, including our own, as we try to understand those people in terms of what we know about ourselves.

That's the pattern of my work. And I'm trying to come up with a theory of each major document, each text. They're always treated as a collection of homogeneous documents with everybody saying the same thing to everybody else, and that's just not true.

*As when people say 'As we read in the Talmud ...'*

Not even that. As in '*The* Rabbis say ...' But the texts aren't all the same. When I worked on *Leviticus Rabbah* [a fifth-century set of discourses built on some verses of Leviticus], for example, I discovered that it wasn't just a matter of commenting on verses of Scripture. It's true that the rhetoric of *Leviticus Rabbah* is a rhetoric of exegesis. But the logic is not a logic of exegesis at all. Through their citations of verses, they're really *saying* things.

Previously, the things people wanted to say were attached to specific texts. In *Genesis Rabbah*, for example, you get straight exegesis. They comment on this verse, they comment on that verse. In the later collections, they're much more discursive. But *Leviticus Rabbah* stands at the turning point between straight exegesis and the kind of straight discursiveness we find in the *Pesiqtas*. It's a point of tension, which makes it very revealing. They are trying to speak discursively while remaining within the framework of exegetical discourse.

*I gather you weren't always approaching the text on this level. Does this approach represent a shift in your methodology?*

To some extent, yes. The shift came around 1970. I had written *A History of the Jews of Babylonia*. In the prefaces to volumes 3, 4, and 5, I signaled that I was unhappy with the existing methods, which were credulous and gullible, but that the questions as I then framed them permitted me to work this way.

In view of the methods I use now, that *History* is a mere curiosity. But it's been accepted into the scholarly canon. I see it quoted, even in those circles which reject the rest of my work.

*I want to talk about those circles for a moment. But first, where did your shift occur?*

In 1970, when I published *Development of a Legend*.

*That was about Yohanan Ben Zakkai, who was also the subject of your first book.*

Yes, but this time around I asked all sorts of critical questions. That book had only one review. Morton Smith, who had been my teacher, listed ten thousand niggling 'errors', but said 'nonetheless, he has proved the following fifteen important propositions'.

After a couple of other books, I decided that the issue to be studied couldn't be people or topics. It had to be documents. If you're going to do anything historical, you've got to start with the bedrock. And the bedrock of the rabbinic canon is the document. That's the irreducible minimum.

When I did *Development of a Legend*, there were some critical odds and ends. A few people had made critical statements before. But these were episodic, not systematic, and were generally ignored. People in the field continued to produce the same gullible tripe they had always been writing.

*What's an example of an episodic critical comment?*

Well, George Foot Moore, writing on Simeon the Righteous, had said, 'This material is all very legendary.' But the normal procedure was like Professor Ephraim Urbach at the Hebrew University, who would say, '*Yesh bazeh tziltzul shel emet*' [this has the ring of truth] or '*Zeh b'vadai lo histori'* [this certainly isn't historical], and you'd want to reply, 'Okay, but how do you *know*?' Urbach says that if you can't prove it's not historical, you have to believe it is. I don't know why. There was no method and no reason, and there still isn't.

You have to remember that rabbinic literature was not written by trained reporters with tape recorders and TV cameras. And yet I can show you a book written as recently as one year ago in Jerusalem where the author, David Rokeach, tells you the motive of a rabbi written about in a story: 'He did this because ...' But where are the letters, the diaries, the *evidence*?

*And so Rokeach, for example, writes about these people as though there were no question that the events in question actually took place?*
Right. But from the data we have, we don't really know that X really said this, or that Y really did that.

*Aren't we simply talking about something as basic as the difference between science and fundamentalism?*
That's my opinion. But the Israelis who work in Talmudic history would say: 'Wait, we also use scientific methods.' My answer to that is: 'Show me. Show me where.'

COMING OF AGE

*We'll come back to the differences between you and the Israeli scholars, but first I'd like to go back to the beginning. You were born in Hartford ...*
In 1932. I was raised in West Hartford, where we were one of the earlier Jewish families. When I started grammar school, there were only four or five Jewish kids enrolled.

*Were you aware of being Jewish?*
Yes, and I'll never forget when it happened. I was in the third grade. We were drawing pictures of the Pilgrims – our New England heritage – and I assumed they were on their way to shul. I didn't want to say 'shul', of course, because the teacher might not know that word. So I asked her how to spell 'synagogue'. And she said rather harshly: 'The Pilgrims weren't *Jews*, they were *Christians*.'

I was deeply offended. 'They couldn't *possibly* be Christians,' I told her. And I never forgave the teacher. I could never get along with her after that.

*What was your Jewish life like at home?*

It was typical second generation, with Yiddish-speaking grandparents and English-speaking parents. My mother learned Yiddish only after she married my father. Her mother was born in New York City, and her grandmother in Odessa. She was not a positive force for Jewishness. Just recently I took her out for supper on her 83rd birthday and she ordered scallops and ham.

But my father was very positive about being Jewish, and he was an active Zionist. For his generation Zionism was everything. He was one of the founders of the New England Zionist Region, and my Jewish memories of childhood are of being bored sitting in the car while my father went to Zionist meetings. He was capable of going to a different Jewish meeting every night of the week.

*He also ran a Jewish newspaper, didn't he?*

Oh yes, the *Connecticut Jewish Ledger*. He founded it in 1929 and ran it until 1953, when he had a stroke. My mother then ran it until 1965, when the staff bought it.

*As a kid, did you have any connection with the paper?*

Are you kidding? My father took it for granted that all of us would work there. In the eighth grade, in the fall, I was bar mitzvahed, and that was the end of my Jewish education, which I had genuinely enjoyed. From eighth grade through twelfth, 1945 to 1950, I had to work at the *Ledger*. So I couldn't go to Hebrew school anymore although I really wanted to.

I worked there every day after school and often on Saturday mornings. There wasn't much Jewish ritual observance in our household. I didn't even know such things existed.

In high school I didn't get to participate in extracurricular clubs or activities. I was always working at the paper. I started as an errand boy. My father hired newsmen from the Hartford *Times*, and they taught me all of the editorial skills from news writing and rewrite to layout. At the end of the school year in June, the news guys were off and I put out the paper myself for four weeks. I did it all, except that I wasn't allowed to sell advertising because I was too young.

*At some point you must have resumed your Jewish education.*

At the end of my junior year, my parents asked me: 'What do you want for your birthday?'

I asked for Hebrew lessons, which I'd never had. So every Saturday morning during my senior year I went to a teacher, Mrs Frieda Wender, who taught me *dikduk* [grammar]. I used to bring my notebook to high school to show everybody that I was learning Hebrew. By the end of the year I had mastered the *binyanim* [Hebrew verb forms].

*So you didn't exactly have a religiously Jewish upbringing.*

No. Except for going to temple, the notion of Jewish observance, even in the Reform sense, couldn't have been more alien. To me, Jewish life meant meetings and organizations and politics and announcement.

*And after high school?*

I went off to Harvard, and I didn't come home for the entire first year. I was afraid that if I left Harvard it wouldn't be there when I got back! I loved it there because everybody was smart.

*Is Harvard where you became interested in ancient Judaism?*

Not yet. I tried everything else first. When I arrived, I went out for the fencing team, and then for the soccer team. Then I decided that God wanted me to be a writer, so I took a creative writing course. I sat next to John Updike. He got an A, and I got a C. From ninth grade through college I had never had less than an A, so I decided that God wanted Updike to be a writer. I was meant for something else.

*But of course you became a writer.*

Well yes, of a different kind. But I couldn't do fiction.

*Did the temptation to write fiction ever return to you?*

No, not in the slightest. I studied American history because I knew the language. My senior thesis was on the Jews of Boston between 1880 and 1914. I was looking for my grandfather, the first Jacob Neusner. It was absolutely typical of the third generation's search for roots. My teacher was Oscar Handlin, and he didn't understand my interest. But I wanted to know who I was and where I had come from.

*What about your Jewish life at Harvard?*

I used to go to services at a Reform temple in Brookline with Herbert Jacob, whose father was a Reform rabbi. We got on the subway every Friday night and went to Ohabei Shalom on Beacon Street. We didn't know from any other form of Jewish observance. We were genuinely pious Reform Jews.

When I was a freshman, I studied with a graduate student, Jonathan Goldstein, who's now at Iowa University. As a favor, he taught me Hebrew, the Book of Ruth. He was remarkably patient and generous with me. I loved him, and I've always been grateful for the help he gave me.

Jonathan Goldstein also kept kosher, and this amazed me. I couldn't believe that anybody in the world kept kosher. Except for my grandmother, I didn't even know such people *existed*.

I had another friend, Henry Sosland, who also kept kosher. I couldn't understand why. He said, 'I want to be a rabbi.'

I said, 'Well, I want to be a rabbi too, but that doesn't mean you have to keep kosher!' I had wanted to be a rabbi from the time I was thirteen. It's the only thing I ever wanted to be.

*You weren't much of a shul-goer, and Jewish observance was the last thing on your mind. So what did being a rabbi mean to you?*

It meant being very Jewish and doing very Jewish things, whatever they might be.

*Short of keeping kosher.*

Right. I believed in God and all that, but who knew that Jews really *did* those things? You'd read about it in books. My grandmother was *frum*, 'feathers-in-the-attic *frum*'. If you keep Shabbas, you get a lot of goosefeathers and you can make a lot of pillows.

*Wait a minute, I don't understand. Is that a metaphor?*

No, she really believed it. She told my mother that if you keep kosher, a lot of goosefeathers will grow in your attic and you'll be able to make pillows. I guess it was part of a Jewish folklore from her region in White Russia.

*And after Harvard you went to JTS?*

No, first I went to Oxford. I studied with Cecil Roth, and I did a thesis on English Jews in America.

*How would you evaluate Cecil Roth?*

By the standards of his day, he was good. He was an antiquarian, and he knew a great deal about many things. He also did a lot of good guessing. But I don't think he had the slightest idea of what it meant to teach or how to do systematic research that had any methodological sophistication.

*Now how did you, a Reform Jew, end up at the Jewish Theological Seminary?*

I was planning to go to Hebrew Union College. But Roth said: 'You'll get a much better education at the Seminary.' I wasn't so sure. I knew that if I went there, I'd have to start keeping kosher and everything else. But by this time I was becoming more traditional.

I was a smoker in those days, and I decided that if I could go through an entire Shabbat without smoking a cigarette, I'd apply. I was successful and the following Monday I sent off the application. I decided that if Paris was worth a mass to King Henry, then a good education was worth this *mishugaas* to me.

I went to JTS in September, and I arrived in the middle of Succot, 1954. On Shabbat, I went to services at the Seminary. I sat down next to Seymour Fox, and I asked: 'What are they up to?'

'Hallel,' he replied.

'Very good,' I said, 'What's *Hallel*?' I just didn't *know*. That was my initiation. As you can imagine, my first year wasn't easy. I had a little Hebrew, but I didn't know anything. Seymour Siegel was our Talmud teacher, and he was superb, a saint. He had the patience to teach us line by line. He loved the students. He was a teacher of Judaism – and by the way, of Talmud.

To keep up, I simply memorized the text. That happens to be a pretty good way to learn the Talmud, because it's such a uniform document. If you know one chapter, you know the rhetoric of fifty.

By the second year I was keeping up. We had Talmud with [Haim Zalman] Dimitrovsky and he was very good. We had Jeremiah with Shalom Spiegel, a great teacher, a truly great man. In the third year I had Shraga Abramson, another great teacher. I was like a sponge and I had wonderful Talmud teachers throughout.

I was also Heschel's assistant. I typed the manuscript of *God in Search of Man*, which I think is his best book. Heschel was my very best influence. I survived because of him.

*Survived? Wait a minute. You just told me about all these great teachers. So what was the problem?*

The pressures at JTS were enormously negative. The students at that time were divided into two groups, the A's and the C's. There were some wonderfully bright people who were quite tolerant of one another, such as Yochanan Muffs, Joe Yerushalmi, Baruch Levine, David Halivni, Shmuel Leiter, Joel Kramer, Neil Gilman, Joel Zaiman, and many others. And then there was a different seminary, composed of kids who were mainly from yeshivas or from Yeshiva

University. They came in order to make a living as rabbis. They couldn't stand us – and they especially couldn't stand me.

*You had come from Harvard and Oxford into this parochial Jewish environment. That must have been a difficult transition.*

It was, but I wasn't alone. But I got it trouble when I started to write for *Commentary*, beginning in my freshman year at JTS. This was the old *Commentary* with Elliot Cohen. I had sent them an article when I was at Oxford. They rejected the article, but they wanted me to write for them. My first article was about the founding of the Student Zionist Organization. I was also writing in many other places, including *The Reconstructionist*. All of this didn't sit too well with the Seminary.

*What was the problem? Was it the chutzpah of a student publishing in Jewish magazines?*

They just didn't like students who wrote. For the most part these people were not publishing scholars. And what they did publish was for other scholars. It was all very political.

As for my fellow students, the graduating class of 1955 had a class will, and they left me 'a text for his commentary'. Meaning: you don't know enough text, but you're busy writing in magazines. They resented it very much. I hadn't gone through the chairs they had sat in, but I was doing all these worldly things.

*How did you get involved in Talmud?*

I had found American history boring, because there was no intellectual challenge. But when I started learning Talmud, I was just stunned by it. I found it unbelievably demanding and engaging. I was interested in the logic of people thinking clearly and rigorously, which you don't see a lot of. I was very impressed by that. I never wanted to do anything else, and I never did.

*Do you still remember the first page of Talmud you ever learned?*

It was Chapter 8 of *Bava Kama,* about indemnity from personal injury. For me, it wasn't talking *about* Jewish anymore. It was *doing* Jewish.

*Around this time you also did a doctorate at Columbia.*

My last two years at JTS were excruciatingly boring, so I did my Ph.D. at Columbia. JTS wasn't thrilled, but I was doing my work and I never missed a class.

I studied with Morton Smith, and my thesis was on the life of Yohanan Ben Zakkai. I received my doctorate in November of 1960, and I was asked to teach at Columbia, beginning in September of that year.

Believe me, there was no happier person on earth. I was thrilled beyond words. I had already been asked to teach at JTS, and with the chutzpah of youth, which thank God I haven't lost, I said: 'I would not accept an appointment at JTS under the present administration.' I really didn't think much of the ethos of the place. They were very offended, and rightly so. But I was right, too.

After teaching at Columbia for one week, I went to the office of the acting chairman to say hello, and I said: 'I'm getting my degree in another week, and I was told that when that happened, I would be made an assistant professor.'

He said, 'Well, it so happens I have something to tell *you*. We decided that we're not going to reappoint you next year.'

*After just one week?*

They said they didn't want anyone in my field. But they immediately brought in David Halivni to teach my courses, so I know that wasn't the problem. I was crushed beyond words. But it got worse. Columbia University had given me a tentative acceptance of my book *A Life of Yonanan*. In December 1960 my father died. I returned from sitting shivah, and in the mail was a letter from the Press informing me that they wouldn't publish my book after all. I was just crushed. It took me four years to get over it.

*How do you explain these abrupt rejections?*

Well, I've since learned that there's a whole tradition at Columbia of old men treating young talent badly. I think the people in charge of Jewish studies, especially Jewish history, were not comfortable with the combination of youth, talent, ambition and independence.

Later, Columbia did the same thing to other people. For me, this was a formative event. The senior people at Columbia did me in. I figured it out because I kept using them for recommendations – and then not getting the jobs or fellowships. When I stopped asking the, my luck suddenly improved. But Morton Smith stood by me in my most trying years.

The bottom line is that the old guys hated the young guys. And I was a successful young guy, so they hated me more than other people. They made my life miserable.

Look, you know about the ones who made it, because you've heard of us. But there are a lot of people you've never heard of, not because they weren't good, but because their spirits were crushed. I still remember them, the ones who didn't survive the hatred and the envy of the old men. They were better men than I.

*Are you implying that this problem is unique to Jewish academic life?*

No. I think it's common in the humanities. In the hard sciences you can replicate results, so politics and personalities play a somewhat smaller role.

At any rate, getting fired in the first week of the first year of my first job was like surviving the atomic bomb: nothing worse can happen to you, so it's an enormously liberating experience.

*What did you learn from that episode?*

Not to take people too seriously, not to depend on people, and to make my own way.

Our generation had a great model not to follow: just do the opposite of our teachers, and we wouldn't make too many mistakes. I decided to make my own way. That was long before I had made anybody in Jerusalem or elsewhere mad at me, but it made it easy for me to deal with the Jerusalem establishment.

TALMUD IN JERUSALEM

*Let's talk about that now. What's the story?*

The story is that you're not supposed to quote my work in Jerusalem. They don't review my books; they never mention them. I'm an untouchable, a pariah from their perspective.

Now I don't mind if people disagree with me, but they can't pretend that I don't exist. Boycotts have nothing to do with scholarship. The Israelis boycott me; they play Arab to my Israel. It's no tribute to their scholarship, such as it is.

*What about the young guys in Jerusalem?*

The young guys are no better than the old guys. They're in a very awkward situation. The young guys can't do anything if they don't work my way, because the rest of the world laughs at them. You cannot approach the sources other than through the critical means that I've devised and still do serious work – and everyone knows it. Everyone in Europe does it my way, and almost everyone in America, even in seminaries and yeshivas. But in Jerusalem, nothing comes out anymore. As far as I know, not one book in Talmudic religion or history has come out in Hebrew, and certainly not in English, for the past fifteen years.

Urbach's *Hazal* [*The Sages*], published in 1969, is the last large and substantial work in Talmudic history or religion to come out of Jerusalem. Mostly they write brief, nitwit articles, or make anthologies or summarize and repeat themselves.

*You've written somewhere that the articles in the Israeli scholarly journals* Zion *and* Tarbiz *could have been published a hundred years ago.*
Absolutely.

*Because?*
Because they're asking the wrong questions, and their methods are all fundamentalist positivism. If the source said it happened, then it happened. But nobody works that way in ancient studies anymore. Nobody, anywhere, except the neo-Orthodox in Jerusalem.

*Is it really that simple? If the Israeli scholars were sitting here in this room, what would they say at this point?*
They wouldn't even sit here. They wouldn't give me the time of day. I've never been invited to lecture at the Hebrew University. Tel Aviv and Bar Ilan and Haifa universities, but not Jerusalem.

Do you know what happened recently? Last November I was invited to give a lecture in July 1984 for the Historical Society of Israel. This is a group that's dominated by the Hebrew University crowd. You also have to understand the phrase 'historical society' has far greater import in Israel than in America. After all, over there history is nothing less than theology.

The occasion for the lecture was a celebration of the fiftieth anniversary of the journal *Zion.* I said fine, I have to be in Israel anyway; it won't even cost you any money. I gave a lot of thought to the lecture, and I decided not to speak too abstractly about methodology. I made up my mind to talk about how Talmudic history was done in *Zion.*

*But you evidently don't think there's much there to celebrate.*
That's what I wrote in the lecture: that the articles are gullible and credulous and fundamentalist. I didn't use quite those words, but you couldn't miss my meaning. I sent it off to them in January because they wanted to translate it into Hebrew.

In March, I got a letter from a junior assistant secretary saying 'We've changed our plans and we don't want foreign guests.' They didn't even acknowledge that I had sent them the paper! They said, 'We're sorry *if* we've inconvenienced you.' But I was the only one was disinvited. I don't think this sort of thing does the Israelis in this field any good. I think it's very bad for their good name.

*They probably wanted a celebration of the magazine.*

But what did they expect? I had never been invited to speak in Jerusalem before. It's the first invitation I ever got from them. When it was withdrawn, I wrote to them and I said: 'Okay, you've shown me who you are and what you are.'

*Does the rest of the world take their work seriously?*

It's not a question of who takes whose work seriously. That's mere politics. Their 'work' isn't coming out. You've read *The Structure of Scientific Revolution*? Kuhn talks about changes in paradigms. When the evidence is different, the questions shift completely. One of the things that makes a difference is *who does the work*. In Israel they do a lot of articles about *pintelach*, little points about this and that.

*Such as?*

Such as what time in the morning Pontius Pilate went to the toilet. Or whose skull did Hillel see floating on the water? Or the day that Rav Shilah hit somebody on the head with a bucket. Or the conception of X in the book of Y. They're at the stage of hunting and gathering, what we in America call 'show and tell'. In the Talmud area, all they're doing is collecting and arranging variant readings, and working on enormously erudite philology that doesn't make much difference to the meaning of the text. There's no critical program, no method and no system.

Now when I talk this way about Israeli scholars, I mean only in this one field, in Talmudic and related historical studies. Israelis do other things very well, but that doesn't do me any good. I have an enormous audience in Israel outside of my immediate area, especially in Bible and history. My recent book, *Judaism: The Evidence of the Mishnah*, is being translated into Hebrew.

But if you went to a lecture in Israel and you raised your hand and asked: 'How do we know if Rav Shimon really said that?' They ask *'Atah talmido shel Noise-nur?'* [Are you a student of Neusner?] In a way, it's a great honor. They've given me credit for everything that's happened in the Western humanities since the Enlightenment!

*Why doesn't this same kind of conflict arise in biblical scholarship?*

Because there you don't have to deal with the modern Orthodox. They reject biblical scholarship out of hand. It doesn't interest them, and they're afraid of it.

But the Talmud they think their own. That's what makes them *them*. I've invaded the sacred preserve, and what's more, I treat it as secular.

And by translating this stuff, I also ruin its mystery. They can no longer ladle out, secret by secret, the way [Saul] Lieberman did, this source and that source. Now, anyone who wants to look can look. And it's true. If you don't like my translation of the Palestinian Talmud, then improve on it. I'll be the first one to applaud. But it's no longer a secret.

There's another dimension to the problem. We in the Diaspora are not supposed to *be* Jewish scholars. We're supposed to be singing Christmas carols on our way to the gas chambers with our goyishe wives. It's bad enough that I work in a Jewish area. But I also work in the holy area, and I publish a lot. And outside of Israel I'm the dominant figure in this field.

*Do you still send students to Jerusalem?*

Sure, all the time. But they don't say they're my students. That's nobody's business. They're there to learn, and we tell them: 'Don't say who you are or what you think about anything. Just learn what there is to be learned, and then come home. Don't ask questions.' We're Marranos.

*And what exactly do they learn there?*

The Israelis do a very good job of language and text teaching. But you've got to be careful, because if you raise your hand and ask 'How do we know that Rabbi Akiva really said that?' they say, 'Oh, you're from Brown!'

*Wait a minute. On the one hand you talk about having an enormous influence. But at the same time you complain that you're not getting a fair hearing.*

It's a paradox. I have an enormous hearing in the scholarly world, in the religious studies and the humanities. My scholarly books sell very well. Outside of Israel, everyone in the academic study of religion knows my work, absorbs it, uses it, and it's a perfectly normal professional transaction. There are not many distinguished universities where I haven't lectured. That's why the Israelis and the parochial types in this country say, 'He writes for the goyim.' They treated Buber and Heschel even worse.

The other side is that I've never been invited to lecture at a rabbinical school in this country or abroad.

*Not even HUC?*

Not in Cincinnati *or* in New York. I'm invited to meals in private homes but not to the campus.

*Not the Reconstructionists?*

I lectured there in their first year, when the place was a disaster. I don't even put that on my resume. I did once give a summer course at JTS, but that didn't work well. After that I became a pariah there, and I haven't been there since. Only one Jewish institution in this country has received me in any way. That's Dropsie, but it's a perfectly secular place.

There *is* a paradox here. The worldly acceptance has been enormous. But on the other side, there is the other world, Jerusalem and the Jewish seminaries and yeshivas, which are very hostile and which don't want to argue with me.

*Do you think that part of this is an antagonism to somebody who's very prolific?*

I don't think that would matter, *if* I were saying things that they wanted to hear. I don't detect any antagonism toward Salo Baron, who is very prolific, because he doesn't upset anybody. He just collects a lot of information. Why get mad at him?

## ON BEING PROLIFIC

*But you do publish an enormous amount, and people tend to focus on that. The other day somebody said to me, 'The problem with Jack is that he writes faster than most people can read.' And somebody else, when he heard I was coming to interview you, said: 'Ask him how he does it? Doe he really use two typewriters at once, one for each hand?' I always think of you in terms of the novelist Joyce Carol Oates, who would probably have a better literary reputation if she published less often. Do you think you're punished for publishing too much?*

Perhaps. But you *can* read one book at a time and listen to one message at a time. I've long ago decided that I'm going to do things my way. I just have more ideas than a lot of people.

*And more energy.*

I guess so.

*How do you publish so much? Do you write all the time?*

No. To me a good working day is three to four hours. I'm in my study by 7:30 or 8 in the morning, and I work until around 10:30 or 11. I also work another hour or two after supper. One reason I'm fast is that I write it in my head before putting it on paper. I'll work on an essay for months in my head. When I go to write it, I just put it down on paper as fast as I can type.

When I was working on Mishnah, tractate *Ohalot*, for example, I was deeply puzzled by the intractability of the central thesis of the tractate. I had memorized the bulk of it and kept repeating the main points to myself. Driving down Hope Street in Providence, I had the bright idea of reversing the predicate and the subject of some of the principal propositions of the tractate. All of a sudden everything fell into place. I was so stunned that I almost drove into a tree.

*Do you think you're prolific in part because you're controversial?*

I once asked Richard Rubenstein how to respond to a particularly virulent and irrational review by Solomon Zeitlin. He said, 'Write another book. The issue is murder, so you affirm life.' My whole career has been an affirmation of life. I don't mean in the abstract, but minute by minute. I used to fear dying young, before I got anything done. I was so glad to pass 30, then 36 – Mozart was my hero. Then 40, now 52. My God, 52. What a gift!

### THE CONTEMPORARY SCENE

*Let's get more concrete. How are you so productive?*

I work hard. I treasure the minutes, but I'm also one of the great *bat-lanim* (time-wasters) of the age. As far as I know, I spend more time with my undergraduates than any other professor at Brown, and I love the time I spend with most of them. I also spend more time with my graduate students than anyone else in graduate education anywhere. Of that I am sure. And I always have time for my colleagues. I spend time, you should pardon me, gossiping on the phone with people I adore, near and far, getting their views on every sort of subject. I can be a real pest.

'Productivity' isn't quantitative. It can mean one book or a hundred. Brahms wrote only four symphonies, whereas Mozart composed ten times that number, and Haydn still more. Who is to say who was the greatest composer of the lot? Each person does what he or she does. God endows us all, and we are judged – and judge ourselves – only by how we use God's gifts. Should I hate Robert Redford because he is handsomer than I am? I have colleagues at least as smart and as hard-working as I am, and they create in media other than books. Why make comparison?

The main thing in writing a log of books is having a log of things you want to say in books. If you have nothing to say in a book, you won't write a book. If you have a lot to say, and if, in addition, you have the capacity and the courage to sit down and write it, then you'll publish. You'll also make a lot of enemies.

*Productivity breeds contempt?*

I once asked Gershom Scholem when the hatred stops. He replied: 'When I turned 40, they got used to me.'

I asked Harry Wolfson, who had been my freshman adviser at Harvard, a man of remarkably honorable character, when 'it' would end. He said to me: 'If you want people to like you, stop writing, stop publishing, stop saying new things. Above all, stop criticizing the work of other people. Then everyone will love you. But if you don't, just go on doing what you're doing, and they'll get used to you.'

I don't think that's how things have worked out so far, but I don't really mind, one way or the other. I don't work to spite anyone, or to impress anyone either, but only to please myself and to say what is welling up and demands to be said.

*How many books have you published?*

If you count each volume, including children's books, anthologies, and everything else, it's probably around two hundred. Maybe more, counting revisions and new editions.

*And how many more are in press?*

Another 50 or so. But that's including each of the tractates of the Yerushalmi and Bavli translations. Still, it's a lot.

*Let's move on and talk a little about the Jewish community. You've complained about a recent obsession with the Holocaust.*

It's not so recent. I've been complaining about it since 1969. Then in 1971 Michael Wyschogrod said it better than I did, with a review of Fackenheim's book in *Judaism*. But I was wrong: I thought the thing would peter out. Instead, it's still going.

A group of Holocaust survivors right here in Providence held a meeting where they debated which concentration camp was worse: 'You didn't go through anything compared to what I went through.' I can't think of anything more grotesque. I think it's equally grotesque for us to be arguing with other ethnic groups that our Holocaust was worse than their Holocaust. I recently read Steve Katz's article in *Modern Judaism* about the 'uniqueness' of the Holocaust. I think it's intellectually vulgar. It comes down to why the Shoah was 'worse' than what the Armenians went through.

Is our blood redder than theirs? It's not a discussion that pays tribute to the human greatness of the Jewish people, to our dignity, or to our sense of self-worth. If you know who you are, you don't have to make statements like that. You don't found the consciousness of who you are on the fact that you've got cancer – or survived cancer. I don't see anything positive in that formulation. Arthur Herzberg has said that the Holocaust is a very easy, accessible Jewish experience, a 'cheap thrill'. He's right. It will always produce an audience. It will always produce a visible, guaranteed reaction. It's exploitation.

*I share your concern. There are many people for whom learning about the Holocaust seems to be their primary Jewish experience.*

It won't last. Why would you want to be Jewish just so you can suffer?

*What else disturbs you about contemporary Jewish life?*

That's easy: the absence of *Ahavat Yisrael*, which I would translate as 'love for oneself as a Jew and for one's fellow Jews'. Everybody has to be special, and nobody wants to respect anyone else. There's a lot of arrogance toward other Jews. The Orthodox are parading around saying: 'We're going to make it. When there are only three-quarters of a million Jews left in America, we'll be them.' I think this is pathetic, and also very dangerous. They believe their own press notices as they write then. The other sects are no more generous in spirit, either. In general, the Jewish community doesn't want to talk to other people. We've always got to be superior, always have to feel persecuted. Otherwise, we can't be Jewish. I think this attitude is disgraceful.

*Do you find this attitude represented in Jewish magazines?*

They have other problems. Take *Commentary*, for example. They're pathetic, bitter enemies of Judaism. They stopped pretending to be Jewish in 1960, when Norman [Podhoretz] took over. By removing the 'Cedars of Lebanon' column and other things, he took the mezuzahs off the doors. A few years later he did his political shift, which I happen to respect and share, but he never did a shift on anything Jewish. The magazine doesn't even pretend that Judaism is a living religion, that Jewish intellectual life has substance and discipline and method and important issues to debate. It in no way takes seriously that the Jews are Jewish *in their minds*. That's why *Commentary* is the most destructive Jewish institution around. It tells people every month that there's nothing important about the Jewish intellect.

That doesn't mean they don't sometimes publish a good article on a Jewish theme. Robert Alter and Jacob Katz are consistently very good. But this is clearly *pro forma*. And by treating it as such with so little else of a Jewish intellectual character of such high quality, they underline the message that the action is somewhere else. Yet they are Jewish. And it's the American *Jewish* Committee. And they want a Jewish audience. It's enormously destructive.

*And the others?*

*Judaism* is dead. [Robert] Gordis killed it. He took a magazine where people could argue about important issues, and turned it into an intellectual embarrassment, a self-celebration of third-rate minds. It's not even boring! It's just show and tell, 'X's view of Y.' Here too there are occasional good articles, but only by accident. It didn't have to be that way. Steven [Schwarzschild], a great man, a moral hero, never should have resigned. Had he known what would happen to the magazine, he wouldn't have left.

It's a great loss, and now we don't have a serious intellectual journal. The *Jewish Spectator* is the closest thing but it's not well supported. We'll see if *New Traditions* can fill the bill. Curiously, *Response* never died. It's odd, it's uneven, but it's always retained the ability to be interesting. I love to print my work there, and also in the reborn *Reconstructionist*. There's a whole new generation.

*Speaking of a new generation, I wanted to mention the havurah phenomenon. Long before there was a 'havurah movement,' you were writing on this topic. What got you interested in it?*

In the late 1950s I had been working on the concept of the *haver* and the *havurah* in the Mishnah. I compared the *havurah* to the *yahad*, that is, to he community formed by the Jews at the Dead Sea, known to us from the Dead Sea Scrolls. I began thinking about the basic principles of social organization of religion that were represented by the early *havurot*, and they seemed to me to solve certain basic problems facing the synagogues and the temples that I knew. So I wrote a few articles and made a number of speeches on the subject. These led to two books: *Fellowship in Judaism, The First Century and Today*, published by Vallentine Mitchell back in 1963, and an anthology called *Contemporary Judaic Fellowship in Theory and in Practice*, published by Ktav in 1972.

*I know that book well because I wrote a long piece for you about Havurat Shalom. You also included articles by Alan Mintz, Art Green, Everett Gendler and Zalman Schachter, if I'm not mistaken. Every now and then somebody comes to interview me about the contemporary havurah phenomenon, and I always tell them to start by reading that book. In most cases they already have.*

You know, people don't really grasp that the things they do, practical things, begin in ideas, commitments, concerns, even yearning. That is to say, practical action begins in reflection, and ideas do matter. Everything we do was thought up by someone, whether it's a Jewish state, which was thought up in a book, or living an ethical life, which was also thought up in a book. The idea of the *havurot* as a renewed form of Judaic social organization began somewhere. In fact, it was in my head.

*To move to the larger Jewish community, do you see any bright spots in contemporary Jewish life?*

Sure, lots of them. I'm basically an optimistic person. The main one is obvious: the fourth generation. There wasn't supposed to be one. We in America know something that Jews haven't yet learned in other parts of the Diaspora – how to transmit 'being Jewish' to free people who have choices. I'm not sure the Israelis have done as well.

*You mean it's working?*

We *know* it's working. By teaching, I'm always 15 years ahead of the Jewish community. As a result, I get a preview of the next generation before the Jewish community sees it. In my classes I'm seeing kids whose *great*-grandparents spoke English without an accent. These kids want to be Jewish, and they're very serious about it, and there are lots of them. That's something we had no reason to expect.

But you can't speak to these people as though they're European, or as though they're inferior, or afraid, or coerced, or as though if you don't tell them every 15 minutes that they're special, that they're the best, and that the world hates them, they'll stop being Jewish. You have to treat them as if being Jewish is normal to their lives, or you won't have anything to say to them. Because it's now perfectly normal to be Jewish in America.

There's a boy in my class who's on the university swim team. He's the most outdoor person you'll ever meet. He spends the summer climbing rocks in Colorado. He's blond and blue-eyed. He's polite and sweet-natured and a first-rate student. But he didn't go to Duke because he thought it was anti-Semitic. I said, 'Gee, David, you could have passed!' He looked at me like I was crazy. He didn't have the *slightest* idea of what I meant. That's a bright spot – one among many.

We in the universities are talking to the Jews as they really are. I don't think the rest of the Jewish world is. They're only interested in the kind of Jews they *want* to see. But we don't have a choice. We see them all as students. The tragedy is the rabbinate. They just didn't keep up, and they've become irrelevant. Their training is irrelevant, their message is irrelevant, their institutions are irrelevant. It didn't have to be that way.

*Who is keeping up?*

I think the federations are. I think they're marvelous. They have a bottom line, and they're very professional about it. Outside of the federations, there's a deep anti-professionalism in the Jewish community. People make things up as they go along ...

*And they call it Judaism.*

Exactly. They're happy, and they don't want to be bothered. The federations, by contrast, have a job to do. There's policy, there's reflectiveness, and there's effectiveness. You may not think that raising money is the whole point, but at least somebody is doing something. Unfortunately, there's still a lot of slovenliness and Jewish self-hatred in the Jewish community. Like coming late to programs, or not making the effort to do something well. But there are plenty of exceptions, and a lot of people who have a sense of honor and commitment.

*More bright spots?*

Among the organizations, Hadassah. As for individuals, Carmi Schwartz and Darrel Friedman from the Council of Jewish Federations. Trude Weis-Rosmarin, editor of the *Jewish Spectator*. And Yitz [Irving] Greenberg is truly good. He spoke recently in Providence about the Holocaust and did a first-rate job. Everybody respected him, including the faculty. It was a talk that wouldn't embarrass you, a talk that was definitely not exploitative. Greenberg has a lot of Jewish dignity. He's a fine man and a great Jew. And he's not alone: there are a lot of fine men and women around. I've also noticed something interesting, and this is another bright spot: the good people know and respect each other.

*Is there anything I should have asked you but didn't? Anything that you'd like to add?*

Only that it's much more worthwhile being Jewish than a lot of people realize. As Heschel used to say, the human materials of the Jewish community are undervalued and underappreciated. We have a great supply of good people. I see their children all the time. They have true Jewish loyalty and commitment, and curiosity as well. Their parents deserve some credit, too, for making these kids into hopeful Jews. That's why, despite some disappointments, I'm optimistic about our future.

# Index

Recently published by Vallentine Mitchell

# Israeli Society, the Holocaust and its Survivors
## Dina Porat
### Tel Aviv University

This collection of twenty essays analyses the encounters of the Yishuv (the Hebrew community in pre-state Israel) and Israeli society with the Holocaust and with its survivors. Sixty years after the end of the Second World War this is still a painful topic, very much at the centre of the agendas of both Israel and the Jewish communities worldwide, focusing on a soul-searching issue: was the tragedy unfolding in Europe part and parcel of public life in the Yishuv, its priorities and anxieties, and did Israeli society embrace the survivors as they deserved? Based on a wide scope of primary sources and on many years of research, the essays deal with a variety of poignant sub-issues, such as the attitudes of David Ben-Gurion, Martin Buber and other leaders, the understanding of the information about the 'Final Solution', relations and tensions between the Yishuv and the Jewish communities and youth movements in Nazi-occupied Europe, rescue plans and their failure, decisions regarding rescue made during a global war, and parallel changes in the attitude to the survivors and in Israeli and Jewish identity. The balanced answers provided in this collection take into consideration the limited resources of a small community under a mandate, and of a young, post-war country flooded by immigration, and the many dominant factors present during a world war and in its aftermath on which the Yishuv and Israel could have no impact, yet could not avoid criticism and pin-pointing of failures and deficiencies.

2007   475 pages
978 0 85303 741 5   cloth   £49.50/$75.00
978 0 85303 742 2   paper   £20.00/$35.00

Recently published by Vallentine Mitchell

# Antisemitism: The Generic Hatred
# Essays in Memory of Simon Wiesenthal
## Michael Fineberg, Shimon Samuels and
## Mark Weitzmann (Eds)

Dedicated to the memory of the 'conscience of the Holocaust', Simon Wiesenthal, to whom it offers a number of personal tributes, this book brings together essays by a wide variety of authors on antisemitism and related forms of intolerance, racism and xenophobia. Starting from the idea that antisemitism constitutes a paradigm case of collective and individual hatred, it examines some of the reasons why it has prospered over the ages and persists in our time, even after well-nigh universal condemnation of the Holocaust. Some authors see it as a virus, always ready to develop and spread, wherever Jewish difference is resented; others emphasize that the antisemitic myths are not grounded in reality but depend rather on a fabrication, an imagined being to whom every kind of vice and perversion can be attributed. Jews, Gypsies, Kurds, Armenians, Tutsis: they can all be made to fit the bill.

Simon Wiesenthal believed not in vengeance but in justice for the victims and played a pre-eminent and, at times, lonely role in tracking down individual criminals and bringing them to trial. But he knew that was not enough. The contributors to this memorial volume, representing a range of cultural, religious and disciplinary perspectives, share that view. They know that so long as the Jewish stereotype is vested with legitimacy, the fight against antisemitism can never be won. Nor can it be defeated so long as it is fuelled by crisis in the Middle East, which has allowed some people to give expression to their antisemitism while denying it, by treating the State of Israel not as a state, with its own particular problems and shortcomings, but as a kind of reified Jew. These are some of the issues addressed by the authors of the essays presented here, along with others, such as antisemitism as a determinant of Jewish identity and the possibility of forgiveness for the perpetrators of genocide. The book thus seeks to understand and learn from this particular paradigm of hatred and to suggest ways of countering it, in the name of the core values of a common humanity.

2007   288 pages
978 0 85303 745 3   cloth   £40.00/$75.00
978 0 85303 746 0   paper   £20.00/£35.00

Recently published by Vallentine Mitchell

# Orthodox Judaism in Britain since 1913
## An Ideology Forsaken
## Miri J. Freud-Kandel

Oxford University
Foreword by Chimen Abramsky

In 1991, just as Jonathan Sacks was acceding to the post of Chief Rabbi, the United Synagogue, the largest synagogal institution in British Jewry, commissioned a report entitled *A Time for Change*. This report identified the significant difficulties in which many of the Orthodox institutions of British Jewry found themselves: the United synagogue, the largest synagogal institution in British Jewry, commissioned a report entitled *A Time for Change*. This report identified the significant difficulties in which many of the Orthodox institutions of British Jewry found themselves: the United Synagogue itself, the Chief Rabbinate, and the *Bet Din* – its religious court. It suggested that the root cause of the problems was a shift away from '*minhag Anglia*, a celebration of the twofold blessing of being Jewish and British'.

This work examines the thought and influence of the three Chief Rabbis whose terms in office began and ended during the twentieth century. It follows the theological shifts that occurred amongst the religious leadership of Orthodox Judaism in Britain and assesses the influence of factors such as immigration and the so-called 'Jacobs Affair' in effecting these changes.

The Jewish community in Britain provides a model of a religious minority group's attempt to secure its survival in the midst of a host society that espouses alternative values derived either from secularism or an alternative religious system. Through an in-depth analysis of the theology of Chief Rabbi Joseph Herman Hertz, this work identifies a paradigm that was established for Jews in Britain of a strong and confident Orthodoxy that champions interaction in the host society. The Chief Rabbinates of Israel Brodie and Immanuel Jakobovits were each influenced in different ways by the burgeoning influence of alternative models for Orthodox Judaism. This work considers how this facilitated the displacement of the community's fervour for unity with religious polarisation; and analyses how its religious leadership adopted a theology which seemed to call on Anglo-Jewry to forsake its ideology of meaningful interaction to secure its religious identity.

2006  236 pages
978 0 85303 713 2  cloth  £45.00/$75.00
978 0 85303 714 9  paper  £19.95/$35.00

Recently published by Vallentine Mitchell

# Identity and Modern Israeli Literature
## Risa Domb
### University of Cambridge

This book explores through literature the long and complex evolution of Jewish identity in Israel and the central role that language, ideology, memory and culture have played in that journey.

Language is possibly the most important component of any collective identity. Indeed, any nation can be better understood through its imaginative literature and never more so than in the case of Israeli literature, whose story runs in parallel with that of the State of Israel and with Zionism. The political task of nationalism directed the course of Israeli literature into a distinct national literature and in turn the literature participated in the formation of the nation. Language became inseparable from identity. But whose Hebrew is it?

Through key texts by such authors as Y.H. Brenner, S.Y. Agnon, Nathan Shaham, Yoram Kaniuk, Aharon Appelfeld, A.B. Yehoshua, Gabriela Avigur-Rotem and Sami Michael, the author explores the connections between language, ideology, memory, culture and identity, and asks whether ideology and identity are on an inescapable collision course.

2006  128 pages
978 0 85303 660 9  paper £18.50/$27.50

Recently published by Vallentine Mitchell

# Confronting the Perpetrators
# A History of the Claims Conference

## Marilyn Henry

### Foreword by Sir Martin Gilbert

At the end of the twentieth century, the world seemed to rediscover Holocaust survivors. Ceremonies commemorating the 50th anniversary of World War II-era events offered occasions for reflection about the war, its heroes and its victims. In the US, broad interest in the Holocaust was sparked by two cultural phenomena: the 1993 opening of the US Holocaust Memorial Museum and the film Schindler's List. The collapse of communism, the opening of archives in eastern Europe and the approach of the millennium - and with it a desire to 'clean the slate' - also sparked a series of confrontations with the past.

Among those confrontations was an extraordinary focus on the material losses and injuries suffered by Nazi victims. Class-action lawsuits filed in American courts against European governments and enterprises, improvised commissions, national historical reviews and international conferences attempted, at century's end, to deal with the material, historical, legal and moral issues stemming from the Holocaust.

These initiatives built on groundwork laid in 1951, when Israel and an ad hoc consortium of voluntary Jewish organizations received an invitation to negotiate with West Germany for 'moral and material amends' for Nazi-era damages. The consortium became the Conference on Jewish Material Claims Against Germany (known as the Claims Conference).

2006  272 pages
978 0 85303 628 9  cloth  £49.50/$79.50
978 0 85303 629 6  paper  £20.00/$35.00